Writing Russian Lives

The Poetics and Politics of Biography in Modern Russian Culture

edited by

Polly Jones

Modern Humanities Research Association
for the
UCL School of Slavonic and East European Studies
2018

Published by

The Modern Humanities Research Association
Salisbury House
Station Road
Cambridge CB1 2LA
United Kingdom
for the
UCL School of Slavonic and East European Studies

© UCL School of Slavonic and East European Studies, 2018
for selection and editorial matter; individual contributions
their contributors

The authors assert their right under the Copyright, Designs and Patents Act 1988 to be identified as the authors of this work. Parts of this work may be reproduced as permitted under legal provisions for fair dealing (or fair use) for the purposes of research, private study, criticism, or review, or when a relevant collective licensing agreement is in place. All other reproduction requires the written permission of the copyright holder who may be contacted at seer@ucl.ac.uk.

This collection also appeared as Volume 96:1 (2018) of
The Slavonic and East European Review

First published 2018

ISBN 978-1-78188-910-7

CONTENTS

Introduction — The Poetics and Politics of Modern Russian Biography
   Polly Jones   1

1. Biography as Archive: Writing the Lives of Scholars in Imperial Russia
   Nathaniel Knight   16

2. Creating a National Biographical Series: F. F. Pavlenkov's 'Lives of Remarkable People', 1890–1924
   Ludmilla A. Trigos and Carol Ueland   41

3. 'Remembrances of a Distant Past': Generational Memory and the Collective Auto/Biography of Russian Populists in the Revolutionary Era
   Ben Eklof and Tatiana Saburova   67

4. Lives and Facts: Biography in Russia in the 1920s
   Angela Brintlinger   94

5. The Antifascist Pact: Forging a First Experience of Nazi Occupation in the Wartime Soviet Union
   Jochen Hellbeck   117

6. 'Life as big as the ocean': Bolshevik Biography and the Problem of Personality from Late Stalinism to Late Socialism
   Polly Jones   144

Notes on contributors   175

Cover image: 'Reading' by Konstantin Makovskii, *c*.1900
<https://commons.wikimedia.org/wiki/File:Reading-Makovsky.jpg>

Introduction

The Poetics and Politics of Modern Russian Biography

POLLY JONES

LIKE many genres, biography came belatedly to Russia. As with other such late arrivals, biography underwent intensive growth in quantity, sophistication, cultural significance and popularity from the era of Nicholas I onwards. It stands today as a dominant force in post-Soviet publishing. Yet studies of Russian biography's poetics and its role as a literary and cultural institution in the nineteenth and twentieth centuries remain thin on the ground, a fact often lamented, yet not fully addressed, in the scattered writings on the subject.[1] The present volume examines modern Russian biography as a literary form, a publishing phenomenon and a cultural force that reveals and contests hegemonic ideas of the role of the individual in society, and of the make-up of the human personality itself.

---

[1] Book-length studies of Russian biography are almost non-existent, with the exception of G. O. Vinokur, *Biografiia i kul'tura*, Moscow, 1927; Dmitrii Zhukov, *Biografiia biografii: razmyshleniia o zhanre*, Moscow, 1980; D. Kalugin, *Proza zhizni. Russkie biografii XVIII–XIX veka*, St Petersburg, 2015, and the series published by Memorial, *Pravo na imia. Biografii XX veka*. Important Russian articles on the form include Boris Tomashevsky, 'Literature and Biography', in Krystyna Pomorska and Ladislav Matejka (eds), *Readings in Russian Poetics*, Cambridge, MA, 1971, pp. 47–55; Iurii Lotman, 'Literaturnaia biografiia v istoriko-kul'turnom kontekste (k tipologicheskomu sootnosheniiu teksta i lichnosti avtora)', in *O russkoi literature. Stat'i i issledovaniia: Istoriia russkoi prozy, teoriia literatury*, St Petersburg, 1997, pp. 804–17; B. V. Dubin, 'Biografiia, reputatsiia, anketa. O formakh interpretatsii opyta v pis'mennoi kulture', in *Slovo, pis'mo, literatura*, Moscow, 2001, pp. 98–119. The 'Lives of Remarkable People' series has attracted the most analysis, though more historical than textual. Several texts are analysed in Zhukov, *Biografiia biografii*; see also G. E. Pomerantseva, *Biografiia v potoke vremeni: ZhZL, zamysly i voploshcheniia serii*, Moscow, 1987; Ludmilla A. Trigos and Carol R. Ueland, 'Literary Biographies in the *Lives of Remarkable People* Series (*Zhizn' zamechatel'nykh liudei*)', *Slavic & East European Journal*, 60, 2016, 2, pp. 207–20; Inna Bulkina, 'The Lives of Remarkable People: Between Plutarch and Triapichkin', *Russian Studies in Literature*, 49, 2013, 2, pp. 87–95. Several excellent studies of Russian concepts of the self shed light on biography but are not intended as direct studies of the genre: Jochen Hellbeck and Klaus Heller, *Autobiographical Practices in Russia = Autobiographische Praktiken in Russland*, Göttingen, 2004; Lidiia Ginzburg, *On Psychological Prose*, trans. Judson Rosengrant, Princeton, NJ, 1991; Laura Engelstein and Stephanie Sandler, *Self and Story in Russian History*, Ithaca, NY, 2000.

The History of Russian Biography

The history of biography is long, with textual narratives of human lives dating back at least to Ancient Greece, if not the Pharaonic era. But it is also relatively short, with recognition (even naming) and theorization of the genre hesitant and partial in many cultures.[2] Biography's very hybridity or 'impurity' — its fusions of art and science, history and literature — long left it excluded from generic taxonomies, or consigned to the unprestigious periphery of the various professions with which it intersected, primarily history and literature.[3] Its galloping mass appeal and its tendencies to either burnish or demolish reputations (the former still much more common) tended to make critics suspicious, or even disdainful, about the idea of subjecting the genre to serious analysis. Biography for much of its history has exhibited a striking disjuncture between its enormous growth, even dominance, within the publishing industry and the halting progress of analysis of the genre, especially before the twentieth century.

Even so, scholars of biography largely agree on the periodization of biography's emergence, noting the particular importance for modern

---

[2] Biography as a term appeared in English in the seventeenth century; in Russia, the term took until the nineteenth century to be established. On the disjuncture between practice and theorization of the genre, see Daniel Madelénat, *La biographie*, Paris, 1984 (whose detailed genre study is intended to address the 'lack of an -ology' of the genre, as he terms it). On the neglect of biography in criticism, especially before the 1950s, see also David Novarr, *The Lines of Life: Theories of Biography, 1880–1970*, West Lafayette, IN, 1986. On the neglect of its poetics, see Ira Bruce Nadel, *Biography: Fiction, Fact and Form*, London, 1984. He points out that most studies of biography are historical rather than textual.

[3] On 'impurity' of biography, see Harold Nicolson, 'The Practice of Biography', *The American Scholar*, 23, 1954, 2, pp. 151–61, and Matthew Josephson, 'Historians and Mythmakers', *VQR Online* <http://www.vqronline.org/essay/historians-and-mythmakers> [accessed 8 August 2017]. On the genre's combination of history and literature, see Madelénat, *La biographie*, and J. Flexner, 'Biography as a Juggler's Art', in James L. Clifford, *Biography as an Art: Selected Criticism, 1560–1960*, London, 1962, pp. 178–84. On the consigning of biography to the periphery of history, see, for example, Josephson, 'Historians and Myth-makers', and Barbara Caine, *Biography and History*, Basingstoke, New York, 2010. Garraty argues that what sets biography apart from history is its central concern with personality, which compels it to move beyond mere fact (John A. Garraty, *The Nature of Biography*, New York, 1964). On the long-standing tendency to ignore biography within literary studies, see Paul Murray Kendall, *The Art of Biography*, London, 1965; Nadel, *Biography*. While many studies of biography present this hybridity as a difficulty, anxiety or tension, others have pointed out that early modern biography was considerably less anxious about the boundaries between truth and fiction, and literature and history, with life narratives drawing liberally on both: Judith H. Anderson, *Biographical Truth: The Representation of Historical Persons in Tudor-Stuart Writing*, New Haven, CT, 1984; Donald A. Stauffer, *The Art of Biography in Eighteenth Century England*, Princeton, NJ, 1941; Naomi Jacobs, *The Character of Truth: Historical Figures in Contemporary Fiction*, Carbondale, IL, 1990.

biography of the works of Plutarch and Suetonius in antiquity, Renaissance portraiture (such as the works of Vasari), the rich culture of biography writing in eighteenth-century England that sprang up around Boswell's seminal *Life of Johnson*, and the Western European polemics around the 'new biography' between World War One and World War Two.[4] These landmarks, while scattered across centuries and countries, were united by their humanist commitment to psychological portraiture and secular subjects. Broadly speaking, they reflected the development of new, and progressively more complex, ideas of the human personality: by the end of the 1920s, André Maurois set the biographer's task as the capturing of its subject's 'coral-reef of diverse personalities'.[5] Equally, however, scholars have often noted the periodic resurgence of elements of hagiography and the writing of 'exemplary lives' — in the Victorian era, and to some extent even after World War Two — which waves of critique, even iconoclasm, have been unable to curtail.[6] Some analyses have gone so far as to see these alternations of heroism and anti-heroism as part of the natural rhythm of the genre.[7]

---

[4] Thorough analyses of at least two millennia of biographical production can be found in Caine, *Biography and History*; Clifford, *Biography as an Art*; Kendall, *Art of Biography*; John A. Garraty, *The Nature of Biography*, London, 1958; Nigel Hamilton, *Biography: A Brief History*, Cambridge, 2007; Catherine Neal Parke, *Biography: Writing Lives*, New York, London, 2002. For a magisterial study of the eighteenth-century English golden age of biography, see Stauffer, *The Art of Biography*. On the 'new biography', see André Maurois, *Aspects of Biography*, Cambridge, 1929; Laura Marcus, *Auto/biographical Discourses: Criticism, Theory, Practice*, Manchester, 1994; Laura Marcus, *Dreams of Modernity*, Cambridge, 2014; Ruth Hoberman, *Modernizing Lives: Experiments in English Biography, 1918–1939*, Carbondale, IL, 1987.

[5] On the development of biography in line with theories of the self, see Clifford, *Biography as an Art*; Madelénat, *La Biographie*; Hermione Lee, *Biography: A Very Short Introduction*, Oxford, 2009; Nadel, *Biography*. On the particular influence of Freud, see Marcus, *Dreams of Modernity*; Hoberman, *Modernising Lives*. Garraty contrasts this more or less uninterrupted progress toward individuality to the supposed effacement of individual personality from Communist biography (in China): John A. Garraty, 'Chinese and Western Biography: A Comparison', *The Journal of Asian Studies*, 21, 1962, 4, pp. 487–89. A similar argument is made by William Ayers, 'Current Biography in Communist China', *The Journal of Asian Studies*, 21, 1962, 4, pp. 477–85.

[6] On the Victorian resurgence of heroic and hagiographic biography, see A. O. J. Cockshut, *Truth to Life: The Art of Biography in the Nineteenth Century*, London, 1974, and Hamilton, *Biography*. On heroic tendencies in twentieth-century biography, even after the 'new biography' critique, see Josephson, 'Historians and Mythmakers', and Peter France and William St Clair (eds), *Mapping Lives: The Uses of Biography*, Oxford, 2002.

[7] Both Lee, *Biography*, and Hamilton, *Biography*, argue that the genre oscillates between these two tendencies over the centuries; Madelénat (*La Biographie*) traces a broad trajectory towards 'modern biography' but points out that even in the present, this type is merely dominant, not exclusive. Anna Makolkin attempts a more systematic classification of the patterning of these tendencies in the genre: Anna Makolkin, 'Probing the Origins

Where, then, does Russia fit in this narrative of the emergence of modern European biography? It was in the mid-nineteenth century that biography started to appear in Russia in a recognizably modern form: a narrative of a life of an individual who was not necessarily a church or state leader, with some attempt at capturing personality as well as great deeds. This emergence, while belated, was preceded and shaped by long traditions of Russian life writing and commemorative tribute. Anna Makolkin observes that the funeral lament was amongst the most important predecessors to Russian written biographies.[8] Hagiography had a particularly long history in Russia, and the *zhitie* narrative shaped early attempts at written biography, before undergoing a renaissance in Stalinist culture.[9] The eighteenth century witnessed publication of large swathes of celebratory narratives of state leaders (especially Peter the Great) and the first attempts at collective biographies and biographical dictionaries. During this period, very early, scattered signs of a less traditional approach to biography could also be discerned, most notably in Radishchev's *Life of Ushakov* (1789).[10] Analyses of the eighteenth century generally concur, however, that biography proper had barely started to emerge by century's end.[11]

In this sense, the desire to give narrative shape to human lives was not entirely a modern invention in Russia (nor indeed in the rest of Europe). However, by the era of Nicholas I, many Russian writers and critics started to perceive biography as a peculiarly under-developed phenomenon in Russian culture, yet one with enormous potential. This was a time, of course, when many genres, including the Russian novel and lyric poetry, were inchoate and unstable; nevertheless, biography seemed especially so.[12] And it is certainly true that, in terms of quantity and complexity of biographical portraiture, Russia lagged behind the culture of life writing that had thrived for much of the seventeenth and eighteenth centuries (and indeed earlier) in England and many other parts of Europe. This shortage of biographies was underscored by the growing numbers of biographical translations — from Plutarch and Suetonius to Byron — published in Russia in the early nineteenth century.

of Literary Biography: English and Russian Versions', *Biography*, 19, 1996, 1, pp. 87–104.
[8] Makolkin, 'Probing the Origins'.
[9] Ibid., and Gareth Jones, 'Biography in Eighteenth-Century Russia', *Oxford Slavonic Papers*, 22, 1989, pp. 58–80.
[10] Ibid.
[11] Ibid., and Dmitri Kalugin, 'Iskusstvo biografii: Izobrazhenie lichnosti i ee opravdanie v russkikh zhizneopisaniiakh serediny XIX veka', *Novoe literaturnoe obozrenie*, 91, 2008.
[12] Ginzburg, *On Psychological Prose*; Simon Franklin, 'Novels without End: Notes on "Eugene Onegin" and "Dead Souls"', *The Modern Language Review*, 79, 1984, 2, pp. 372–83.

This under-development of Russian life-writing has, variously, been attributed to the unusually long-standing influence of the Orthodox church, the relatively late advent of the Petrine reforms and the halting progress of change to autocracy thereafter.[13] Closely connected to Russia's distinctive history of church and state is the often noted fact that concepts of privacy and individuality developed along very different lines to Western Europe.[14] Dmitrii Kalugin suggests that Russia by the mid-nineteenth century did finally start to develop ideas of personality that enabled the development of biography proper, while Boris Dubin links the growth in both biography and photography — as 'individual' arts *par excellence* — to increasingly individualized conceptions of the self in the twentieth century.[15] However, others have argued that notions of the personality, or *lichnost'*, remained radically different from Western understandings, making it inevitable that biography and autobiography would develop a distinctive — even unique — trajectory in nineteenth- and twentieth-century Russia.[16]

While established biographical practices of the eighteenth century, such as the production of biographical dictionaries, continued into the next century — notably with Bantysh-Kamenskii's five-volume *Dictionary of Notable People of the Russian Land* (1836) — the previously scattered signs of a distinctively modern biography started to coalesce during and just after the era of Nicholas I. The first full biographies appeared in Russia in the 1840s, with literary writers — who at the time were, in Lotman's words, asserting their 'right to a biography' while emerging as a profession in their own right — a particularly popular subject.[17] Viazemskii's biography of Fonvizin (written in the 1830s but first published 1848) and Annenkov's biography of Pushkin (1855) were key landmarks in the evolution of this literary biography, and indeed in the history of Russian biography more generally.[18] As Nathaniel Knight shows in his article for this volume, other professionals, such as scholars, were also eager to use and adapt

---

[13] Jones, 'Biography'; Makolkin, 'Probing the Origins'; Dmitri Kalugin, 'Soviet Theories of Biography and the Aesthetics of Personality', *Biography*, 38, 2015, 3, pp. 343–62.

[14] Derek Offord, 'Lichnost': Notions of Individual Identity', in Catriona Kelly and David Shepherd (eds), *Constructing Russian Culture in the Age of Revolution, 1881–1940*, Oxford, 1998, pp. 13–25; Nikolai Plotnikov, 'Ot "individual'nosti" k "identichnosti" (istoriia poniatii personal'nosti v russkoi kul'ture)', *Novoe literaturnoe obozrenie*, 91, 2008, pp. 64–83; Hellbeck and Heller, *Autobiographical Practices*.

[15] Kalugin, 'Iskusstvo biografii', and 'Soviet Theories'; Dubin, 'Biografiia'.

[16] Offord, 'Lichnost''; Anatoly Pinsky, 'The Origins of Post-Stalin Individuality: Aleksandr Tvardovskii and the Evolution of 1930s Soviet Romanticism,' *Russian Review*, 76, July 2017, 3, pp. 458–83.

[17] Lotman, 'Literaturnaia biografiia'.

[18] For analyses of these texts, see Zhukov, *Biografiia biografii*.

biographical form to articulate their emergent professional identities in this period. More generally, intelligentsia biographies of the time were a crucial testing ground for new ideas of *lichnost'*, reflecting and fostering the development of potentially radical notions of autonomy and agency.[19]

Akin to the rapid evolution of the Russian novel, many of the institutions in biography that had taken several centuries to form in Western Europe emerged in a few short decades in the mid- to late-nineteenth century. A market for biography quickly formed, and its mass, cross-class appeal became swiftly apparent. Publishers spurred fandom by creating new biographical series, most notably 'The Lives of Remarkable People' (LRP), founded in 1890 under the editorship of Florentii Pavlenkov (see article by Ludmilla Trigos and Carol Ueland, and on the later Soviet reincarnation of the series, the article by Polly Jones). Various sub-genres of biography began to thrive, with Dmitrii Merezhkovskii making a notable contribution to the broader development of the *biographie romancée*, though documentary biography remained by far the most common type.[20]

Biography also began to play a key role in the key mid- to late nineteenth-century project of articulation of Russian national identity, echoing processes of nation-building through biography (especially biographical dictionaries and collective biographies) in Western Europe and America of the same period.[21] As in other cultures, this emergent biographical canon of great Russian men often obscured as much as it revealed about the history of the nation. To take one example (analysed in this issue by Ben Eklof and Tatiana Saburova), the biographies of a whole generation of revolutionaries — the 'populists' of the 1870s and 1880s — emerged into the public eye only after a long delay of several decades. By the time that they did, however, this collective project of remembrance and generational identity was already starting to fall out of step with the emergent state narrative of the pre-Revolutionary period.

This issue's Stalinist and post-Stalinist case studies, of Stalinist biographical investigation (by Jochen Hellbeck) and post-war Bolshevik biography (by Polly Jones), illustrate that interest in biography did

---

[19] Kalugin, 'Iskusstvo biografii'; Ginzburg, *On Psychological Prose*; Heller and Hellbeck, *Autobiographical Practices*.

[20] Temira Pachmuss, *D. S. Merezhkovsky in Exile: The Master of the Genre of Biographie Romancée*, New York, 1990.

[21] Keith Thomas, *Changing Conceptions of National Biography: The Oxford DNB in Historical Perspective*, Cambridge, 2005; Ian Donaldson, 'National Biography and the Arts of Memory: From Thomas Fuller to Colin Matthew', in France and St Clair, *Mapping Lives*, pp. 67–82; Parke, *Biography*, pp. 111–24.

not disappear after the Revolution. After a brief but intensive period of attempted reinvention of the genre by formalist and other avant-garde literary critics (analysed in Angela Brintlinger's article), published biographies of the Stalin era became predominantly hagiographic and often lacked a sense of personality.[22] Despite the dashing of the radical hopes of the 1920s and this impoverishment of the form under Stalin, biography nonetheless remained intensely important to the Soviet regime. Life narratives of ordinary citizens and Soviet heroes were assigned crucial roles in propaganda and local party work.[23] As such, they endured heavy interference in both content and form, but also enjoyed a prominence and prestige that may seem paradoxical given the communal orientation of Marxist-Leninist ideology; indeed, histories of biography often assume that the form thrives in democracies but cannot exist in any meaningful way in a 'totalitarian' system.[24] However, this Stalinist *and* post-Stalinist obsession with biography, as several articles in this issue contend, makes sense in the context of the regime's incessant attempts to transform individual citizens into exemplary Soviet subjects.[25]

The Uses of Biography in Russia
When Maksim Gor'kii restarted the LRP series, he explicitly described biographies of the 'remarkable' as a key guide to life: 'our goal,' he wrote to Romain Rolland in 1918, 'is to inculcate in young people love and faith in life. We need to teach people heroism.' The series, which continued to be framed quite explicitly in these edificatory terms, went on to recruit a number of the most celebrated Western European biographers, including

[22] Katerina Clark, *The Soviet Novel: History as Ritual*, 3rd edn, Bloomington, IN, 2000; Claude Pennetier and Bernard Pudal, 'Stalinism: Workers' Cult and Cult of Leaders', *Twentieth Century Communism*, 1, 2009, 1, pp. 20–29.
[23] Jochen Hellbeck, 'Galaxy of Black Stars: The Power of Soviet Biography', *American Historical Review*, 114, June 2009, 3, pp. 615–24; Igal Halfin, 'From Darkness To Light: Student Communist Autobiography During NEP', *Jahrbücher für Geschichte Osteuropas*, 45, 1997, 2, pp. 210–36; Igal Halfin, *Terror in My Soul: Communist Autobiographies on Trial*, Cambridge, MA and London, 2003.
[24] Madelénat argues that a 'totalitarian' system, such as the Soviet state, used biography in a different way, for disinformation and active falsification of the past, than liberal political systems (*La Biographie*, p. 188). See also, Josephson, 'Historians and Mythmakers'; Hamilton, *Biography*.
[25] This apparent paradox is analysed in Hellbeck, 'Galaxy of Black Stars', and id. *Revolution on My Mind: Writing a Diary under Stalin*, Cambridge, MA and London, 2006. Eastern European analyses include Catherine Epstein, 'The Politics of Biography: The Case of East German Old Communists', *Daedalus*, 128, 1999, 2, pp. 1–30; Josie McLellan, 'The Politics of Communist Biography: Alfred Kantorowicz and the Spanish Civil War', *German History*, 22, 2004, 4, pp. 536–62.

André Maurois, Stefan Zweig and Irving Stone. The fact that the series was cosmopolitan both at the moment of its foundation and in this ongoing recruitment of authors serves as a reminder that the use of biography for education and edification was far from exclusive to the Soviet context; rather, it may be seen as typical of the genre, and had by no means been eliminated by the twentieth century.[26]

Indeed, analysts of biography have often expressed frustration that the genre may never fully disentangle itself from its roots in celebration and commemoration, or from the assumption that it should somehow be socially or culturally 'useful'.[27] In 1954, well after his significant contribution to the 'new biography' in England, Harold Nicolson diagnosed a number of lingering 'contaminations' of the genre, notably the pressure on biography to be commemorative or didactic.[28] This suspicion of biography's significant extra-textual functions was one of the key reasons that it was not viewed as a branch of literature for most of its history (another, of course, was the genre's persistent wariness of departing from factual evidence).[29]

The unusually intense pace of social and political change in nineteenth- and twentieth-century Russia meant that the uses of biography changed repeatedly (sometimes polemically) during the period, although its fundamental use for the study of 'remarkable' lives endured throughout. From what has been said already, it is evident that biography fulfilled multiple functions for the imperial and Soviet state, from the education and 'subjectivization' of citizens, to the delineation of a canon of 'remarkable' historical actors and — related to both these goals — the articulation of Russian and Soviet identities at a time when they were in considerable flux.

Yet our authors also explore the ways in which biography was deployed to fulfil agendas different from — and sometimes, in opposition to — those

---

[26] André Maurois (in Maurois, *Aspects of Biography*) offers a complex combination of 'new biography' principles and an unstinting belief in biography's capacity for moral improvement through emulation of heroes: 'certainly it is a wholly admirable thing to put lofty examples before men, and especially young men but they will not strive to imitate them unless these models are true to life', p. 23.

[27] On biography's 'uses', see Edwin Paxton Hood, *The Uses of Biography: Romantic, Philosophic, and Didactic*, London, 1852; France and St Clair, *Mapping Lives*. See also Josephson, 'Historians and Mythmakers'.

[28] Nicolson, 'Practice of Biography'.

[29] Nadel, *Biography* and Hoberman, *Modernising Lives*, both call for biography to be read as literature. Yet even such a distinguished and prolific analyst of biographical form as Leon Edel repeatedly warned biographers to borrow from fiction, but not lapse into it (or, put differently, to produce at most novelistic, not novelized, texts): Leon Edel, *Writing Lives: Principia Biographica*, New York and London, 1987; Leon Edel, *Literary Biography: The Alexander Lectures, 1955–56*, London, 1957.

of the state. The articles by Trigos and Ueland, and by Saburova and Eklof, both dramatize biographers' and publishers' attempts to grant the 'right to biography' to figures outside the canon of the time. The eclecticism of Pavlenkov's LRP — which endures to this day in the post-Soviet series — was partly the result of his cosmopolitanism and impressive breadth of learning, which his series was intended to disseminate to the newly literate masses. However, as Trigos and Ueland show, the choice of subjects and *raznochintsy* authors for the series was subtly political, reflecting the publisher's long-term and often controversial leftist sympathies. Pavlenkov was at once an establishment figure and an individual close to the margins; this study of LRP's earliest incarnation offers much insight into this biographical publisher's own complex biography. A similar, though more focused, attempt to 'smuggle' a personal agenda into biographical publishing can be traced in Eklof and Saburova's study of populist biographies. While Vera Figner was, for a time at least, a canonical figure with a clear 'right' to a biography, she had to coax her lesser-known colleagues, such as Nikolai Charushin, to write their biographies, and persuade Soviet publishers to publish them. Her populist colleagues came to see biography as a way to consolidate the collective memory of their movement and generation, an impulse that became more urgent given their long prohibition in the late imperial period and the suspicion that came to surround them not long after the Revolution.

These kinds of struggles played out on an ever more uneven field as the Soviet monopoly on publishing tightened, and the criteria for biographical narrative firmed up (though remaining subject to periodic bouts of anxiety and revision). Jones's study of the particularly sensitive realm of Bolshevik biography reveals the careful editing and tight censorship surrounding the state's most elevated heroes, while Hellbeck demonstrates that even Soviet biographies that were never intended for public circulation — such as narratives of World War Two suffering gathered from citizens by various state commissions — were produced in a controlled discursive environment (albeit one sometimes punctured by raw trauma).

Publishing biographies was, of course, not always, or not only, a political act; it was also, increasingly, a sound commercial decision. Biography's popularity in today's book market has often been noted, and its astronomical growth shows no signs of stopping.[30] The case studies

[30] Nadel, *Biography*, notes it is the most popular non-fictional genre in Western markets. Lucy Riall similarly points to the immense popularity of biography, and the conservatism of a great deal of this commercial biography, especially of political figures. Lucy Riall, 'The Shallow End of History? The Substance and Future of Political Biography',

here offer insight into an earlier period of Russian biographical production, when economic capital and cultural capital jostled more evenly. Some of the biographies in question were evidently produced with no thought of turning a profit: Nathaniel Knight's study of scholarly biographies emphasizes that they were difficult to read, even for the highly specialist audience for whom they were intended, but that was partly their point, inasmuch as their erudition advertised the skills of the profession. Some of the experiments in literary biography analysed by Angela Brintlinger were also never intended (or suitable) for mass consumption, though the works of Tynianov were amongst the most popular and best-selling biographies of the 1920s.

On the other hand, LRP, as analysed by Ueland and Trigos and by Jones, was a publishing phenomenon in all three of its incarnations: late imperial, Soviet and post-Soviet. Pavlenkov, as Ueland and Trigos argue, deserves considerably more attention not only as one of the first mass publishers of biographies, but also as one of the genre's pioneering entrepreneurs, who found a way to produce and sell huge print-runs of accessible biographical texts, hooking many readers on the series for life. The lasting contribution of LRP to the importance of series in Soviet and post-Soviet Russian reading practices cannot be overstated.[31] Jones's comparative study of LRP and Politizdat reveals that the extensive post-Stalinist changes to their Bolshevik biographies were driven fundamentally by concerns about popularity and sales: the failure of biographies to appeal to a mass audience meant not only a depletion of propaganda efficacy, but also wastage of state money in producing books that failed to sell (which, given Soviet methods of allocating print-run budgets, also meant that other, potentially more profitable texts had lost out too).

Theory and Practice of Russian Biographical Writing
Although biography has been 'used' in all the above ways throughout its existence, often attracting suspicion for pursuing (or being deployed for) aims other than the dispassionate investigation of the human personality, it has nonetheless attracted growing critical attention and aesthetic analysis, especially since the 1960s.[32] Earlier, the first major modern

---

The Journal of Interdisciplinary History, 40, 2010, 3, pp. 375–97. On the post-Soviet market for biography, see Bulkina, 'The Lives of Remarkable People'.

[31] Stephen Lovell, *The Russian Reading Revolution: Print Culture in the Soviet and Post-Soviet Eras*, Basingstoke, 2000.

[32] Particularly striking is the increase in references to 'art' and 'form' in titles of studies of biography from the 1950s onwards. See Nadel, *Biography*; Clifford, *Biography as an Art*;

intervention in the form — the Europe-wide attempts to articulate the principles of a radically 'new biography' after World War One — was largely motivated by the desire to liberate biography from its 'use' as a guide to human behaviour or a source of national pride, and to shift its purpose to that of creating vivid, aesthetically sophisticated portraits; the increased attention to inner life propelled an unprecedented borrowing of methods from fiction.[33] More recently, the very hybridity of biography has made its delicate, sometimes fraught combinations of history and literature, its 'strange amalgam of science and art', increasingly interesting as the notions of strict generic boundaries and positivist truth claims seem ever more antiquated.[34]

The case studies in this issue illustrate Russian biography's distinctive, if under-appreciated, contribution to the broader development of modern biographical theory and form. Angela Brintlinger's analysis of the intense biographical debates and daring biographical experiments of the first decade after the Revolution shows that critics such as Eikhenbaum, Tynianov and Vinokur were engaged in discussions as intense as those that attended the emergence of a 'new biography' in 1920s Britain, France and Germany. Indeed post-Revolutionary iconoclasm and experimentation, and the wholesale rethinking of social and aesthetic categories in the early Bolshevik years, made the Russian discussions perhaps more urgent and far-reaching. Brintlinger immerses us in a time pregnant with possibility, when the future of biography — and, indeed, its imagined past — was thrown open to radical reimagination. In this febrile atmosphere, some biographers pushed biography towards fiction and even fantasy, much as Strachey, Woolf and Nicolson were attempting in England at the time. But others, perhaps the majority, attempted to forge a more direct, unmediated connection to biographical 'fact' and draw life writing closer to real life, seeking revolutionary new formulations of the relationship between everyday life (*byt*), history and the individual (*lichnost'*).

This latter current of post-Revolutionary biographical practice reflected, most obviously, the broader documentary turn of the 1920s, which Hellbeck argues remained in the later attempt to generate reams of documentary evidence about wartime lives.[35] Yet it also linked back to a longer tradition

---

Kendall, *Art of Biography*.

[33] Marcus, *Auto/Biographical Discourses*, and *Dreams of Modernity*; Hoberman, *Modernising Lives*.

[34] Clifford, *Biography as an Art* (quotation p. ix); Jacobs, *Truth to Life*; Michael Lackey, *The American Biographical Novel*, London, 2016.

[35] Elizabeth Astrid Papazian, *Manufacturing Truth: The Documentary Moment in Early*

of biography as documentary compilation, which can be traced in Russian practice as well as the broader history of the genre. Biography's tendency towards inelegant compilation of evidence — in the Boswellian vein — was one of the major targets of critics such as Strachey and Maurois in the 1920s. However, the 'paralysis' of biographers, and the 'cluttering' of their texts, by documents without due consideration for aesthetic arrangement featured just as prominently in Western biographical criticism from the 1950s to the 1980s.[36] Nathaniel Knight's study of nineteenth-century scholarly biographies identifies compilation of documents as the key feature of this sub-genre, but argues that scholars' biographers never in fact intended to capture their personality, but rather aimed to create a monument to assiduous research and to fashion a text-as-archive for future generations of the profession to mine: in the case of Nikolai Barsukov's twenty-two-volume 'biography' of Mikhail Petrovich Pogodin, a truly forbidding one that amply merits the use of Leon Edel's term, the '*omnium gatherum* life'.[37] Brintlinger's study of the myriad strands of post-Revolutionary biographical thought suggests that this mentality was by no means abandoned; indeed, she draws attention to the preponderance of unmediated documentary material in 1920s biographies by Veresaev, Feider and others.

More broadly, the case studies in this issue suggest that the biographer's art — and indeed, his very identity as a creative personality — was often overlooked, primarily due to the historical and educational functions that biography was called upon to fulfil.[38] The fact that populist revolutionaries themselves became the main biographers of the movement is one of several Soviet-era examples of state marginalization fuelling a 'historical turn' amongst tight-knit communities.[39] Eklof and Saburova argue that the consequence of this collaboration was an effacement of authorial *and* textual individuality: so important was the imperative to preserve, and

Soviet Culture, DeKalb, IL, 2009.

[36] Edel, *Writing Lives*, p. 14; Kendall, *Art of Biography*, p. 121 ('for the art of biography, precariously perched between the demand of fact and the hope of illumination, this ambience of mass attack on mass materials, of fact triumphant, has already posed, as we shall see, the threat of paralysis'); Nadel, *Biography*.

[37] Edel, *Writing Lives*, p. 98.

[38] Lotman, 'Literaturnaia biografiia' offers a fascinating analysis of the oscillations between biographers' anonymity and celebrity in different periods. Nadel, *Biography*, also argues that the biographer has not generally been appreciated as a professional, let alone a creative, writer.

[39] Denis Kozlov, 'The Historical Turn in Late Soviet Culture: Retrospectivism, Factography, Doubt, 1953–91', *Kritika: Explorations in Russian and Eurasian History*, 2, 2001, 3, pp. 577–600.

indeed mythologize, the memory of the movement that authors freely borrowed tropes from one another's texts, generating a collective (auto) biography rather than an individual one. Many of the biographers in Pavlenkov's pre-Revolutionary biographical series were historians in a more strictly professional sense. They saw their mission as the careful, lucid presentation of lives whose details were not yet familiar to the mass readership; their texts' biographical form drew very little attention, either from their own authors or the texts' critics. As biography raced towards ever greater popularity in the late nineteenth century, several of the series' authors became full-time biographers, their careers solidified by the potentially (though not actually) infinite expansion of the serial form and the public's constant thirst for life stories. It was only in the late socialist and post-Soviet period, though, that LRP began to produce biographies that merited serious aesthetic analysis, although as Jones argues, the seemingly conservative Politizdat publishing house had pioneered literary, and even fictional, techniques earlier.[40]

It was also historians, led by the distinguished historian Isaak Mints, who organized the vast archive of World War Two biographies analysed in Jochen Hellbeck's article; Hellbeck shows how these oral historians *avant la lettre* conscientiously and professionally gathered detailed testimony. Yet they also limited the boundaries of biographical discourse by posing questions, about collaboration or trauma for instance, in particular ways that were intended to reconstruct and consolidate post-war Soviet identities rather than allowing war-time biographies to spiral out of control.

Despite the prevalence of historical concerns and historical writers, literary writers and literary technique made an important contribution to Russian biography in both the nineteenth and twentieth centuries, albeit perhaps not as significant as that of modernist and later postmodernist literary writers in the West. In the mid-nineteenth century, it was above all literary biography, often written by literary colleagues of the subject, that first pushed the genre to public attention, although without making major formal breakthroughs. In the post-Revolutionary decade analysed by Brintlinger, the constellation of literary critics and literary writers trained in Vengerov's literary seminar, briefly revitalized biography and sketched out a number of highly innovative paths for the genre, including a convergence with the novel or even an appropriation of the genre. For Eikhenbaum,

[40] Zhukov, *Biografiia biografii* offers detailed analysis of several later LRP texts, including celebrated biographies by Leonid Grossman. For close analysis of multiple LRP literary biographies, see the special forum on the series in *Slavic & East European Journal*, 60, 2016.

the principal theorist of this potential new relationship between novel and biography, the realization of these ambitious theories proved difficult. However, the works of his contemporary Tynianov traversed effortlessly the full spectrum of the genre, from strictly documentary texts to highly experimental fantasies.

It is generally assumed that this kind of textual experimentation ceased with the advent of Stalinism and Socialist Realism, even though biography publication continued apace. However, Jones argues that Soviet publishers and propagandists were all too aware in the post-war period of Bolshevik biography's failure to evoke personality (and thus its failure to attract or captivate readers), and increasingly called for a rethinking of biographical approaches. They came to view literary expertise and even fictionalization as the key solution to the problem. This study of late Stalinist and post-Stalinist biographies of Bolsheviks argues that their two main publishers were in their own way, and for their own pragmatic aims, just as preoccupied with the problems of personality and narrative form as Western biographical criticism of the same period.

In 1973, one of Molodaia gvardiia's most senior biography editors, Sergei Semanov, observed to literary colleagues at a Soviet roundtable that there was an 'undoubted boom in the distribution of biographical literature. This boom needs thinking through, deep analysis'.[41] The late socialist years indeed witnessed an explosion of biographies that was at least the equal of the 'rampant' Western 'boom' of biography that critics really started to notice from the 1960s onwards; moreover, the late Soviet adoption of literary techniques often ran ahead of the slow evolution of the biographical novel, and biographical experimentation more generally, in Western Europe and America (the experimentation described in Jones's article was one of the first signs of this literary turn).[42] During the last Soviet decades, a rich debate about biography as a genre — and, unavoidably, about the nature of

---

[41] 'Zhizn' i deiatelnost'. Nereshennye problemy biograficheskogo zhanra', *Voprosy Literatury*, 1973, pp. 16–93.

[42] Hamilton, 'Biography, p. 191; Kendall, *Art of Biography*, p. 115. On the slow rise of the Western biographical novel, see Michael Lackey, 'The Rise of the Biographical Novel and the Fall of the Historical Novel', *A/b: Auto/Biography Studies*, 31, 2016, 1, pp. 33–58; Irving Stone, 'The Biographical Novel', in Gertrude Clarke Whittall, Poetry and Literature Fund (eds), *Three Views of the Novel*, Folcroft, 1977 (1957); Carl Bode, 'The Buxom Biographies', *College English*, 16, 1955, 5, pp. 265–69. On biographical experimentation more broadly, see Kendall, *Art of Biography*, p. 115; Sally Cline, *Life Writing: A Writers' and Artists' Companion: Writing Biography, Autobiography and Memoir*, London, 2013; Lackey, *American Biographical Novel*; Hamilton, *Biography*; Kendall, *Art of Biography*; Jacobs, *Truth to Life*.

personality and individual identity — unfolded across Soviet media and in the literary and historical professions.[43]

One of the origins of this late socialist biographical obsession was the Soviet authorities' early appreciation for the unique propaganda potential of biography and the correspondingly close attention that they paid to producing and policing its texts. Another factor was the increasing expertise, skill and professionalization of biographers themselves, as its social utility and cultural popularity continued to grow and granted them relatively secure careers. One of the key outcomes of this Soviet-era rise in biography consumption is the post-Soviet craze for life stories, reflected in the current proliferation of biographical books (including the still wildly popular LRP series), magazines and TV programmes, a phenomenon that still awaits its historian.

---

[43] Examples of this growth of critical attention to biography in late socialism are legion, but some examples include the roundtable on the genre, 'Zhizn' i deiatelnost''. Zhukov, *Biografiia biografii*; Iurii Lotman, 'Biografiia zhivoe litso', *Novyi Mir*, 10, 1985, pp. 228–36, argues explicitly for the 'sense of the individual' to be captured in unique biographical forms. Most notably perhaps, the 1966 founding of an almanac, *Prometei*, as an offshoot of LRP, offered more than two decades of critical analysis of the genre and many experiments with the form.

1

Biography as Archive:
Writing the Lives of Scholars in Imperial Russia

NATHANIEL KNIGHT

HISTORIANS of nineteenth-century Russian intellectual life cannot delve far into their research without encountering Nikolai Barsukov's monumental biography of Mikhail Pogodin. Stretching over twenty-two dense volumes, Barsukov's work offers far more than its title promises — an account of the life and work of the Moscow historian. A middling scholar known for his reactionary views and inflated ego, Pogodin would hardly seem to merit such a feat of biographical research.[1] Yet scholars consider Barsukov's work indispensable: the biography overshadows its own subject. In his introduction, Barsukov admits that he had not actually wanted to write about Pogodin initially — there were other scholars who elicited his admiration and curiosity more deeply. When asked whether he would consider writing a biography based on the historian's voluminous personal papers, Barsukov had hesitated. He was ultimately convinced to take on the project by the realization that Pogodin had been tightly connected with key figures in Russian scholarly and literary circles for almost half a century. He could not tell the full story of Pogodin's life without touching on the life and work of the scholars he most admired.[2] The result was a work that went beyond the bounds of ordinary biography to encompass an entire era.

Barsukov's ability to encapsulate such a broad swathe of the intellectual life surrounding Pogodin was predicated on a distinctive approach to sources and narrative. Rather than constructing his own synthetic narrative, Barsukov builds his account directly from the sources through

---

[1] For a characterization of Pogodin as a proponent of 'official nationality', see Nicholas Riasanovsky, *Nicholas I and Official Nationality in Russia, 1825–1855*, Berkeley, CA, 1959. A. G. Tartakovskii suggests, with some justification, that a reappraisal of Pogodin's image may in fact be overdue. See his *Russkaia memuaristika i istoricheskoe sosnanie*, Moscow, 1997, p. 107.

[2] Nikolai Barsukov, *Zhizn' i trudy M. P. Pogodina*, 22 vols, St Petersburg, 1888–1910, 1, pp. iii–vii. The specific individuals Barsukov mentions are the Metropolitan Filaret, Prince P. A. Viazemskii and the archeographer P. M. Stroev.

extended excerpts from the primary texts — letters, diaries, articles and literary works. The result is something like a curated archive, a structured succession of documents that opens up a world of ideas, associations and events. Barsukov's voice as author is subdued and restrained. He sets the stage, provides the background, choreographs transitions to the next scene, but it is the documents themselves that tell the story.

Few of Barsukov's contemporaries were able to match his feat of scholarly endurance, but Barsukov's approach to sources and narrative was not unique. Other biographies of scholars written in the second half of the nineteenth century show similar qualities. Is it possible, therefore, to speak of a distinct genre of biography written by, for, and about scholars? If so, what would be its defining features? These are the questions this article sets out to explore. To approach the problem, I have examined a series of biographies of scholars in fields ranging from history to oriental studies, literary criticism, philosophy and statistics published in the period from the 1850s to the years just before the outbreak of World War One.[3] The biographies were selected in part with the goal of attaining a representative sample of scholars from a variety of fields active across a broad chronological period. Works that illustrate a range of biographical approaches and methodologies were also included, as were landmark works that shaped the development of the biographical tradition in Russia and served as models for subsequent writers. In examining these biographies, I have focused on four specific points: the authors' use of source materials; style and structure of the biographical narrative; views of personality and the inner life of the individual; and the degree to which the authors expressed an independent critical perspective. While this analysis reveals a wide range of characteristics and approaches, certain common patterns

---

[3] In addition to Barsukov's biography of Pogodin, the works examined include E. F. Shmurlo, *Metropolit Evgenii kak uchenyi: Rannie gody zhizni*, St Petersburg, 1888; N. K. Kozmin, *Nikolai Ivanovich Nadezhdin: Zhizn' i nauchno-literaturnaia deiatel'nost*, St Petersburg, 1912; N. N. Veselovskii, *Vasilii Vasil'evich Grigor'ev po ego pis'mam i trudam: 1816–1881*, St Petersburg, 1887; V. V. Grigor'ev, *Zhizn' i trudy P. S. Savel'eva*, St Petersburg, 1861; A. N. Pypin, *Belinskii: ego zhizn' i perepiska*, 2nd edn, St Petersburg, 1908; V. V. Grigor'ev, 'T. N. Granovskii do ego professorstva v Moskve', *Russkaia beseda*, kn. 3, ot. 5, 1856, pp. 17–46; kn. 4, ot. 5, pp. 1–57; M. P. Pogodin, *Nikolai Mikhailovich Karamzin po ego sochineniiam, pis'mam, i otzyvam sovremennikov*, 2 vols, Moscow, 1866; P. P. Pekarskii, 'O zhizni i uchenykh trudakh akademika Konstantina Ivanovicha Arsen'eva', in *Sbornik otdeleniia russkogo iazyka i slovesnosti Imperatorskogo Akademii Nauk*, vol. 9, 1872, pp. 1–78; N. A. Popov, *V. N. Tatishchev i ego vremia: epizod iz istoii gosudarstvennoi, obshchestvennoi i chastnoi zhizni v Rossii, pervoi poloviny proshedshego stoletiia*, Moscow, 1861; V. I. Lamanskii, *Mikhail Vasil'evich Lomonosov: Biograficheskii ocherk*, St Petersburg, 1864.

were evident, supporting my view of the lives of scholars as a distinctive genre of biographical writing.

The term 'scholarly biography' can be understood to encompass two interrelated meanings: on the one hand biography of and about scholars, and on the other biographies written using scholarly methods and approaches. Both of these dimensions are pertinent to this study. As scholarly biographers drew on their critical skills and knowledge of their fields to depict the lives of their predecessors, they contributed to the establishment of scholarship as a personal vocation and to the creation of disciplinary traditions. In the first decades of the nineteenth century, when the university system was just emerging and definitions of scholarly fields remained ambiguous it was not always clear who could be considered a scholar and under what circumstances. Was the Metropolitan Evgenii Bolkhovitinov first and foremost a cleric who pursued scholarship as an amateur pastime, or was scholarship his true vocation undertaken under the cover of ordination? Was Nikolai Nadezhdin primarily a scholar, a journalist, a bureaucrat or all of the above? Biographies helped to trim back this ambiguity, casting into sharper relief the scholarly identities of their subjects by justifying their 'right to a life' through their contributions to the creation of knowledge within their fields. In the process biographies modelled career trajectories showing how scholars were formed through education and hard work, how research interests coalesced, how professional success and advancement was achieved, how setbacks were overcome. At a time when disciplinary identities had only recently started to crystallize, biographies of scholars provided a grounding in the past, formative moments and foundational figures to whose intellectual legacy readers were the heirs.

The particular tasks confronting biographers of scholars gave rise to a distinctive approach that set these works apart from the burgeoning memoir literature and other developing forms of biographical writing. In contrast to the canonical intelligentsia biography with its focus on the realization of personality (*lichnost'*) as an end in itself, scholarly biographies concentrated less on the internal life of the subject and the formation of the individual.[4] Rather, they direct the reader's attention toward the development of knowledge and insight, the attainment of professional recognition, the production of major works — achievements

---

[4] On the role of personality in nineteenth-century Russian biography, see D. Ia. Kalugin, 'Iskusstvo biografii: izobrazhenie lichnosti i ee opravdanie v russkikh zhizneopisaniiakh serediny XIX veka', *Novoe literaturnoe obozrenie*, 91, 2008, pp. 84–113.

that justified the subject's status as a person of note within a disciplinary tradition.

Biography in Russia
Biographical writing would not have been unfamiliar to Russian readers in the first half of the nineteenth century. Several literary forms had introduced readers to the practice of 'life description' (*zhizneopisanie*). The first was the tradition of Orthodox saints' lives, to which educated Russians were exposed from an early age. Even such seemingly secular and Westernized intellectuals as Alexander Herzen and Mikhail Bakunin attested to the reading of saints' lives as a formative influence.[5] Russian readers were also familiar with the biographical legacy of classical antiquity exemplified by Plutarch, Livy, Tacitus, Suetonius and Nepos, most of whose works had been published in Russian by the first decades of the nineteenth century.[6] Those Russians who had the means or the occasion to travel abroad may well have also encountered contemporary biographical literature — landmark works like Boswell's *Life of Johnson* and Condorcet's *Life of Voltaire*, which helped to make biography a thriving enterprise by the start of the nineteenth century.[7] To this might be added the tradition of Russian memoir writing which was a well-established, if not widespread, genre by the end of the eighteenth century.[8]

Given the general familiarity with the idea of biographical writing, it is striking how little this genre of literary activity was practised in actuality before the 1850s.[9] Apart from a few encyclopaedic collections of the lives

---

[5] Margaret Ziolkowski, *Hagiography and Modern Russian Literature*, Princeton, NJ, 1988, pp. 18–19.
[6] Plutarch's 'Lives', for example, appeared in Russian in 1810 under the title, *Plutarkhovy sravnitel'nye zhizneopisaniia slavnykh muzhei*. Cornelius Nepos's *Excellentium Imperatorum Vitae* was published as early as 1748 under the title, *Korneliia Nepota Zhitiia slavnykh Generalov v pol'zu iunoshestva*. Updated translations appeared in 1808 and 1816. Catherine the Great was evidently disturbed by Tacitus's descriptions of Roman tyrants and rejected Denis Fonvizin's proposed translation, but by 1803 a Russian edition had appeared. See Andrew Kahn, 'Readings of Imperial Rome from Lomonosov to Pushkin', *Slavic Review*, 52, 1993, 4, pp. 745–68.
[7] For a good overview of British biography in the nineteenth century, see Juliette Atkinson, *Victorian Biography Reconsidered: A Study of Nineteenth-Century 'Hidden' Lives*, Oxford, 2010.
[8] On the tradition of memoir writing, see A. G. Tartakovskii, *Russkaia memuaristika: XVIII–pervoi poloviny XIX v*, Moscow, 1991.
[9] On Russian biography in the eighteenth century, see W. Gareth Jones, 'Biography in Eighteenth-Century Russia', *Oxford Slavonic Papers*, 22, Oxford, 1989, pp. 58–81. Of the works listed in Jones's bibliography of biographical works printed in Russia before 1800, the vast majority are translated works. The lack of interest applies not only to the

of noteworthy individuals, substantial biographical works are almost entirely absent, particularly in the period prior to 1820.[10] In 1808, Mikhail Kachenovskii noted in his journal, *Vestnik Evropy*, the lack of works that might shed light on the lives of 'eminent people of the eighteenth century'. Foreign sources, he insisted, could not be trusted while 'our own historical accounts' either did not exist or were completely unknown.[11] The complaint that Russians were insufficiently attentive to the lives of their forefathers was a common refrain within Pushkin's circle of friends in the 1820s and 1830s. In a note in the first book of *Evgenii Onegin*, written in 1825, Pushkin declared his intention to write a complete biography of his illustrious ancestor Abram Gannibal. In Russia, he wrote, 'where the memory of noteworthy people soon disappears due to the lack of historical accounts, the strange life of Gannibal is known only through family legends'.[12] Ten

practice of biography in the early nineteenth century, but also to the historiography. With the exception of very recent work by Dmitrii Kalugin — the article cited above and his monograph, *Proza zhizni: russkie biografii XVIII–XIX veka*, St Petersburg, 2015 — I have found little in the way of comprehensive critical discussions of biography as a genre. Dmitrii Zhukov's *Biografiia biografii: razmyshlenie o zhanre*, Moscow, 1980 is a short impressionistic work, and cannot be considered a full treatment of the topic. Iurii Lotman's essay, 'Literaturnaia biografiia v istoriko-kul´turno kontekste (K tipologicheskomy sootnosheniiu teksta i lichnosti avtora)', in his *Izbrannye stat´i v trekh tomakh*, Tallinn, 1992, vol. 1, pp. 365–76, is a brilliant theoretical discussion of one aspect of autobiographical writing. A. G. Tartakovskii's works have provided much helpful information, but his interest in biographical writing is primarily in connection to the memoir literature. Likewise, P. A. Zaionchkovskii's well-known bibliography of biographical source materials extends only to memoirs and diaries. P. A. Zaionchkovskii, G. A. Glavatskikh, E. A. Akimova (eds), *Istoriia dorevoliutsonnoi Rossii v dnevnikakh i vospominaniiakh*, 5 vols, Moscow, 1976–1989. As far as I have been able to ascertain, there is no comprehensive bibliography of nineteenth-century Russian biographies. The closest equivalent, S. A. Vengarov's *Kritiko-biograficheskii slovar´ russkikh pisatelei i uchenykh (ot nachala russkoi obrazovannosti do nashikh dnei)*, 6 vols, St Petersburg, 1889–1904, while an ambitious and valuable endeavour, was never completed, and is not, strictly speaking, structured as a bibliography. In recent years the society 'Memorial' has sponsored a major biography project which resulted in an annual workshop and a substantial publication. See T. B. Pritykina (ed.), *Pravo na imia: Biografika XX veka. Cheteniia pamiati Veniamna Iofe: Izbrannoe. 2003–2012*, St Petersburg, 2013. Most of the works in this volume, however, focus on the twentieth century, particularly the history of the Gulag and dissident movement and none, as far as I can see, examine the history of biography as a genre over a broader historical time span.

[10] Most notably, N. I. Novikov's *Opyta istoricheskogo slovaria o rossiiskikh pisatelei*, St Petersburg, 1772, and D. N. Bantysh-Kamenskii's *Slovaria dostopamiatnykh liudei russkoi zemli*, 5 vols, Moscow, 1836–1847. The main exception to the overall trend is Radishchev's 'Zhitie Ushakova' (1789). See Jones, 'Biography in Eighteenth-Century Russia', pp. 67–70.

[11] Preface to 'Vypiska iz zhizni Kniazia Shakhovskogo', *Vestnik Evropy*, 17, October 1808, p. 11.

[12] A. S. Pushkin, *Polnoe sobranie sochinenii v desiati tomakh*, Moscow and Leningrad, 1949, vol. 5, pp. 513–14.

years later, reminiscing on his meeting with Griboedov in the Caucasus, he returned to the theme: 'What a pity that Griboebov did not leave memoirs! His friends might take up the cause of writing his biography, but here wonderful people disappear without leaving any trace of themselves. We are lazy and lacking in curiosity.'[13]

The first among Pushkin's friends to take up biography as a literary pursuit was Prince Petr Andreevich Viazemskii. In the early 1820s, Viazemskii was asked to write a short biographical portrait of his friend, the poet I. I. Dmitriev, to serve as the introduction to a new edition of his works. The endeavour was ultimately successful, but revealed in the process some of the challenges facing a writer of biography in an atmosphere of pervasive censorship. The initial draft, which touched on a number of controversial issues, could only appear in print after rigorous and extensive editing.[14] Nonetheless, Viazemskii's appetite for biography was whetted, and he soon threw himself into a second project on the late-eighteenth-century playwright, Denis Fonvizin. Initially Viazemskii had envisioned an article on Fonvizin, but in the autumn of 1830, confined to his family estate of Ostaf'evo by the cholera epidemic raging through the country, with his research materials and an excellent library at hand, Viazemskii set to work, and in a burst of inspiration produced a book-length biography, arguably the first of its kind in Russian literary history.[15] For reasons that remain obscure, however, Viazemskii was in no rush to see his book appear in print. Although it was given censorship approval in 1835, it was not published until 1848.

By the late 1840s, interest in biography had grown substantially. Memoirs began to appear with greater frequency both on the pages of 'thick journals' and as separate publications, and biographical essays,

---

[13] Ibid., vol. 6, p. 668.

[14] Karamzin, among others, warned Viazemskii about 'your wont [*okhota*] to play at Voltaire [*vol'terstvovat'*] and tweak a stone wall. Because of this the censor will never pass all that is good and very good'. 'Pis'ma N. M. Karamzina k kniaziu P. A. Viazemskomu (1810–1826)', *Starina i novizna: istoricheskii sbornik*, book 1 of 2, 1897, p. 121.

[15] Viazemskii makes precisely this claim in his introduction, referring to his book as 'just about the first attempt in Russia at something like biographical literature'. *Polnoe sobranie sochineniia Kniazia P. A. Viazemskogo t. 5, 1848: Fon-Vizin*, St Petersburg, 1880, p. vii. Tartakovskii concurs with Viazemskii's assertion calling the book 'the first monograph about a major Russian writer, and as the first study of the literary-social movement in Russia'. See *Russkaia memuaristika i istoricheskoe soznanie*, p. 97. M. I. Gillel'son in his biography of Viazemskii, places more emphasis on the Fonvizen biography as the first serious study of the history of eighteenth-century Russian theatrical comedy, but does not dispute its significance as a biography. See M. I. Gillel'son, *P. A. Viazenskii: zhizn' i tvorchestvo*, Leningrad, 1969, pp. 202–15.

while still not common, started to make an appearance. Much of the interest in biography was directed toward literature. Most notably, in 1849 Pushkin's widow granted permission for a new edition of the poet's works that would include a biographical sketch. The task was entrusted to the writer Pavel Annenkov, who took up the cause with such enthusiasm that the sketch expanded into a free-standing biography constituting the first volume of the new edition of Pushkin's works. Despite the modest title — 'Materials for the Biography of A. S. Pushkin' — Annenkov's work was a literary biography in the fullest sense. He looked with scepticism on 'those archaeologists and researchers who, having freed themselves from the labour of thought, replace it with the task of the simple collection of documents, identifying variants between texts [...] and other such preparatory work'. On the contrary, Annenkov aimed to 'generalize facts, draw from them definitions and, relying on their content, to arrive at positive conclusions'.[16] Annenkov's biography, which appeared in early 1855 just weeks before the death of Nicholas I, was influential not just with regard to its style, but also with regard to the practice of biographical research. In his efforts to assemble as much material as possible, Annenkov reached out to a wide range of individuals associated with Pushkin in the hope that they would share reminiscences and documents. Thus the biography of the great poet became a collaboration that served to heighten interest in the practice of biography and demonstrate how it could be undertaken.

The desire to preserve memory, to encapsulate in print the character and deeds of outstanding individuals, which began to be expressed in literary circles in the 1820s and 1830s, was present among scholars as well. The expansion of Russian universities and the reinvigoration of the Academy of Sciences under Sergei Uvarov brought together a critical mass of scholars and set in motion the establishment of academic schools, as charismatic teachers trained the generations of scholars who would succeed them. Yet when philologists, historians, geographers, statisticians and natural scientists, lacking, perhaps, the literary inclinations of a Viazemskii or Annenkov, took up the task of memorializing their mentors, they applied the outlook and methodologies of their scholarly fields, endowing their biographical narratives with a distinctive flavour.

Nikolai Karamzin represents a revealing transitional figure in this regard. Best known to posterity as the author of the monumental *History of the Russian State*, the first comprehensive narrative of Russian history,

[16] P. V. Annenkov, *Materialy dlia biografii A. S. Pushkina*, Moscow, 1984, pp. 14–15.

BIOGRAPHY AS ARCHIVE

Karamzin was also a seminal figure in Russian literary circles and an important poet and prose stylist in his own right. His name was among those most frequently mentioned by Pushkin and his friends in the 1830s as deserving of a biography. An early attempt to publish a collection of Karamzin's letters in 1837, however, fell afoul of censorship. The publication could not be permitted, the censorship committee declared, since some of the letters concerned 'persons of the Imperial house and certain state affairs', while others were related to 'many individuals of our time, who have only recently passed away, or are still alive'.[17] Under such restrictions, a biography was unthinkable. By the late 1840s, however, the atmosphere had changed, and discussions revived of the prospects for a biography of Karamzin. The individual who ultimately took up the challenge, however, was not one of the Karamzin's literary associates, but rather a historian, none other than Mikhail Pogodin.

It is not surprising that Pogodin would aspire to the position of Karamzin's biographer. Perhaps more than any of the historians of his time, Pogodin saw himself as an heir to Karamzin, pursuing the study of Russia's past in his tradition. Yet, the very aura of reverence which Pogodin cultivated toward Karamzin limited his options as a biographer. In the preface to the biography, he rejected outright the possibility of a strong narrative voice that would, in his view, place the subject of the biography in the shadow of the author. 'Karamzin', he wrote,

> represents such an elevated, unique and astonishing figure in the history of Russian life [...] that any admixture to his biography, whatever form it might take, would seem to me an inappropriate obstacle, an impermissible distraction. [...] And so, setting aside any thought of authorial pride, ignoring in advance the howls that will emanate from the opposing camp, I took it upon myself to seek out in the writings and letters of Karamzin, characteristic features expressing the essence of his nature. [...] I turned with my questions to his contemporaries, recalled everything I myself had heard and learned of since an early age, and in conveying the information attained, I concealed myself behind the scenes, behind the curtains, appearing on the stage only in cases of necessity for explanation and elaboration.[18]

In setting out his principles of biography, emphasizing an authorial voice restrained to the point of inaudibility and a historian's sensitivity

[17] Quoted in Tartakovskii, *Russkaia memuaristika i istoricheskoe soznanie*, p. 81.
[18] M. P. Pogodin, *Nikolai Mikhailovich Karamzin*, vol. 1, pp. i–ii.

to the primacy of the sources, Pogodin was setting an example for his own biographer, Nikolai Barsukov, whose methodology and goals were remarkably similar.

Sources: The Archeographic Biography
As the examples above suggest, assembling source materials posed a challenge for biographers of nineteenth-century scholars and literary figures. In most cases the biographies were written relatively soon after the death of their subjects. Source materials necessary for a detailed biographical narrative — letters, manuscripts, official documents, and so forth — were rarely accessible in well-organized archival collections. Barsukov's biography of Pogodin represents a best case scenario. Pogodin himself was scrupulous in preserving his correspondence and papers and passed to his heirs a massive personal archive that served as the foundation for the biography. Seeing the value of this collection, Pogodin's widow began to solicit a biographer and through intermediaries was directed to Barsukov. As a condition for accepting the assignment, Barsukov insisted that he be given possession of the complete archive until the work was finished. Basing himself at the country estate of his friend and benefactor Count S. D. Sheremetev, he put a team of assistants to work cataloguing the collection and writing out topical excerpts.[19] Assembling the book was largely a matter of arranging the excerpts, adding additional materials from printed sources and writing transitional passages.

Nikolai Kozmin, Nadezhdin's biographer, describes a scenario that was probably much more common: 'the fate of Nadezhdin's papers was no less sad [than that of Nadezhdin himself],' he wrote. 'Partly lost, partly rotted or burned, they were unknown to historians of literature.'[20] After his death in 1856, Nadezhdin's library and papers had been dumped in a cathedral basement where they remained abandoned to the forces of decay until the 1880s. Another part of the collection, in private hands in Nadezhdin's native Riazan', was in rapid danger of suffering a similar fate. If was only through protracted negotiations that Kozmin was able to gain access to the documents. Other biographers, such as Aleksander Pypin and E. F. Shmurlo, report a similar process of painstaking correspondence and negotiation in order to assemble the sources for their accounts. In all of these cases, despite the efforts of the biographers, significant gaps remained in the documentary record.

---

[19] Barsukov, *Zhizn' i trudy Pogodina*, vol. 1, pp. vi–vii.
[20] Kozmin, *Nikolai Ivanovich Nadezhdin*, p. vi.

The challenge of assembling documents contributed to a distinct sense of purpose among scholarly biographers. Rather than merely providing an entertaining and edifying account of the life of a great man, the biographers sought to make new material available to other scholars, drawing into the realm of intellectual scrutiny new facts and documents. In this regard, scholarly biography was not far removed from the archeographic enterprises that thrived in Russia throughout much of the nineteenth century. Interest in the discovery and collection of ancient documents, which had been developing in Russia since the early eighteenth century, was given official sanction in the 1830s with the establishment of an Archeographic Commission. The Commission along with its regional affiliates supported scholars throughout the empire as they scoured monastery libraries, government offices and noble estates in search of undiscovered historical texts shedding new light on Russia's past.[21] In addition to locating documents, scholars such as K. F. Kalaidovich, P. M. Stroev and A. Kh. Vostokov pioneered the scholarly publication of chronicles, laws, treatises and other historical texts. Pogodin was an active participant in the archeographic movement, assembling a formidable collection of manuscripts and books which he donated to the Imperial Public Library in St Petersburg.[22] Barsukov, in turn, had written a biography of Stroev before turning to Pogodin, and as a professional archivist had participated in major publications of historical sources. Other authors were tied to archeographic projects through their biographical subjects: Metropolitan Evgenii was a participant in the Rumiantsev circle, a seminal forum for archeographic research, and collaborated with Stroev in his final years. Even in cases where there was not a direct connection to the archeographic movement, scholarly biographers could not be unaware of the work of the archeographers and were undoubtedly touched by their sense of mission to expand the realm of knowledge by publishing previously hidden documents.

Narrative through Compilation
The imperative to bring to light new sources drew writers of scholarly biography toward a particular style of narration. Barsukov provides

---

[21] N. L. Rubinshtein, *Russkaia istoriografiia*, Moscow, 1941, pp. 212–22. On the earlier history of Russian archeography, see V. P. Kozlov, *Rossiiskaia arkheografiia kontsa XVIII–pervoi chetvert XIX v.*, Moscow, 1999.
[22] On Pogodin's connections with Stroev, see Barsukov, vol. 2, pp. 365–70 and *passim*. Pogodin's activities as a collector and publisher are briefly described in G. B. Mozhaeva, 'M. P. Pogodin', in *Istoriki Rossii: Biografii*, ed. A. A. Chernobaev, Moscow, 2001, p. 142.

the clearest illustration. His account consists of individual chapters, each roughly five to seven pages, exploring a particular theme within a set chronological framework. Chapter seventeen of volume seven, addressing relations between the Moscow Slavophiles and Westernizers in the early 1840s, is typical in its style of narration. Barsukov starts with Belinskii's letters showing the critic's disapproval of friendly relations between the Moscow Slavophiles and Westernizers. Turning to Pogodin, Barsukov discusses his relations with the Slavophiles and quotes diary entries documenting visits with the Aksakov family. Pogodin's diary also illustrates N. M. Iazykov's role as an additional point of contact with the Slavophiles. Discussion then turns to Stepan Shevyrev, whose letters show his more militant stance in polemicizing with the Westernizers.[23] Roughly 75 per cent of the chapter's 161 lines of text consist of direct quotations, and neighbouring chapters follow a similar pattern.

For a historian of Russian cultural and intellectual life, this is a treasure trove of useful information — all the more so since the volumes are thoroughly indexed, making it easy to locate the sections most relevant to particular topics. As a free-standing work of scholarship, however, Barsukov's approach has its drawbacks. The interpretive voice of the author, while not completely absent, is largely submerged under the weight of documentary evidence. To be sure, one can make inferences based on the choice of documents and the way in which they are presented, but a clear line of argumentation structuring the presentation is largely absent. As a result, there is a stream of consciousness quality to the narrative. Topics appear and disappear for little apparent reason depending on the documents available within a given time period. Barsukov presents the documentation roughly as it was produced: it is up to the reader to decide what it means.

Elements of Baruskov's narrative style can be found to varying degrees in other scholarly biographies. Nikolai Veselovskii, for one, employs a similar approach in his biography of the orientalist Vasilii Grigor´ev. Veselovskii maintains a restrained authorial voice and relies heavily on direct quotations extending at times over entire pages. Of the text in a sample chapter, 65 per cent consists of direct quotation.[24] Veselovskii's style may be connected to the context and the subject of his work. Grigor´ev was an outspoken and often controversial figure who left a rich epistolary legacy after his death in 1884. Rather than taking it upon himself

---

[23] Barsukov, *Zhizn´ i Trudy Pogodina*, 1893, vol. 7, pp. 107–12.
[24] Veselovskii, *V. V. Grigor´ev*, pp. 76–83.

to summarize and analyse Grigor'ev's opinions directly, it may have been easier for Veselovskii to let his subject present his views as much as possible in his own words. Veselovskii's reticence may have been accentuated by the fact that he was writing only a few years after Grigor'ev's death when many of his colleagues, students and family would have still been alive. A critical narrative casting judgment on Grigor'ev's ideas and actions may have alienated people upon whose support Veselovskii depended.

If Veselovskii had any doubts about his approach to Grigor'ev, however, he had the option of following Grigor'ev's own practice as a biographer. In 1860, Grigor'ev had published a biography of his close friend and fellow orientalist Pavel Stepanovich Savel'ev, who had died the previous year. The close connection between the two men sets Grigor'ev's biography apart somewhat from the other works in the genre. Some sections of the work read more like a memoir, and Grigor'ev's grief at losing his closest friend is palpable throughout. Nonetheless, in large sections of the book, particularly concerning periods when the two men were separated, Grigor'ev relies heavily on Savel'ev's correspondence. Like Barsukov, Grigor'ev included long excerpts from his sources. In a sample chapter from the biography of Savel'ev, 53 per cent of the text consists of direct quotation.[25] Unlike Barsukov, however, Grigor'ev kept the focus solidly on his subject: he did not attempt to use his sources to depict the times more broadly or portray Savel'ev's social milieu. As a result, the narrative appears more streamlined and coherent than Barsukov's meandering account, although the chronological framework still necessitates some sudden shifts of topic.

Petr Pekarskii's biography of Konstantin Arsen'ev, published in 1872, also coincides with Barsukov's style of narrative. Pekarskii's account is largely based on unpublished materials received from Arsen'ev's son soon after his father's death in 1865. Like Barsukov, Pekarskii hews closely to his sources and refrains from argumentation or analysis. Pekarskii's biography of Arsen'ev differs from Barsukov and others mainly in the author's reliance on a single source, Arsen'ev's unpublished memoirs. A sample chapter consists of 60 per cent direct quotation. Another chapter, describing a difficult period in Arsen'ev's life when he was accused of freemasonry and lost his teaching position, contains an even higher proportion of quotation.[26]

---

[25] Grigor'ev, *P. S. Savel'ev*, pp. 71–76.
[26] Pekarskii, 'O zhizni i trudakh akademika Konstantina Ivanovicha Arsen'eva', pp. 9–14, 24–38.

At first glance, Aleksandr Pypin's biography of Vissarion Belinskii appears consistent with the approach of Barsukov and the other biographers. In his introduction, Pypin states his intention to rely as much as possible on direct documentary evidence:

> In my work I have set for myself [...] the task of beginning to sort through the factual material trying in so far as it is possible to elaborate the external facts and events of Belinskii's inner life in the form in which he himself expressed them, in his direct impressions and remembrances. I had to give preference to this method of narration, which has the particular virtue of conveying to readers the personal testimony of a number of historical figures, because the letters which I used have been collected for the first time. Almost without exception they were unpublished and could hardly be published any time soon. In recounting the biography, it was necessary to make available at the same time its sources.[27]

The archeographic impulse that informed Barsukov's work was clearly a factor for Pypin as well. Yet in his narrative Pypin applies a different style characterized by a much stronger analytical voice. Chapter four of the Belinskii biography, covering the period from 1836 to 1838, illustrates well Pypin's method. In an extended introductory section, Pypin establishes the central theme and interpretive framework that would structure the chapter as a whole. His task in this section was to address and explain one of the vexing aspects of Belinskii's intellectual development — his 'reconciliation with reality' and embrace of conservative values under the influence of Hegelian theory. At the same time, it was precisely during this time that Belinskii's material circumstances reached their lowest ebb: for much of the period Belinskii was living in dire poverty. One might hypothesize that these two factors could be interrelated, but Pypin argues to the contrary:

> It would be wrong to sort out who among the friends of the [Stankevich] circle were favoured by external material conditions and who were not, and to draw conclusions from this about their opinions: Neither the lordliness [*barstvo*] of Stankevich nor the poverty of Belinskii forced them to look differently on things, on reality, on social relations.[28]

It was, in fact, the power of philosophical idealism itself and the logical progression of its postulates that drew Belinskii and his comrades into

---

[27] Pypin, *Belinskii*, pp. vi-vii. Pypin's biography was originally published in 1876.
[28] Ibid., pp. 132.

their period of 'reconciliation'. The result was a painful state of disjuncture between their abstract ideals and the attitudes toward the surrounding world to which they were accustomed.

It was only having articulated this central idea and established a framework for the discussion that followed that Pypin turns to the particulars of Belinskii's life. In the pages that follow, describing Belinskii's relations with members of the Stankevich circle, his growing friendship with Bakunin, and the circumstance of his conservative turn, Pypin quotes extensively from letters and other sources. In a sample of fourteen pages following the introductory section, roughly 43 per cent of the text consists of direct quotations, mainly from Belinskii's letters.[29] Yet these quotations are carefully framed such that they illustrate and elaborate upon points already articulated. Thus while Pypin's use of quotations is extensive, it does not approach the scale of Barsukov's work in which the excerpts themselves carry most of the weight of the narration. Pypin's professional profile as a literary critic, editor and social commentator as well as a scholar of Russian literature may have predisposed him to a more analytical and literary approach to biographical narrative. Moreover, the lack of a direct personal connection with Belinskii, and the passage of nearly thirty years since Belinskii's death, may have allowed Pypin more freedom to adopt a critical stance.

Evgenii Shmurlo's biography of Metropolitan Evgenii Bolkhovitinov also differs substantially from Barsukov's model in his sources and narrative style. Shmurlo defended his biography of Bolkhovinitov for his Master's degree at St Petersburg University in 1888 under the direction of Konstantin Bestuzhev-Riumin, and the academic orientation of the work distinguishes it from the other biographical works. Not the least of its distinguishing features are its discursive footnotes which often extend for the better part of the printed page. Shmurlo's footnotes open additional possibilities for discussing and quoting source materials. Often he relegates extended quotations to the footnotes while relying on paraphrasing and synthesis for the body of his text. When Shmurlo does quote his sources it tends to be in smaller excerpts grammatically integrated into the structure of his sentences. In other respects, however, Shmurlo's narrative is closer to Barsukov than to Pypin. Opening his fourth and final chapter, for example, Shmurlo moves straight into biographical narrative without attempting to establish a broader conceptual framework or overarching theme. Taking as his starting point Bolkhovitinov's move to St Petersburg

---

[29] Ibid., pp. 32–46.

in 1800, Shmurlo recounts the sad family circumstances that led Evgenii to leave his home in Voronezh, move to St Petersburg, and enter the monastic clergy.[30] In addition, like Barsukov, Shmurlo does not focus exclusively on his biographical subject. Rather, he provides contextual information about the people and trends that Bolkhovitinov encountered. For example, to prepare for a discussion of a memorandum Evgenii wrote on the Jesuits, Shmurlo plunges into a detailed account of the activities of the order in Russia following its suppression by the Pope in 1773.[31] Shmurlo's biography is a study of 'life and times' in the manner of Barsukov, but because he wove a synthetic narrative rather than relying on direct quotation he is able to maintain a greater degree of control over the text and avoid the sudden shifts to which Barsukov was prone.

Representations of the Self
Biographers, by definition, are obliged to account for the individuality of their subjects. Yet for nineteenth-century scholarly biographers, capturing the unique qualities of individual personality posed challenges. In early biographical writing, as Dmitrii Kalugin points out, individual lives tended to be set against a standard array of moral qualities and virtues, the fulfilment of which constituted the attributes of a worthy life.[32] By the mid-nineteenth century, however, a new approach emerged informed by the Romantic cult of the individual that highlighted the development of a unique personality as an end in itself. Pavel Annenkov's 1857 biography of Nikolai Stankevich, who died at a young age before his considerable talents could bear significant fruit, exemplifies this shift toward personality.[33] In Annenkov's narrative Stankevich appears as an artist whose sole masterpiece is himself, his admirable and inimitable character meticulously crafted through a process of introspection, self-education and dialogue.[34]

While the striving for individuality may have been a growing preoccupation within literary and philosophical circles by the mid-nineteenth century, it is not a theme that is reflected strongly in biographies

---

[30] Shmurlo, *Metropolit Evgenii kak uchenyi*, pp. 267–75.
[31] Ibid., pp. 283–89.
[32] D. Ia. Kalugin, 'Iskusstvo biografii', pp. 88–94.
[33] P. V. Annenkov, 'Nikolai Vasil′evich Stankevich: Biograficheskii ocherk', *Russkii vestnik*, February 1857, vol. 7, pp. 441–90, 695–738; March 1857, vol. 8, pp. 357–98. Annenkov's biography was republished in a slightly abridged form together with Stankevich's correspondence as a separate volume the following year.
[34] See Kalugin, 'Iskusstvo biografii', pp. 94–101 for discussion of this point. See also Dmitry Kalugin, 'Soviet Theories of Biography and the Aesthetics of Personality', *Biography*, 38, 2015, 3, pp. 343–62.

of scholars. To be sure, Shmurlo uses the word personality (*lichnost'*) in defining his own task and in assessing the work of others. A biography of Bolkhovitinov, he notes, should provide an acquaintance with the personality (*oznakomlenie s lichnost'iu*) of the learned monk. However, it is not entirely clear how Shmurlo understood the meaning of this term. Judging from the context it is plausible that he used it merely to denote the object of biographical research, a life broadly construed, without implying any specific philosophical or psychological meaning. In a similar way, he uses such phrases as 'to sketch the image' (*narisovat' obraz*), 'to characterize' and 'to describe the activity'.[35] But for a scholar like Shmurlo, committed to rigorous documentation and careful use of sources, an inward looking treatment raised methodological problems. To characterize personality the historian needs to look beyond the sources and take risks, synthesizing, speculating, drawing on intuition and insight to piece together a representation of the subject that rises above the texts on which it was based.

If this task proved daunting for Shmurlo, it was all the more formidable for someone like Barsukov for whom the textual basis of the biographical narrative was paramount. Throughout the many volumes of Barsukov's opus, Pogodin himself seems oddly absent. People and events around him are described in detail, his movements and actions are dutifully recorded, yet Podogin's own perceptions and emotions remain opaque. Even in the first volume describing Pogodin's childhood which, one might expect, would focus more directly on the development of the individual, the descriptions tend toward the external elements. The reader learns in detail where Pogodin went, whom he met, what he read and wrote, but little about his interior life. Barsukov's treatment of Pogodin's years in the gymnasium is a case in point. Modern readers tend to regard adolescence as a critical period in the formation of an individual's personality and worldview, a time of emotional turmoil, wild enthusiasms, testing of boundaries and tentative forays into romantic entanglements. But if Pogodin went through such a stage, it remained beyond the gaze of his biographer. Instead we learn (from Pogodin himself) that the school had filthy floors, the students were fed watery soup and clothed in garments made of cloth better suited for canvas bags, but that in the end all was for the best: 'They studied in need, but not without benefit, under the old-time patriarchal regime,

---

[35] Shmurlo, *Metropolit Evgenii kak uchenyi*, pp. i–xi. These phrases appear in the first pages of Shmurlo's introduction and sporadically throughout the book.

whose kindheartedness made up for all of its shortcomings.'[36] After a long and detailed description of the school curriculum with characterizations of the various teachers based on Pogodin's reminiscences, Barsukov appears to make a gesture toward generalization, but quickly backs away:

> These are the conditions in which Pogodin's gymnasium years passed. What then did he derive from the gymnasium? Pogodin himself will answer this question for us: 'A decent knowledge of the Latin and German languages. Good knowledge of algebra, geometry and trigonometry. A general knowledge of natural history: an acquaintance with botanical terminology, knowledge of how to identify stones, reviewing various animals in Blumenbach's [catalogue] and so forth.'[37]

If adolescent life held any deeper lessons for Pogodin, they went unspoken.

Pypin's biography of Belinksy, again, stands in contrast to Barsukov. In the chapter described above devoted to Belinskii's period of 'reconciliation' the central thread, the tension driving the narrative, is his internal struggle. Pypin writes:

> In the letters of this time, however fragmentary they are, more than a few examples can be found of the difficult spiritual struggle by which Belinskii paid the price for the convictions he had acquired. [...] It is understandable if he were persuaded of or came himself to imagine theoretical doubts or contradictions, backed by strong and compelling arguments, he would fall into despair [...]: theoretical concessions were for him not a switch of an algebraic formula, but entailed a renunciation of the most deeply held convictions [...]. Naturally, this renunciation was too hard for him, and his calm was restored only when this ferment of contradictions was resolved by the fall of one system and the triumph of another.[38]

Belinskii and Pogodin were of course very different individuals — diametrically opposed in their political views and in agreement only in their mutual contempt. Yet the stylistic differences between their biographers transcends the contrast between the individuals. Pogodin may not have approached the 'furious Vissarion' in the intensity of his views, but he was no stranger to strong feelings, and another biographer might have highlighted them in a very different way.

---

[36] Barsukov, *Zhizn' i trudy*, vol. 1, p. 23.
[37] Ibid., p. 24.
[38] Pypin, *Belinskii*, p. 147.

Other scholarly biographies fall between Barsukov and Pypin with regard to views of the individual, but most tend toward Barsukov's external approach. Veselovskii vividly portrays his protagonist Grigor'ev's emotional upheavals in the course of his turbulent career, but almost always he was able to use Grigor'ev's own words drawn from his letters to express his emotional state. Savel'ev, in contrast, was more reserved in his self-expression, and Grigor'ev as his biographer chose to focus more on his professional activities and scholarly achievements, filling in more intimate details largely on the basis of his personal recollections. N. K. Kozmin, writing a half century after his subject's death, did not have the luxury of relying on personal testimony, but was able to use Nadezhdin's correspondence and published writing to good effect to trace his intellectual development and personal travails. A large segment of Kozmin's account is devoted to Nadezhdin's stormy and ultimately futile romance with Elizaveta Sukhovo-Kobylina (who later gained recognition writing under the pen-name Evgenia Tur). Thus his emotional and psychological state is highlighted, but always through the prism of his own writing.[39] Similarly, Pekarskii, in relating a particularly difficult and traumatic period in the life of his subject, Konstantin Arsen'ev, refrains almost entirely from direct narration relying on excerpts from Arsen'ev's memoirs and other sources to convey both the events themselves and Arsen'ev's emotional response.[40]

Critical Perspectives
Whether they emphasized external influences or internal development, the authors of the scholarly biographies shared a tendency to avoid critical assessments of their protagonists. While none of these works could be termed a eulogy, the desire to memorialize and commemorate tended to override any urge to subject the protagonist's actions and ideas to scrutiny. It is hard to avoid the suspicion that Barsukov was not particularly fond of Pogodin, yet he scrupulously maintains his neutrality, leaving more explicit pronouncements to his sources. Veselovskii also withholds judgment yet is able to arrange his sources such that a positive view of Grigor'ev emerges. And one would certainly not expect Grigor'ev, writing the biography of his friend Savel'ev soon after his death, to have adopted a critical stance.

In another instance, however, Grigor'ev was not so tactful, and the reaction that he provoked reveals the strength of the cultural

---

[39] Kozmin, *Nikolai Ivanovich Nadezhdin*, pp. 457–506.
[40] Pekarskii, 'O zhizni i trudakh akademika Konstantina Ivanovicha Arsen'eva', pp. 26–38.

standard against speaking ill of the dead. As a student at St Petersburg University in the 1830s, Grigor´ev had known Timofei Granovskii, the future professor of medieval history at Moscow University, and the two kept up a correspondence for several years after their paths diverged. When Granovskii died in 1855, Grigor´ev was approached regarding the availability of this correspondence. Rather than turning the letters directly over to Granovskii's friends, however, Grigor´ev chose to publish them himself in a biographical essay. But the image Grigor´ev painted of the revered professor was anything but complimentary. Moscovites were enthralled with Granovskii, Grigor´ev suggested, because they had never encountered the phenomenon of an 'artist professor' whose theatrical style and exaggerated manners served as camouflage to conceal his lack of intellectual and scholarly depth. Granovskii, his former friend reported, had been a lazy student, lounging about in cafes by day and the theatre by night while his more serious comrades toiled at their studies. Grigor´ev specifically contrasted the rigorous training he and Savel´ev had received in Oriental languages under Osip Senkovskii with Granovskii's lacklustre education. Without a solid base of fundamental knowledge, Granovskii fell under the sway of poorly digested Western philosophy which he was never able to properly contextualize. It was no accident that for all his popular acclaim as a lecturer at Moscow University, Grigor´ev concluded, his actual contributions to scholarship were minimal.[41]

Appearing in the Slavophile journal, *Russkaia beseda*, a year after Granovskii's death, Grigor´ev's article stirred up a whirlwind of controversy in Moscow society. A series of angry articles appeared personally attacking Grigor´ev and calling into question his scholarly credentials. Notwithstanding an article by Savel´ev stalwartly defending his friend and fellow orientalist, the damage was done — in Moscow, Grigor´ev was *persona non grata*. The price to be paid for a hostile biography could not have been clearer.[42]

Biographers like Pypin, Shmurlo and Kozmin, writing several decades after the deaths of their subjects, had more opportunity for critical engagement, but even in these cases notes of criticism were muted at best. Shmurlo expressed at the outset his admiration for Metropolitan Evgenii, though he acknowledged and tacitly concurred with critical assessments in

---

[41] Grigor´ev, 'T. N. Granovskii do ego professorstva v Moskve'.
[42] The controversy surrounding Grigor´ev article on Granovskii is recounted in Veselovskii, p. 143–53. An account from the opposite perspective can be found in Boris Chicherin, *Vospominaniia: Moskva sorokovykh godov*, Moscow, 1991, pp. 186–87.

the historiography.⁴³ His own criticisms of Bolkhovitinov tended to focus on his scholarly works, highlighting places in which Evgenii's findings had been superseded by more recent scholarship.⁴⁴ Nadezhdin's biographer, Kozmin, was even more committed to a positive portrayal of his subject. Nadezhdin's reputation among Russian intellectuals had been quite low and his intellectual contributions had long been neglected. Kozmin endeavoured to set the record straight and make the case for Nadezhdin's significance as a major Russian thinker. It is perhaps no accident that Kozmin ends his account not with Nadezhdin's death in 1856, but rather with his brief exile in 1837 following the Chaadaev affair. Defending his integrity in the period following his return from exile and his entrance into the state bureaucracy becomes more problematic.⁴⁵ Aleksandr Pypin had no such challenges in his biography of Belinskii. While still politically sensitive when Pypin's book first appeared in the 1870s, Belinskii was already revered as a heroic figure in liberal intellectual circles. There was no need for Pypin to justify or to condemn Belinskii: it was enough for him to explain his difficult and often contradictory personality. From his detached but critical perspective, Pypin was able to probe most deeply into the inner life and intellectual development of his subject.

Scholarly Biography as a Genre
The distinctive features of Russian scholarly biographies — patchwork narratives pieced together from excerpts, lack of internal perspective, a tendency toward a hagiographic view of the 'great man' — are by no means unique to the Russian cultural milieu. To a degree, these features were mainstays of the classic Victorian biography — the 'fat two volumes' in Lytton Strachey's words, 'with their ill-digested masses of material, their slip-shod style, their tone of tedious panegyric, their lamentable lack of selection, of detachment, of design' by means of which English men of

---

[43] Evgenii had been criticized by Metropolitan Filaret who noted the depth of Evgenii's knowledge but the 'inactivity of his reflective powers which was frequently and sharply manifested'. Shmurlo, while seemingly not pleased with Filaret's assessment, did not attempt to refute it, suggesting that he may have recognized that it contained a grain of truth. Shmurlo, *Metropolit Evgenii kak uchenyi*, p. 28.

[44] For example, Shmurlo criticized Bolkhovitinov's assertion in his description of Voronezh that the city had been founded in the twelfth century. It was only much later when the region came under the control of the Muscovite state that such a city could be founded. See Ibid., p. 230.

[45] Nadezhdin was condemned in particular for his role in the persecution of Old Believers and Sectarians while working in the Ministry of Internal Affairs. See Thomas Marsden, *The Crisis of Religious Toleration in Imperial Russia: Bibikov's System for the Old Believers, 1841–1855*, Oxford, 2015, pp. 89–92 and *passim*.

note were ushered into oblivion.⁴⁶ Victorian biographers were particularly sensitive to any hint of scandal and impropriety. Not only did Lord Byron's biographer, Thomas Moore, refrain from including sensitive material from his subject's handwritten memoirs, he was accused, probably unfairly, of burning the offending manuscript lest other less tactful biographers come across the compromising information.⁴⁷ Just as Grigor'ev's unflattering portrait of Granovskii revealed the limits of acceptable criticism, so the scandal surrounding James Anthony Froude's sympathetic but revealing biography of Thomas Carlyle showed the capacity of British readers for outrage in the face of what was perceived as indecency and betrayal.⁴⁸ Given these parallels, and the diversity of approaches and methods among the works we have examined, does it make sense to mark them as a distinct phenomenon grouped under the rubric of scholarly biography?

Perhaps the best way to justify the utility of the classification would be to consider what these works are not. Most notably, scholarly biography can be distinguished from literary biography, a genre that can be understood variously as biography of literary figures, by literary figures, or using literary methods. Shaped by artistic sensibilities as well as historical knowledge, the literary biography aims not merely to inform and educate but also to evoke aesthetic admiration reminiscent of, if not equivalent, to the pleasure evoked by the works of the subject. As Virginia Woolf put it, literary biography seeks to meld 'the granite-like solidity of facts' with the 'rainbow-like intangibility of personality' into a seamless whole, thereby encapsulating what is most distinctive about the individual.⁴⁹

Of the works we have examined, Pypin's biography of Belinskii falls most clearly into the realm of literary biography. While Pypin was not a writer of fiction (nor was Belinskii), his ability to penetrate beneath the surface of external fact revealing the underlying dynamics and applying them to the trajectory of Belinskii's intellectual development sets his work apart from the other examples we have seen of scholarly biography.

Scholarly biographies, in contrast, seek not so much to entertain or to edify as to stand as a monument, a repository of documentary evidence to fix and preserve the life and works of the scholar for future reference and for posterity. Sections of Barsukov's biography of Pogodin make interesting

⁴⁶ Quoted in Leon Edel, *Writing Lives: Principia Biographica*, New York and London, 1984, p. 194.

⁴⁷ John A. Garraty, *The Nature of Biography*, London, 1957, pp. 91-92; Atkinson, *Victorian Biography Reconsidered*, p. 18.

⁴⁸ Garraty, *The Nature of Biography*, pp. 95-96; Atkinson, *Victorian Biography Reconsidered*, pp. 21-22.

⁴⁹ Virginia Wolff, 'The New Biography', in *Granite and Rainbow*, New York, 1958, p. 149.

reading to be sure, but the prospect of an ordinary reader ploughing through all twenty-two volumes seems almost unthinkable. The indexes provided at various intervals are the obvious mode of access for scholars seeking not a holistic portrait of an individual but rather particular data on points of literary and cultural history. A reader might find Grigor'ev's biography of Savel'ev easier fare, but given its detailed discussions of numismatics and archaeology, it too would seem to be of value primarily to readers with a specialized interest in these areas. Shmurlo's biography of Bolkhovitinov, a dissertation subsequently published as an academic monograph, while potentially of interest to an audience of historically-minded general readers was presented for a learned audience cloaked in all the attributes of formal scholarship.

In one respect, however, scholarly and literary biography share an important parallel. In both genres, the qualities that enable an individual to, as Iurii Lotman puts it, 'possess a biography' are shared to varying degrees by the author and subject.[50] While Pavel Annenkov's literary gifts did not approach those of his illustrious subject, it was precisely his credentials as a *littérateur* that made him an appropriate biographer in the eyes of Pushkin's family. Pypin's background as a socially engaged literary critic as well as his ties to Chernyshevskii (a cousin) and the journal *Sovremennik*, in which Belinskii had published, made him an ideal and obvious candidate to write the first full biography. For a scholar to claim entitlement to write a biography meant, in many respects, to claim rights to a lineage, either fraternal, as in the case of Grigor'ev and Savel'ev, or as an heir preserving the legacy of an intellectual predecessor for subsequent generations.[51] The audacity of Pogodin's gesture in claiming for himself the position of Karamzin's biographer is all the more striking in this regard.

The relationship between writer and subject in scholarly and literary biography presupposes a certain proximity, not only professionally, but also chronologically. Thus, scholarly biography can also be distinguished from historical biographies which require a more specialized range of skills on the part of the biographer and in which the lineage between biographer

---

[50] Lotman, 'Literaturnaia biografiia', p. 365.
[51] This phenomenon of biographical dynasties can be seen particularly clearly in the field of Orientology. P. S. Savel'ev had recently completed a biography of Osip Senkovskii at the time of his death. Savel'ev was the subject of a biography by V. V. Grigor'ev whose biography in turn was written by N. N. Veselovskii. Veselovskii died in 1918 and several years later a biographical sketch was published by the major Russian orientologist, V. V. Bartol'd about whom an extensive biographical literature exists. On the various schools of Russian oriental studies, see David Schimmelpenninck van der Oye, *Russian Orientalism: Asia in the Russian Mind from Peter the Great to the Emigration*, New Haven, CT, 2010.

and subject is more tenuous. In Nil Popov's magisterial biography of Vasilii Tatishchev published in 1861, it is historical argument rather than biographical narrative that serves as the organizing principle. Popov's chapter on the succession crisis of 1730 begins with a long discourse on the political ideology of autocratic power stretching back to the mid-sixteenth century. Only after almost thirty pages of detailed historical analysis does the reader happen upon the phrase: 'at that time, Tatishchev was living in Moscow.'[52] While Popov may have identified to some degree with Tatishchev as a historian, it is the historical context rather than the individual that stands at centre stage.

The close proximity of author to subject in scholarly biography also tended to preclude their use for didactic purposes to edify or instruct the reader. Authors of scholarly biography tended to accept implicitly the life and work of their subject as an end in itself. This sets them apart from a didactic tradition extending back to Plutarch in which biographical narratives exemplified specific virtues from which the reader was to draw inspiration.[53] British biographical literature of the nineteenth century was particularly rich in didactic 'lives'. Works like George Lillie Craik's *The Pursuit of Knowledge Under Difficulty* or Samuel Smiles's *Self-Help* used biographical narrative to trumpet the virtues of industriousness, self-reliance and moral responsibility. While authors like Smiles focused primarily on well-known individuals, didactic biography could validate the lives of the obscure as vehicles for the articulation of virtue and as objects of emulation.[54] In the Russian context, saint's lives functioned in a similar manner by illuminating the ability of the saint through extraordinary feats of will and endurance to exemplify universal models of virtuous conduct.[55] There is little evidence of a secular equivalent to the didactic biography in Russia before the establishment of the series, 'Lives of Remarkable People' (ZhZL), by Florentii Pavlenkov in 1890.[56] It could be argued that the genre of revolutionary biography and autobiography that arose in the years before the start of World War One and flourished

[52] Popov, *V. N. Tatishchev i ego vremia*, pp. 67–93. In his introduction (pp. 2–4) Popov accounts for the apparently absence of the subject of his biography in much of the narrative by the difficulties he encountered in locating sources as well as his lack of expertise in the many areas of science and administration in which Tatishchev was active.

[53] This was the concept behind Plutarch's famous 'Parallel Lives' in which biographies of Greek and Roman historical figures were paired in order to illustrate exemplary virtues and vices.

[54] This theme is treated in detail in Juliette Atkinson's *Victorian Biography Reconsidered*.

[55] Lotman, 'Literaturnaia biografiia', p. 366.

[56] See Carol Ueland and Ludmilla A. Trigos's contribution in this issue, 'Creating a National Biographical Series: F. F. Pavlenkov's "Lives of Remarkable People", 1890–1924'.

in the 1920s embodied elements of both the didactic and the hagiographic tradition in a new cultural context.[57]

Didactic biographies also presuppose a broad audience to be morally uplifted by examples of virtuous lives. This was less the case for scholarly biography, which delved unabashedly into arcane and specialized branches of knowledge and placed little importance on accessibility for the masses. What, then, was the function of scholarly biography, given that it seems to fulfil so few of the roles commonly ascribed to biography in other contexts? For all their variety, scholarly biographies served a common purpose in the construction of disciplinary traditions. By highlighting the achievements of their noteworthy predecessors, scholarly biographers articulated the boundaries between the scientific and mundane and set in place genealogies of knowledge in relation to which practitioners could orient themselves and validate their status. Scholars merited biographical attention through their contribution to an ever expanding body of disciplinary knowledge which both authors and readers could claim as their heritage.

Imperial Russian scholarly biographies illustrate the difficulties authors can encounter in establishing an optimal position with regard to their biographical subject. One might envision an ideal of respectful distance in which the author is far enough removed from the subject to allow rigorous critical analysis, but not so distant that the capacity for empathy is lost and the biography turns into an indictment. For the biographers examined here, with the possible exception of Pypin, finding this golden mean, particularly with regard to critical engagement, proved to be a challenge. Barsukov's biography of Pogodin may represent an extreme example, but the trends he exemplified reverberated throughout the genre of Russian scholarly biography. There is reason to suppose that these tendencies continued into the Soviet period as Soviet scholars endeavoured to create an intellectual genealogy for their fields without seeming to depart overtly from the obligatory framework of Marxist-Leninist thought.[58] Extensive use of primary sources while refraining from detailed critical engagement proved an effective tool for Soviet scholars in creating a useable past.

The challenges faced by Russian scholarly biographers reflect a dilemma that all historians face in their explorations. As one encounters figures

---

[57] Igal Halfin has made an argument somewhat to this effect in *From Darkness to Light: Class Consciousness and Salvation in Revolutionary Russia*, Pittsburgh, PA, 2000.

[58] For a more detailed description of this trend, see Nathaniel Knight, 'Salvage Biography and Useable Pasts: Russian Ethnographers Confront the Legacy of Terror', *Kritika: Explorations in Eurasian History*, 1, 2000, 2, pp. 365-75.

from the past they come alive in the imagination through the power of empathy. Writers respond not just intellectually but also emotionally to the encounter with their subjects: antipathies and attachments take shape driving inquiries and endowing representations with life and colour. One hopes that these emotional entanglements can be confined and restrained by a grounding in sources and an aspiration toward dispassionate critical inquiry. Yet to purge the biographical endeavour entirely from its emotive dimensions is unlikely to lead to a satisfactory outcome. A reader will sooner tolerate advocacy than indifference.

2

Creating a National Biographical Series: F. F. Pavlenkov's 'Lives of Remarkable People', 1890–1924

LUDMILLA A. TRIGOS and CAROL UELAND

THE publisher Florentii Fedorovich Pavlenkov (1839–1900), founded the series 'Biograficheskaia biblioteka: Zhizn′ zamechatel′nykh liudei' (The Biographical Library: Lives of Remarkable People — hereafter, ZhZL) in 1890 as an inexpensive publication geared toward a mass readership. The series gained nationwide popularity and survived even after Pavlenkov's death in 1900 until 1924, and then was reinvigorated by Maksim Gor′kii, who in 1929 specifically sought 'to repeat the Pavlenkov biographies in a condensed form'.[1] Though Gor′kii had begun discussing the possibility of publishing a biography series as early as 1916, due to the economic and political conditions immediately after the 1917 revolutions and the 'book famine' immediately thereafter, it took him some time to garner the resources necessary to find a home for the series. The first volume of the series as we know it was published in 1933 by Zhurnal′no-gazetnoe ob′edinenie, but the series was eventually taken up by the Molodaia gvardiia press, where it continues to be published to the present day. Close to 2,000 biographies have been released since the series' inception. In the post-Soviet era, the series has 'swallowed up' every other biographical series that came before.[2] The publication's longevity has been remarked upon by many Russian writers and critics, who claim that it is the longest running biography series in world literature. During the Soviet era, the series became a cultural barometer and, after returning to private ownership in the post-Soviet period, continues unabated in its significance to the present day. This article will examine the interrelationship between the history of Pavlenkov's development as a writer and publisher and his creation

---

[1] Sergei Semanov, 'Samaia znamenitaia na svete', in V. F. Iurkin (ed.), *Zhizn′ zamechatel′nogo izdatel′stva: 'Molodaia gvardiia' – 75 let*, Moscow, 1997, p. 196.

[2] Inna Bulkina, 'The Lives of Remarkable People: Between Plutarch and Triapichkin', *Russian Studies in Literature*, 49, Spring 2013, 2, p. 88.

of Russia's first biography series at a crucial point in the development of Russian literary culture. It was Pavlenkov's series that fostered the notion of a national biographical tradition during the pre-Revolutionary era, and would have a significant impact on the development of later biography writing during the Soviet era and beyond.[3]

Models for Serial Biographies

Keith Thomas differentiates three types of collective biography: group biography, universal biography and national biography. The most influential model for group biography, originating in the classical era, was Plutarch's *Lives*.[4] The genre proliferated throughout modern Europe and was frequently motivated by the desire of a particular group to assert its importance in a given culture. Thomas indicates that group biographies are part of a process of developing a national biographical tradition but are limited in terms of audience appeal to select elites, as well as in their primary motive, which was to bolster the group identity of particularly upper-class segments of society. Another type of collective biography is the universal biography, which draws on heroes from many different cultures and backgrounds, presenting a synthesis of information in a dictionary or encyclopaedic form, such as Louis Moréri's *Le Grand Dictionnaire Historique* (1673). The third form is national biography, which came to the fore in the late eighteenth and early nineteenth centuries as a vehicle for the establishment of national identity.[5] As Catherine Parke suggests, 'there is much to be learned about a particular period by studying the ways it

---

[3] In addition to the ZhZL series, Pavlenkov published two other biographical collections by the famous pedagogue V. P. Ostrogorskii: *20 biografii obraztsovykh russkikh pisatelei. Dlia chteniia iunoshestva*, St Petersburg, 1891, which went through eight editions, and *Khoroshie liudi. Sbornik rasskazov*, St Petersburg, 1891, which had five editions. See N. Rassudovskaia, *Izdatel' F. F. Pavlenkov*, Moscow, 1960, p. 95. In his biography of Pavlenkov, Vladimir Desiaterik (p. 299) cites these collections along with Ostravinskii's biography collections for children and youth, *Iskry bozhi. Biograficheskie ocherki* (Novikov, Belinskii, Shchepkin, Zhukovskii, Ershov, Seriakov, Cervantes, Swift), and A. Pavlov's *Biografii obraztsovkikh russkikh pisatelei* as some of Pavlenkov's first publications in the genre of biography. See V. Desiaterik, *Pavlenkov*, Moscow, 2006, p. 299.

[4] For a discussion of Plutarch as a model for biography, see Ludmilla A. Trigos and Carol Ueland, 'Introduction' to special forum, 'Literary Biographies in the *Lives of Remarkable People* Series (*Zhizn' zamechatel'nykh liudei*)', *Slavic & East European Journal*, 60, Summer 2016, 2, pp. 207–20.

[5] Keith Thomas, *Changing Conceptions of National Biography: The Oxford DNB in Historical Perspective*, Cambridge, 2005, pp. 2–11. For a discussion of the relationship between the rise of nationalism and the establishment of national biography, see also Catherine N. Parke, *Biography: Writing Lives*, New York, 1996, and Barbara Caine, *Biography and History*, Basingstoke, 2010.

tells lives and the purposes it conceives for biography'.[6] She emphasizes that there is a direct connection between life-writing and commercial, technological, cultural and imperial expansion, and highlights the fact that collective biographies, dictionaries of biography and other multi-volume works of biography play an important role in the formation of national identity by narrating 'national history through the lives of its major participants'.[7] Other scholars have also pointed to the relationship between national and collective biographies, nation-building and the print revolution. Similar processes took place earlier in France, for example, as they did in Russia in the late nineteenth century.[8]

Although biography series (issued either as dictionaries, encyclopaedias or as collective biographies) had existed in Western Europe, especially in France and England, from the late 1600s to the mid-1700s,[9] in Russia, all three types of collective biographies only began to appear in the late eighteenth century, an early example being N. I. Novikov's *Opyt istoricheskogo slovaria o rossiiskikh pisateliakh* (1772).[10] N. Rudakov, a contemporary reviewer for the *Zhurnal ministerstva narodnogo prosveshcheniia*, dates the true beginning of biographical interest in Russia to the 1790s, with the publication of the first Russian biographical dictionary from 1790–98 in fourteen parts, *Slovar' istoricheskogo ili sokrashchennoi biblioteki zaliuchaiushchei v sebe: zhitie i deianie patriarkhov, tsarei, imperatorov i korolei, velikikh polkovodets, i t.d.* (a second edition of three volumes of the dictionary was published in 1807–11). At the beginning of the nineteenth century there had been several attempts to assemble a dictionary of biographies of writers, church fathers and Russian military commanders.[11] In the 1830s, D. Bantysh-Kamenskii's well-known work, *Slovar' dostopamiatnykh liudei russkoi zemli* appeared, as well as A. Tereshchenko's *Opyt obozreniia zhizni*

---

[6] Parke, *Biography*, p. 9.
[7] Ibid., pp. 11–13.
[8] See Caine, *Biography and History*, pp. 47–65, and Thomas, *Changing Conceptions*, especially pp. 2–18.
[9] For a discussion of series of collective biographies that participated in the formation of a 'canon of great Frenchmen', see David A. Bell, *The Cult of the Nation in France: Inventing Nationalism, 1680–1800*, Cambridge, MA, 2001, pp. 127–39. The first series according to Bell was Jean Du Castre D'Auvigny in 1739, and was published in 26 volumes over the course of thirty years.
[10] Dmitrii Zhukov, *Biografiia biografii. Razmyshlenie o zhanre*, Moscow, 1980, p. 26.
[11] Cf. 'Novyi opyt istoricheskogo slovaria o rossiiskikh pisateliakh', *Drug prosveshcheniia*, 1805, and a volume published by N. Grech in 1812 in N. Rudakov, 'Zhizn' zamechatel'nykh liudei. Biograficheskaia biblioteka, F. Pavlenkova — Piat' desiat tri vypuska biografii russkikh deiatelei', *Zhurnal ministerstva narodnogo prosveshcheniia*, August 1895, pp. 497–519 (citation p. 498) September 1895, pp. 158–79.

sanovnikov, upravliavshikh inostrannymi delami v Rossii and V. N. Berkh's *Zhizneopisanie pervykh rossiiskikh admiralov*. These collections focused on distinguished members of the military and church hierarchy and did not attempt to popularize biographies of a broad range of 'great men', as per the model provided by Thomas Carlyle. Carlyle expanded the canon of possible 'great men' to include literary figures, as seen in his lectures on 'The Hero as Poet' (1840) and 'The Hero as Man of Letters' (1840).[12] In 1865–66, two Russian publications — *Portretnaia gallereia russkikh deiatelei* (1865–69) by A. E. Münster, comprising up to 200 biographies, and *Russkie liudi, zhizneopisania sootechestvennikov, proslavivshikhsia na poprishche nauki, dobra i obshchestvennoi pol′zy* (2 vols, 1866), with forty biographies — by the publisher and bookstore owner M. Vol′f, began the popularization of works that featured a broader range of great men from Russian society. From the late 1860s there was no significant development in the expansion of collective biographies or series until the appearance of ZhZL in 1890. On 2 January 1890, Pavlenkov remarked in a letter to S. N. Krivenko, the populist and editor of *Russkoe bogatstvo*, that 'our literary material is pitifully poor: biography, it appears has been completely forgotten'.[13] Yet this 'poverty' provided him with a new market to explore and an opportunity to reinvent the serial biographical tradition for a mass audience. At the same time, the conditions in book publishing in the mid-nineteenth century intersected with Pavlenkov's development as a writer-translator-publisher and ultimately led to the conception of ZhZL.

The New Russian Reader and the Book Market in the Late Nineteenth Century

Scholars such as Jeffrey Brooks, Stephen Lovell, Beth Holmgren and Louise McReynolds have analysed the publishing market boom in Russia in the late nineteenth century that was initiated by several important factors. The mass circulation press expanded due to increased literacy, specifically amongst so-called 'middle' readers who demanded very specific types of works. Both Brooks and Holmgren discuss the varieties of popular

---

[12] For Carlyle's notion of great men as movers of history, see Thomas Carlyle, *On Heroes, Hero-Worship and the Heroic in History*, Berkeley, CA, 1993.

[13] Desiaterik, *Pavlenkov*, p. 300. For a useful discussion of the history of biography in Russia, see Zhukov, *Biografiia biografii* and Anna Makolkin, 'Probing the Origins of Literary Biography: English and Russian Versions', *Biography*, 19, Winter 1996, 1, pp. 87–104. Both authors discuss the variety of influences (for example, the *zhitie*, Plutarch's *Parallel Lives* and in some cases, European biographies) on Russian writers who were drawn to biography during the nineteenth century.

literature available to the semi-literate and newly literate audience, ranging from saints' lives to *lubok* literature and periodicals (e.g. inexpensive illustrated magazines, daily 'kopek' newspapers and other serialized novels, such as adventure stories and potboilers).[14] Brooks points to the discomfort that many educated Russians felt with the development of these forms of popular culture and the growing 'divergence between high and low culture'; the educated elite (including critics, pedagogues, authors of high literature) expected to be solely responsible for creating a common culture that would be accessible to all Russians, although 'the desired character of the general culture differed among educated Russians of different political persuasions'.[15] Lovell has noted the stratification of the Russian reading public, and emphasizes that at this point in time it was not homogenous:

> By the 1860s Russia's 'active readers' numbered in the hundreds of thousands, and they could not remotely be seen as a single homogeneous 'public'. They included, as always, an elite of 'serious' readers, but also a sub-elite that depended on digests and surveys to make sense of new literary and scholarly developments. More numerous still were readers who required from books and periodicals that blend of entertainment, escape, and practical and moral guidance that tends to be characteristic of modern 'popular' literature.[16]

A variety of commercial and non-commercial publishers catered to these new groups of readers. The commercial publishers and their products were looked down upon by the majority of the educated elite and liberal and radical social activists, who sought to supply another type of literature to these emerging audiences. These sponsored publications came from a variety of institutions whose aim was mass education, stemming from the Orthodox Church (such as the Synod Publishing Commission, which

---

[14] See Jeffrey Brooks, 'Readers and Reading at the End of the Tsarist Era', in William Mills Todd, *Literature and Society in Imperial Russia, 1800–1914*, Stanford, CA, 1978, pp. 97–150 and *When Russia Learned to Read: Literacy and Popular Literature, 1861–1917*, Princeton, NJ, 1985, and Beth Holmgren, *Rewriting Capitalism: Literature and the Market in Late Tsarist Russia and the Kingdom of Poland*, Pittsburgh, PA, 1998. See also Stephen Lovell, *The Russian Reading Revolution: Print Culture in the Soviet and Post-Soviet Eras*, Basingstoke, 2000, especially pp. 10–14. For more detailed information on the circulation of newspapers, see Louise McReynolds, *The News under Russia's Old Regime: The Development of a Mass Circulation Press*, Princeton, NJ, 1991.

[15] Brooks, *When Russia Learned to Read*, pp. 295–96.

[16] Stephen Lovell and Birgit Menzel (eds), *Reading for Entertainment in Contemporary Russia: Post-Soviet Popular Literature in Historical Perspective*, Munich, 2005, p. 16.

issued a series called the 'Parish Library'), and various state commissions established in the 1870s to oversee public readings and which subsequently published their own booklets (for example, the Standing Commission for Popular Readings had published more than 100 titles in 10,000-copy print runs). However, these books were not held in high esteem by critics, either for their content or for their artistry.[17] Another important sponsor was the military which, through the publisher V. A. Berezovskii, provided military propaganda, training materials and other items such as the series, 'Soldiers' Library', which had hundreds of titles, particularly stories featuring the bravery and valour of soldiers in both war and peace.[18] For many members of the intelligentsia, the educational and enlightenment aims of publishing were incompatible with the profit motive of the commercial press.[19] In researching reading habits during this period, scholars have focused primarily on high literature until close to the end of the Soviet era. More recently, there has been a rediscovery of products of popular, or boulevard, literature from the publishing boom that took place from 1890 up until the 1917 revolutions. Pavlenkov and his publications remain understudied in the history of Russian print culture of the time specifically because he and they do not fit neatly into the categories designated by Western and Soviet scholars.

Pavlenkov as Author and Publisher

Unlike many other publishers of his time, who were either already a part of the literary mainstream or whose families were merchants or had been involved in publishing for generations, Pavlenkov was from a gentry family in Tambov. He came to publishing after training at the Mikhailovskii military academy, where he became disillusioned because of widespread corruption amongst its officers. Following the frustrations of his military career, Pavlenkov was keen to become a teacher at a *gymnasium*, but did not find that path open to him. He found himself increasingly influenced by his former mathematics and mechanics instructor at the military academy, Petr Lavrov, as well as other Russian radicals of the 1860s, including Vissarion Belinskii, Nikolai Chernyshevskii, and especially Dmitrii Pisarev, with whom he became personally acquainted in 1865. These figures called upon their generation to become socially and politically engaged by promoting progress based on not only Russian but

---

[17] See Brooks, *When Russia Learned to Read*, pp. 312–13.
[18] Ibid., p. 315.
[19] For an extended discussion, see ibid., pp. 295–352.

also Western European progressive thought.[20] In response, Pavlenkov looked for a role in which he could make a productive, positive impact in spreading knowledge and enlightenment among the masses and found it in publishing. Pavlenkov was also influenced by Western European enlightenment thinkers. For example, John Stuart Mill attested to the seminal role that could be played in society by a publisher who was not merely focused on commercial success:

> It is necessary to look at a publisher as an enlightener of the people, since we are obliged to him for the appearance of many compositions which never would have otherwise seen the light; publishers, imparting a particular direction to their activities develop, so to speak, a taste for one or another branch of science or literature, create readers, enable the dissemination of literacy.[21]

Echoing Mill, Belinskii commented, 'Is it necessary to say what a great influence a bookseller-publisher can have upon the successes of literature?'[22] Pavlenkov was undoubtedly inspired by these two men when he founded the ZhZL series in 1890, and he included biographies on them both in his series (Belinskii in 1891 and Mill's in 1892).[23]

Pavlenkov played a variety of roles in the publishing industry; he began as an author and translator, then a publisher, and in 1866 a bookshop owner. He started writing even before he resigned his military commission, authoring critiques of Russian military law and articles on the new technology of photography. Pavlenkov's first published book was his own translation of a work by the French physicist A. Ganot: *Polnyi kurs fiziki s kratkim obzorom meteorologichskikh iavlenii A. Gano, professor fizicheskikh i matematicheskikh nauk* ('Complete Course of Physics with a Short Review of Meteorological Manifestations of A. Ganot, Professor of Physics and Mathematics', 1864). It sold 4,000 copies, a large quantity

---

[20] Desiaterik, Pavlenkov's biographer in the post-Soviet ZhZL series, cites both Belinskii (who in 1836 'literally foretold the appearance of of Pavlenkov's series') and P. L. Lavrov (Pavlenkov's professor at the Mikhailovskii artillery academy). Desiaterik, *Pavlenkov*, p. 298.

[21] John Stuart Mill, quoted in E. A. Dinershtein, *I. D. Sytin*, Moscow, 1983, p. 3.

[22] Rassudovskaia, *Izdatel' F. F. Pavlenkov*, p. 3.

[23] M. I. Tugan-Baranovskii, *D. C. Mill': ego zhizn' i ucheno-literaturnaia deiatel'nost'*, St Petersburg, 1892. Desiaterik speculates that a number of factors influenced Pavlenkov's decision to found the series, and specifically cites the influence of Belinskii and Lavrov (Desiaterik, *Pavlenkov*, p. 298).

for a science textbook at the time, as noted by Arlen Blium.[24] Pavlenkov concentrated on publications on popular technology and science before expanding into other areas. He valued progressive thought in all arenas, so much so that he endeavoured to give mass readers access to the most up-to-date, comprehensible information about technological developments, such as electricity, the camera and astrophysics. He also sought to make literary works and political thought, both Russian and European, accessible to the masses, even at great personal risk. His first literary publication was the collected works of the radical critic D. I. Pisarev. His timing was, however, unfortunate. After the height of the most 'liberal' period of tsarist censorship in the early 1860s, the regime once again tightened controls following the attempted assassination of Alexander II in April 1866. It was no easy task at that time to collect and publish the works of Pisarev, whose works were banned from circulation. In November 1866 Pisarev was released from prison by the tsar in a conciliatory gesture to the intelligentsia to celebrate the marriage of the tsarevich. The articles that Pavlenkov hoped to republish had been written and published either anonymously or under an alias while Pisarev was in prison.[25] In the new political climate following the assassination attempt, some of these articles were read as a call for opposition to the tsarist regime.

Pavlenkov's efforts included submitting the articles under different titles to other cities where the censors were more lenient than in St Petersburg and then presenting the approvals to the St Petersburg Censorship Committee as a fait accompli. When the volume was banned and brought to court, Pavlenkov argued his own case and brought a stenographer to document the proceedings. These proceedings also detailed his speeches, which summarized the contents of the forbidden articles.[26] His willingness to prioritize getting the larger project into print even at the cost of excisions of material enabled him to obtain censorship approval for the publication of several volumes of Pisarev's writings, though not without omissions.[27]

---

[24] A. Blium, *F. F. Palvenkov v Viatke*, Kirov, 1976, p. 8.
[25] Rassudovskaia, *Izdatel' F. F. Pavlenkov*, p. 28.
[26] Blium, *Pavlenkov*, pp. 10–11.
[27] For example, 'Bednaia russkaia mysl'' was excised from the second volume, which was then permitted to be released without it (cf. Blium, *Pavlenkov*, p. 10). Another article that Pavlenkov could not get reprinted in his second edition of the collected works was on the poet Heinrich Heine. Heine was one of the foreign writers most frequently banned by the tsarist authorities for perceived blasphemy and advocacy of revolution. Although Pavlenkov never published his collected works, Heine's biography was one of the earliest in the ZhZL series, and when Gor'kii revived the series, it was the first biography in the Soviet ZhZL series. For more on Heine, see Marianna Tax Choldin, *A Fence around the*

Ironically, it was not Pavlenkov's publishing activity but rather his personal involvement with the Pisarev family that led to his detention and subsequent exile. Pavlenkov acted on behalf of Pisarev's family after the writer's untimely death by drowning in July 1868, organizing a collection to fund a graveside monument and also to assist Pisarev's mother and sister. For the authorities this was the last straw. Pavlenkov was arrested in September 1868 as he went to collect the leaflets he had had printed to announce the collection. For this unsanctioned act he was imprisoned in the Petropavlovsk fortress, then sent into indefinite exile in Viatka and banned from publishing. From that moment on, Pavlenkov was branded as a revolutionary, a dangerous adversary of the tsarist government, and was kept under surveillance for the rest of his life, despite the fact that he had no direct connection to any specific political organization.

Before leaving St Petersburg, Pavlenkov transferred full ownership of his bookshop to M. P. Nadein and gave V. D. Cherkasov, his close childhood friend, control of his publishing business. However he managed to continue to run the business from exile secretly and by proxy with the support of acquaintances in Viatka who had ties to typographers and progressive circles, such as the young seminarian N. P. Kuvshinskii, the writer M. E. Selenkina and the bookseller, library-owner and publisher, A. A. Krasovskii. As Blium has emphasized, the Viatka period was crucial for the development of Pavlenkov's thinking about what kinds of books he wanted to publish, as well as which techniques he would use to ensure that the books could pass the censor. Pavlenkov employed a variety of devices, including releasing books under other titles, publishers and/or printers' names, or else anonymously. Although Pavlenkov's publishing business was located in St Petersburg, he continued to submit material to censors in other cities, such as Moscow or Kiev, who were reputed to be more liberal. He sometimes submitted the same material with a new title, a new introduction and a softening of any controversial passages, although in later printings he often restored the original content. He was well aware of the changing laws regarding publishing and knew the ways in which the length of a work could be used to avoid preliminary censorship. Vladimir Korolenko described Pavlenkov as something of a rogue, who was not above such practices as bribery, or an illicit trip back to St Petersburg while still in exile to shore up his publishing firm. In his own writing, Pavlenkov was skilled in the use of Aesopic language and other oblique referencing, such as paraphrasing, hints, omissions and the use of visual materials to

Empire: Russian Censorship of Western Ideas under the Tsars, Durham, NC, 1985, pp. 43–47.

provide satirical commentary on the written text. These were the methods that he would follow for the rest of his career.[28]

Even though Pavlenkov was for all intents and purposes officially banned from publishing until the late 1870s, whilst in exile he was responsible for the publication of thirty-four new books, plus a partial republication of Pisarev's collected works, each volume printed by a different St Petersburg typographer.[29] He received governmental permission to work as a translator, and continued working on a variety of translations while also planning several publishing projects, which he would bring to fruition as soon as he had regained his freedom. During this time, in a letter to N. K. Mikhailovskii, Pavlenkov sketched out his visionary idea for a new publishing project: 'a *biographical library*, [Thomas] Carlyle and [Gabriel] Tarde, taken generally in aggregate, must evoke faith in humankind in the hearts of the reading youth.'[30] The subtitle, *Biograficheskaia Biblioteka F. F. Pavlenkova*, would later appear under the title of each of the biographies issued in the series, 'Zhizn′ zamechatel′nykh liudei'.

Upon his return to St Petersburg in 1877, he was able to regain his right to publish and went back to publishing progressive works more or less openly. In 1879, he was again arrested and imprisoned, first in St Petersburg and then in Vyshnevolotsk prison until he was exiled to western Siberia in 1880. Pavlenkov, along with his friends and associates petitioned the government, insisting that he had been wrongfully arrested, never put to trial and had committed no crimes whatsoever. After a personal appeal to the Minister of the Interior, Count Mikhail Loris-Melikov, he was finally released from exile in Ialutarovsk in 1881 and allowed to return to St Petersburg where he resumed his publishing work.[31] Pavlenkov's publishing ventures found a ready place in the now burgeoning market, and he produced a variety of educational materials, popular science texts and literary collections that became an integral part of lending libraries in urban and provincial areas. In the late 1880s and early 1890s, Pavlenkov managed to revive his business, primarily through publishing various types of series, often under the rubric *biblioteka*. Pavlenkov's company published eleven of these, ranging from ZhZL to the 'Popular Science Library' (edited by Lunkevich) and the 'Popular Law Library'. As many publishers realized, serial publications offered a solid means of financial success, as they often

---

[28] For more detail, see Blium, *Pavlenkov*, pp. 34–35, and Korolenko quoted in Rassudovskaia, *Izdatel′ F. F. Pavlenkov*, pp. 21–22.

[29] See Blium, *Pavlenkov*, pp. 25–26, 85–87.

[30] Pushkinskii dom. Rukopiznyi otdel. Arkhiv N. K. Mikhailovskogo, f. 181, op. 1, ed/khr. 510, as cited in Rassudovskaia, *Izdatel′ F. F. Pavlenkov*, pp. 48–49. Emphasis added.

[31] See Desiaterik, *Pavlenkov*, pp. 176–216.

involved subscription-buying, book collection and multiple editions and printings. Also popular and profitable were Pavlenkov's collected editions of Pushkin, Pisarev, Shelgunov and Uspenskii, illustrated libraries of Pushkin, Lermontov and Gogol´, illustrated novels of Dickens and Scott, and abridged translations of Hugo and Cervantes. These authors later became biographical subjects for the ZhZL series, and their translators, editors and commentators would subsequently become some of Pavlenkov's biographers.

Pavlenkov and Biography
In the 1880s, Pavlenkov had already made forays into biography, publishing translations of Gaston Tissandier's *Les Martyrs de la science* (1879) and Henri Joly's *Psychologie des grandes hommes* (1884). In the introduction to Tissandier's volume, Pavlenkov wrote that 'the lives of the great scientists must awake in us a striving for work, presenting us examples of perseverance and unwavering energy, which make up the secret of success and sometimes the secret of genius'.[32] According to his contemporaries, Pavlenkov saw the era of 'great reaction' as an important time for providing positive role models to the young readers of his day. Now that Pavleknov had reinvigorated his publishing business and was turning substantial profits he could achieve his long-held ambition of creating a biographical library, as first conceived in Viatka, which would fulfil his dream of spreading enlightenment.

The critic E. A. Solov´ev, Nikolai Mikhailovskii and many other liberals and radically-inclined thinkers of the day were inspired to write something for the series, as evidenced by Pavlenkov's correspondence; his list of authors and subjects would become a veritable who's who of progressive thought. Pavlenkov's contemporary and close friend, N. A. Rubakin, commented on the striking circumstance that many of Pavlenkov's associates were members of revolutionary movements:

> As the Department of Police attested in those times, the large majority [of Pavlenkov's co-workers [authors and translators] comprised the 'untrustworthy element' [*raznochintsy*] who one way or another had attracted police surveillance to themselves. Besides that, among them were several political exiles (for example, N. S. Tiutchev), and political prisoners (V. Lichtenshtadt) and émigrés (L. Shishko, N. Konchevskaia, Kh. Rappoport, E. Lazarev-Laier, etc, etc). Of course, many of these people worked for Pavlenkov under pseudonyms or completely anonymously.

[32] Rassudovskaia, *Izdatel´ F. F. Pavlenkov*, p. 48.

All the same, their names, for the literary fellowship of their time and in general for the intelligentsia was undoubtedly an 'open secret'.[33]

To name just two revolutionary luminaries, Vera Zasulich wrote a biography of Voltaire under the pseudonym I. M. Karenin; People's Will member, journalist and poet Petr Filippovich Iakubovich authored a biography of Nekrasov. According to Rubakin, who was writing his recollections of Pavlenkov in 1928 for the Soviet reader, Pavlenkov strove to show readers 'an international intelligentsia', which would enable readers to form their own judgments about world culture, and in each small book wanted to 'provide a social, historical, ethical and scientific evaluation of each *intelligent*'.[34] Though Rubakin emphasized that Pavlenkov had an unbiased approach, on closer examination, the figures that Pavlenkov selected for the 200 biographies either belonged to a list of forbidden authors, whose works at one point were considered too dangerous for distribution to the mass reader, or who espoused ideals that were alien to the principles of orthodoxy, autocracy and nationality propounded by the tsarist government. For Pavlenkov, this was a means of making inaccessible historical figures and their dangerous ideas more available and widely known.

It was an unprecedented undertaking of massive scope. To grasp fully the breadth of Pavlenkov's vision, we employ Roger Chartier's methodology of describing the formal, pictorial and substantive elements of this body of texts to identify how readers could 'appropriate the object of their reading'.[35] Pavlenkov originally envisioned a library that would include 200 biographies by category, divided into a 'Foreign Division' and a 'Russian Division' (see fig. 1).[36] The ten categories of biographies were representatives of world religions; political and national heroes; scientists; philosophers; philanthropists and enlighteners/educational activists; explorers; inventors and people with broad social initiatives; writers; artists; musicians and actors. The biographies were usually seventy to ninety pages in length. On occasion two similar figures would be published together in the same book, while certain biographies were collective in nature, such as

---

[33] N. A Rubakin, 'Iz istorii bor′by za prava knigi' (Rukopis′). Gosudarstvennaia Biblioteka im. Lenina. Otdel rukopisei, f. 358 (N. A. Rubakin), p. 211. In some ways, this group can be seen as analogous to the 'Grub Street' discussed by Robert Darnton in *The Literary Underground of the Old Regime*, Cambridge, MA, 1982.

[34] Rubakin, 'Iz istorii', cited in Rassudovskaia, *Izdatel′ F. F. Pavlenkov*, p. 49.

[35] Roger Chartier (ed.), *The Culture of Print: Power and the Uses of Print in Early Modern Europe*, Oxford, 1989, p. 4.

[36] 198 biographies actually came out in 193 booklets, according to E. Gorelik, *Katalog ZhZL 1890–2010*, Moscow, 2010, p. 46.

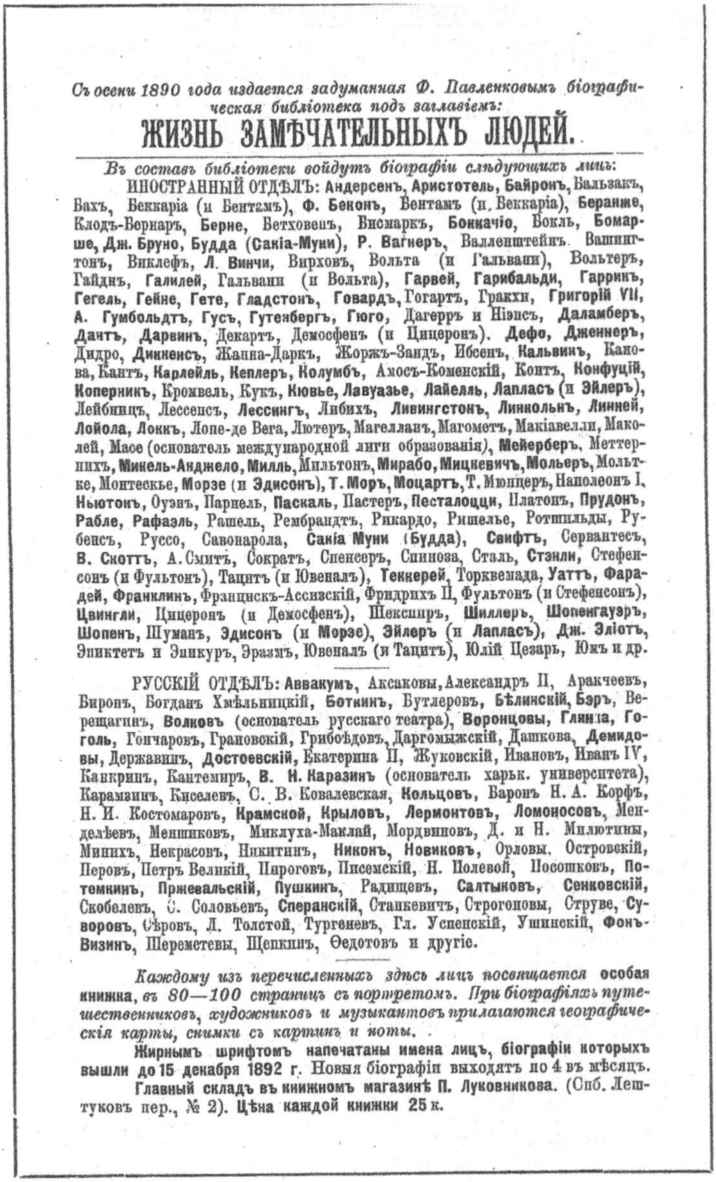

Съ осени 1890 года издается задуманная Ф. Павленковымъ біографическая библіотека подъ заглавіемъ:

ЖИЗНЬ ЗАМѢЧАТЕЛЬНЫХЪ ЛЮДЕЙ.

Въ составъ библіотеки войдутъ біографіи слѣдующихъ лицъ:

ИНОСТРАННЫЙ ОТДѢЛЪ: **Андерсенъ, Аристотель, Байронъ,** Бальзакъ, Бахъ, Беккарія (и Бентамъ), **Ф. Беконъ,** Бентамъ (и Беккарія), **Беранже,** Клодъ-Бернаръ, **Берне,** Бетховенъ, Висмаркъ, **Боккачіо,** Бокль, **Бомарше, Дж. Бруно, Будда (Сакіа-Муни), Р. Вагнеръ,** Валленштейнъ. Вашингтонъ, Виклефъ, **Л. Винчи,** Вирховъ, Вольта (и Гальвани), Вольтеръ, Гайднъ, **Галилей,** Гальвани (и Вольта), **Гарвей, Гарибальди, Гаррикъ, Гегель, Гейне, Гете, Гладстонъ, Говардъ,** Гогартъ, Гракхи, **Григорій VII, А. Гумбольдтъ, Гусъ, Гутенбергъ, Гюго,** Дагерръ и Ніэпсъ, **Даламберъ, Дантъ, Дарвинъ,** Декартъ, Демосфенъ (и Цицеронъ). **Дефо, Дженнеръ,** Дидро, **Диккенсъ,** Жанна-Даркъ, Жоржъ-Зандъ, Ибсенъ, **Кальвинъ,** Канова, Кантъ, **Карлейль, Кеплеръ, Колумбъ,** Амосъ-Коменскій, Контъ, **Конфуцій, Коперникъ,** Кромвель, Кукъ, **Кювье, Лавуазье, Лайелль, Лапласъ (и Эйлеръ),** Лейбницъ, Лессепсъ, **Лессингъ,** Либихъ, **Ливингстонъ, Линкольнъ, Линней, Лойола, Локкъ,** Лопе-де Вега, Лютеръ, Магелланъ, Магометъ, Макіавелли, Маколей, Масе (основатель международной лиги образованія), **Мейерберъ,** Меттернихъ, **Микель-Анджело, Милль,** Мильтонъ, **Мирабо, Мицкевичъ, Мольеръ,** Мольтке, Монтескье, **Морзе (и Эдисонъ), Т. Моръ, Моцартъ,** Т. Мюнцеръ, Наполеонъ I, **Ньютонъ,** Оуэнъ, Парнель, **Паскаль,** Пастеръ, **Песталоцци,** Платонъ, **Прудонъ, Рабле, Рафаэль,** Рашель, Рембрандтъ, Рикардо, Ришелье, Ротшильды, Рубенсъ, Руссо, Савонарола, **Сакіа Муни (Будда), Свифтъ,** Сервантесъ, **В. Скоттъ,** А. Смитъ, Сократъ, Спенсеръ, Спиноза, Сталь, **Стэнли,** Стефенсонъ (и Фультонъ), Тацитъ (и Ювеналъ), **Теккерей,** Торквемада, **Уаттъ, Фарадей, Франклинъ,** Францискъ-Ассизскій, Фридрихъ II, Фультонъ (и Стефенсонъ), **Цвингли,** Цицеронъ (и Демосфенъ), Шекспиръ, **Шиллеръ, Шопенгауэръ, Шопенъ,** Шуманъ, **Эдисонъ (и Морзе), Эйлеръ (и Лапласъ), Дж. Эліотъ,** Эпиктетъ и Эпикуръ, Эразмъ, Ювеналъ (и Тацитъ), Юлій Цезарь, Юмъ и др.

РУССКІЙ ОТДѢЛЪ: **Аввакумъ,** Аксаковы, Александръ II, Аракчеевъ, Биронъ, Богданъ Хмѣльницкій, **Боткинъ,** Бутлеровъ, **Бѣлинскій, Бэръ,** Верещагинъ, **Волковъ** (основатель русскаго театра), **Воронцовы, Глинка, Гоголь,** Гончаровъ, Грановскій, Грибоѣдовъ, Даргомыжскій, Дашкова, **Демидовы,** Державинъ, **Достоевскій,** Екатерина II, Жуковскій, Ивановъ, Иванъ IV, Канкринъ, Кантемиръ, **В. Н. Каразинъ** (основатель харьк. университета), Карамзинъ, Киселевъ, С. В. Ковалевская, **Кольцовъ,** Баронъ Н. А. Корфъ, Н. И. Костомаровъ, **Крамской, Крыловъ, Лермонтовъ, Ломоносовъ,** Менделѣевъ, Меншиковъ, Миклуха-Маклай, Мордвиновъ, Д. и Н. Милютины, Минихъ, Некрасовъ, Никитинъ, **Никонъ, Новиковъ,** Орловы, Островскій, Перовъ, Петръ Великій, Пироговъ, Писемскій, Н. Полевой, Посошковъ, **Потемкинъ, Пржевальскій, Пушкинъ,** Радищевъ, **Салтыковъ, Сенковскій,** Скобелевъ, С. Соловьевъ, **Сперанскій,** Станкевичъ, Строгоновы, Струве, **Суворовъ,** Сѣровъ, Л. Толстой, Тургеневъ, Гл. Успенскій, Ушинскій, **Фонъ-Визинъ,** Шереметевы, Щепкинъ, Ѳедотовъ и другіе.

Каждому изъ перечисленныхъ здѣсь лицъ посвящается **особая книжка,** *въ 80—100 страницъ съ портретомъ. При біографіяхъ путешественниковъ, художниковъ и музыкантовъ прилагаются географическія карты, снимки съ картинъ и ноты.*

Жирнымъ шрифтомъ напечатаны имена лицъ, біографіи которыхъ вышли до 15 декабря 1892 г. Новыя біографіи выходятъ по 4 въ мѣсяцъ.

Главный складъ въ книжномъ магазинѣ П. Луковникова. (Спб. Лештуковъ пер., № 2). **Цѣна каждой книжки 25 к.**

Fig. 1. Advertisement for 'Lives of Remarkable People', 1892

those on the Demidovs, the Rothschilds, the Aksakovs and the Vorontsovs. Each biography featured a title with its subject name and the subtitle: *Life and XXX Activity* (*Zhizn′ i literaturnaia deiatel′nost*, or *Zhizn′ i nauchnaia deiatel′nost′*, etc.). Pavlenkov often disguised the political activism of Western and Russian figures by using the subtitles to label their activities as primarily 'literary'.

Given the censorship restrictions on writing about Russian rulers only Ivan IV and Peter I appeared in the series, though advertisements from *Russkoe bogatstvo* in 1896 promised biographies of Alexander II and Catherine the Great.[37] Although some entries Pavlenkov planned for inclusion never appeared for similar reasons — for example, on Radishchev — he managed to get biographies of controversial Western figures, such as Cromwell and Metternich, through the censor, although he was unable to publish a biography of Marx.[38] Considering the strictness of the era's censorship, the fact that Pavlenkov included the biographies of Russian writers and political thinkers with revolutionary inclinations (Pisarev, Belinksii and Herzen) is remarkable; moreover, they were a great success with the public.[39]

The first two biographies came out at the end of 1890; the first biography in the series is usually considered to be the biography of Ignatius Loyola, by A. A. Bykov (although this was not the first to pass the censor), followed by Victor Hugo by A. N. Paevksaia. In 1891, fifty-eight biographies were published, including those of Columbus, Mozart, Jonathan Swift, Alexander Humboldt, Gogol′, Galileo, Darwin, Kramskoi, Schopenhauer, Abraham Lincoln, and Carl Linnaeus. The largest single group was the scientists, but particularly striking was the inclusion of the category of religious thinkers and activists, including Catholic, Protestant and non-Christian figures who were little known in Russia at that time, and who would later disappear altogether in the Soviet series, though some were eventually reintroduced in the post-Soviet incarnation of ZhZL. In the series, 'heroes', there were 140 non-Russians and sixty Russians. Pavlenkov's series was thus a hybrid of the universal and national biography. The numbers reflect Pavlenkov's clear preference for the need to introduce more world figures, but over the history of the series the proportions were constantly in flux. Even one of the authors in Pavlenkov's series, Evgenii Soloviev, remarked on its significance and emphasized its importance for Russian national identity. 'I am very glad,' he wrote in a letter to Pavlenkov, 'that you are especially concerned about the strengthening of the Russian division. This

---

[37] See *Russkoe bogatstvo*, 1896, 3, p. 183.

[38] See Desiaterik, *Pavlenkov*, especially pp. 316–26, on the controversies over the biographies of Cromwell, Katkov, Metternich and Marx. Marx's biography was never published, but the censor eventually passed the others after 1905.

[39] Rassudovskaia, *Izdatel′ F. F. Pavlenkov*, p. 52.

is really necessary. It would be unfortunate if there weren't [biographies of] Dobroliubov, Pisarev, but most of all, Herzen. [...] Let us not give up hope that the biographical library will be enriched with Herzen. The success would be striking.'[40] Many contemporary reviewers also focused more on the national component than on the biographies of foreigners. This emphasis on reviewing the biographies of their countrymen would indicate that, at least among the critics, there was a need for the establishment of a canon of great Russians.

The main task of the biographer was to relate the major facts of the subject's life and activities. Most biographies followed a conventional chronological format, narrating a life from birth and childhood through the subject's most productive period of activity and ending with their death. This exposition did not vary significantly from one type of biography to another, although Pavlenkov sometimes included illustrations for biographies of artists and excerpted musical transcriptions of composers' most famous works. The books were produced in 8,100-copy print runs and totalled more than 1.5 million copies. The volumes were inexpensive, priced at 25 kopeks each. Brooks has demonstrated that books priced over 30 kopeks were not intended for a lower class audience, thus the pricing, paperback covers and the length of the books in Pavlenkov's series demonstrates that they were largely intended for the mass reader rather than the educated audience.[41]

Unlike his predecessors, Pavlenkov instituted a biographical series rather than producing individual biographies, biographical dictionaries or an encyclopaedic form, which relied on short entries for each figure and a fixed alphabetical ordering principle. Pavlenkov was building on his earlier reputation as a publisher, as attested to by Rubakin: 'I remember, in 1877–1881, when I was working in the library of my mother, readers would ask me: "Do you have Pavlenkov publications?" They asked for them not by their titles but by the name of the publisher. That kind of interest on the part of readers did not occur then with any other publishers.'[42] The publication of multiple series served as a great source of revenue for the savvy publisher, and indeed has become one of the 'staples of the business of publishing'.[43] Stephen Lovell has remarked upon the 'cultural impact' and continued importance of *seriia* in the Soviet era, which organized reading for the less

---

[40] Desiaterik, *Pavlenkov*, p. 303.
[41] Brooks, 'Readers', pp. 105, 145.
[42] Rubakin, 'Iz istorii', p. 222.
[43] Robin Myers, Michael Harris and Giles Mandelbrote (eds), *Lives in Print: Biography and the Book Trade from the Middle Ages to the 21st Century*, New Castle, DE and London, 2002, p. vii.

experienced reader and made it a routine activity. He also emphasizes the special importance of the subscription edition, which played an important part in introducing new readers to the 'world of books'.[44]

Since Pavlenkov chose to issue the biographies as a *library*, that is, as a series, which the reader could purchase and read in any order, both visual and internal similarities were paramount. Pavlenkov's innovation was to develop a template to signal to the reader that there were certain typical visual and contextual features that could be expected from volume to volume despite having multiple authors. The uniform physical format of the Pavlenkov series, with the subject's and author's names, accompanied by a photograph or engraving on the frontispiece (see fig. 2), made them instantly recognizable and constitutes one feature that unites all the permutations of the series over time, although the Pavlenkov series had soft rather than hard covers. This brand recognition was only taken to the next level in the Soviet era series as late as 1962, when the cover became a standardized format with artwork designed by Iu. Arndt.[45] Though ZhZL had competitors at the turn of the century — 'The Library of Famous Writers', 'The People's Library' and 'Travels' — ZhZL took first place among them.[46] Pavlenkov's series greatly contributed to the habit of Russian readers to subscribe to a series, rather than to purchase individual books. Pavlenkov was a shrewd businessman and deliberately undercut the pricing of his competitors in order to get these volumes and others that he produced to the largest possible audience.

A total of seventy-eight biographers took part in the series, the majority of whom were Russians who knew multiple foreign languages and came from St Petersburg and the provinces. Some biographers had earlier worked on their subject's collected works for Pavlenkov's press and had written biographical notes which they then developed into longer biographies, a practice inspired by the German scholarly tradition.[47] The largest group of biographers were *raznochintsy*, and included teachers, translators, lawyers and bureaucrats, who were generally categorized as the 'democratic

---

[44] Lovell, *Reading Revolution*, p. 62.

[45] *Katalog ZhZL 1890–2010*, p. 110.

[46] V. F. Iurkin, 'Dukhovnoe zaveshchanie', cited in Iurkin, *Vremia i knigi. Molodaia gvardiia v epokhu peremen*, Moscow, 2010, p. 112.

[47] See Roger Paulin, 'Adding Stones to the Edifice: Patterns of German Biography', in Peter France and William St Clair (eds), *Mapping Lives: The Uses of Biography*, Oxford, 2002, pp. 103–14. This trajectory can be seen in A. S. Skabichevskii's work on A. S. Pushkin for the publisher. For an analysis of Skabichevskii's and later Pushkin biographies in the series, see Angela Brintlinger, 'The Remarkable Pushkin', *Slavic & East European Journal*, 60, 2016, 2, pp. 221–40.

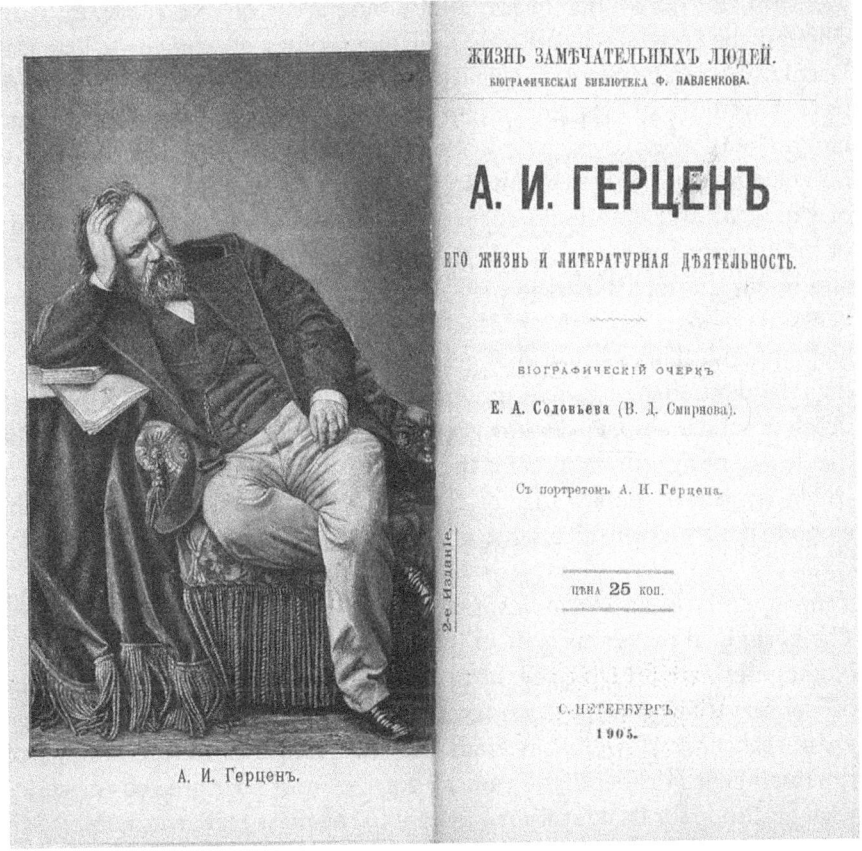

Fig. 2. Frontispiece and title page of ZhZL's biography of Herzen, 1905

intelligentsia' by one of Pavlenkov's own biographers.[48] Many of them were people Pavlenkov met when he was exiled in Viatka and Siberia or serving time in the Vyshnevolotsk transit prison, as Rubakin noted. One group of biographers were generalists who worked in any genre, others were subject specialists who were willing to become popularizers (the most famous of these was Vladimir Solov′ev who wrote the biography of Mohammed for the series) and a third group was made up of memoirists who wrote on the basis of their own personal relationships, or memoirs of their subjects, such as the doctor of mathematics, Elizaveta Litvinova, who wrote the biography of her friend Sofiia Kovalevskaia. Pavlenkov's last commissioned biographer, P. F. Iakubovich, (writing under the pseudonym

---

[48] Gorbunov, *Pavlenkov*, p.153.

Mel′shin) authored the series' 200th biography on Nekrasov in 1907. Though the series included only four biographies of women — Princess Dashkova, George Sand, Sofiia Kovalevskaia and George Eliot — there were a number of women among the biographers.[49] According to one biographer, Pavlenkov's circle worked as a 'family *artel*″ and thought of his enterprise not only as an intellectual place of refuge but also as a source of financial and emotional support.[50] Pavlenkov attended to the needs of his authors and made sure to pay them more than sufficient advances and honoraria to cover their costs of living. He also sent his authors any necessary books, journals or other materials for the composition of their biographies.[51] Though some biographies in the series were criticized for their tendentiousness, while others were faulted for unevenness in their depth of scholarship, Pavlenkov gave his authors a great deal of freedom in the degree of interpretation and their views of their subject.[52] The project, which continued publishing for fourteen years after Pavlenkov's death, embodied a true collective sense of purpose.

Contemporary Reactions to the Series

The periodical press was split in its assessment of the series. Pavlenkov's biographies were criticized by the periodicals that served as the mouthpiece of conservative groups, such as the *Zhurnal ministerstva narodnogo prosveshcheniia*. However, journals that reflected the divergent views of the intelligentsia (liberal and radical) for the most part greeted the series with gratitude for its educational benefit to the mass reader, as reflected in reviews in *Russkaia mysl′*, *Russkoe bogatstvo*, *Obrazovanie* and *Russkaia shkola*. One reviewer in *Obrazovanie* opined:

> Recently, Mr Pavlenkov had the happy thought to give us an entire biographical library, beautifully composed and inexpensively priced.

[49] Pavlenkov was acquainted with a number of very well educated women who were pedagogues, translators, writers and doctors, who became authors of biographies in the series. They included A. N. Annenskaia, M. A. Beketova (Blok's aunt), E. F. Litvinova, A. N. Paevskaia, M. V. Sabinina and M. V. Vatson. A few were also members of revolutionary groups such as Vera Zasulich (who wrote under a pseudonym) and S. E. Usova. For more information on these talented individuals, see Gorbunov's cameo portraits of members of Pavlenkov's artel′ in *Pavlenkov* (unnumbered pages between pp. 128–29) and the *Katalog*, pp. 56–60.

[50] Gorbunov, *Pavlenkov*, pp. 143–44.

[51] Ibid., pp. 152–62, 176–80.

[52] Kharkov University professor A. S. Viazigin, who wrote the ZhZL biography of Grigorii V while still a graduate student, later became a member of the nationalist rightist group the Black Hundreds. Ibid., p. 157.

These little booklets will be of great use to the Russian public. One famous thinker said, that opening a great work, he experiences the same feeling as if he walked in a splendid church, beneath the great vaults, taking in each one with involuntary veneration. Isn't this the same feeling we experience when we read the life of remarkable people? We need great graves [*mogily*] if there is no greatness among the living. Such reading has an enormous significance also for the youth.[53]

Contemporary psychologist Evgenii Lozinskii also spoke of the pedagogical benefits that would redound to the advantage of Russian youth upon reading the biographies from Pavlenkov's library in an article in *Russkaia shkola*.[54] Yet even among all the positive reviews, there was a common refrain: the biographies suffered from a lack of general editorship, which would have set a consistent standard for the ways that the subjects would be treated, would have carefully checked for factual inaccuracies and inconsistencies and would have monitored the text for clarity in writing and argumentation.

The readership of the original series greatly extended beyond its intended original audience. Famous Russian writers and critics spoke of their high estimation of ZhZL biographies. Nikolai Leskov and Il´ia Repin both commented on how they were carried away by reading ZhZL biographies (of Buddha and Aristotle, respectively).[55] The philosopher Nikolai Berdiaev, the historian Vladimir Vernadskii and writers Ivan Bunin and Aleksei Tolstoi read the biographies in their youth.[56] Meanwhile, the preeminent Russian religious philosopher and biographer of Mohammed in the series, Vladimir Solov´ev, wrote of his expectation to be included in the series upon his death.[57]

Upon Pavlenkov's death, obituaries written in a variety of journals extolled Pavlenkov's importance as a publisher and the benefit that the masses received from his publications. In an obituary published in *Russkoe bogatsvo*, Korolenko wrote:

---

[53] N. L. L., 'Zhizn´ zamechatel´nykh liudei. Biograficheskaia biblioteka F. Pavlenkova. V. G. Belinskii. N. V. Gogol´, M. E. Saltykov. 1891 g. po. 25 k.', *Obrazovanie*, 2, 1892, pp. 177–82 (p. 177).

[54] G. Pomerantseva, *Biografiia v potoke vremeni: ZhZL, zamysly i voploshcheniia serii*, Moscow, 1987, p. 24. See Evgenii Lozinskii, 'Geroi i geroichestvo v vospitanii', *Russkaia shkola*, 1, January 1911, pp. 5, 13–14.

[55] Desiaterik, *Pavlenkov*, p. 312.

[56] *Katalog ZhZL*, p. 5.

[57] Desiaterik, *Pavlenkov*, p. 312.

> Beginning with the works of D. I. Pisarev [...] book after book, the deceased produced a mass of publications, sometimes with the greatest of labour. To number them all in connection with the slowly changing conditions of the press would mean to write a biography of the deceased, and this work, probably will be done. The list would be long, the biography — full of engrossing interest.[58]

Pavlenkov's rank and status among publishers and his critical importance in the literary culture of the late nineteenth century was demonstrated in an obituary by P. Mertsalov in the competing publication catalogue/journal issued by the bookseller and publisher, Vol′f: *Izvestiia po literature, naukam i bibliografii knizhnykh magazinov tovarichestva M. O. Vol′f*.[59] Mertsalov points to the location of Pavlenkov's grave in Petersburg's Volkovo cemetery in the section accorded to literary greats, near to the graves of Pisarev, Dobroliubov and Afanasiev, as a sign of the honour accorded to him:

> though not a writer, nor a scholar nor a social activist, all the same he etched his name in the history of Russian culture [...] a publisher, enriching literature with an array of useful compositions, a publisher, bringing the light of knowledge through the perspective of popular works to the most diverse societal groups is worthy of being placed with the best proponents of native culture.[60]

Twenty-nine years later, Rubakin emphasized the importance of Pavlenkov's legacy, specifically in reference to ZhZL not just to their contemporaries, but to later generations: 'Not one of Pavlenkov's works, in my observance, can compare with the enormous influence that was shown on readers of all Russian strata, classes and ranks as the "Biographical library" or "Zhizn′ zamechatel′nykh liudei" published by Pavlenkov.'[61] Rubakin's assessment resonates in the observation of Roger Chartier:

---

[58] Ibid., p. 354.

[59] P. Mertsalov, 'F. Pavlenkov i ego zaslugi dlia russkoi kul′tury', *Izvestiia knizhnykh magazinov tov. M. Vol′f*, 3, February 1900, 5, pp. 74–76. For an analysis of how the publication strove to market books while also purveying high Russian culture, see Holmgren, *Rewriting Capitalism*, pp. 117–49 (p. 119).

[60] Mertsalov, 'F. Pavlenkov', p. 74.

[61] Desiaterik, *Pavlenkov*, p. 312; the quote is from N. A. Rubakin (p. 326). This comment by Rubakin has been repeatedly (ritualistically) cited in all the Soviet and post-Soviet publications on ZhZL.

To a greater extent than has been thought, widely distributed texts and books crossed social boundaries and drew readers from very different social and economic levels. Hence the need for the precaution of not predetermining their sociological level by dubbing them 'popular' from the outset.[62]

In the Soviet period, readers of the series spanned several social strata, from the designated youth audience of Molodaia gvardiia to the Soviet intelligentsia.

The Revival of ZhZL and the Rehabilitation of Pavlenkov
It is beyond the scope of this article to discuss in depth the central role played in the history of Soviet biography by Gor´kii's incarnation of ZhZL. Suffice it to say that during the Soviet era, it predominated and became the standard by which all other publishers measured the successes and failures of the genre. When rival presses sought to create their own biography series, they had to contend with the examples that ZhZL provided and to define how their series would be different and improve upon it, as Polly Jones's article in this collection demonstrates. What is curious for our purposes is how little Pavlenkov entered into Soviet histories of Russian biography and print culture. One would expect Pavlenkov to be taken up, like Chernyshevskii and Dobroliubov had been, for inclusion in Soviet cultural mythology as a forefather of the Bolsheviks. His lack of centrality is surprising for several reasons. First, Pavlenkov's progressive credentials and exile experiences made him ripe for mythification in the Soviet era. Secondly, Pavlenkov's orientation towards mass publishing and education and his own involvement in writing and publishing innovative primers to help the less literate in society would surely secure him a leading position in the pantheon of educators and progressive publishers. Thirdly, one would expect Pavlenkov's apparent single-minded dedication to publishing and his almost monastic life in pursuit of his goals to appeal to the Soviet notion of self-sacrifice for the betterment of the masses. In the thirty years of his publishing venture under difficult censorship conditions (including one decade of that period in exile), he released more than 750 different titles, totalling more than 3.5 million copies. Pavlenkov bequeathed the money that his press earned (over 3 million rubles) to the establishment of more than 2,000 village libraries and the founding of two self-help funds for writers and scholars.[63]

[62] Chartier, *Culture of Print*, p. 4.
[63] Desiaterik, *Pavlenkov*, p. 364.

Though Pavlenkov's enterprise was mentioned in some general histories of late nineteenth-century Russian publishing,[64] Pavlenkov's name did not play a large part in early Soviet discussions of Russian reading history. The first short but scholarly monograph on Pavlenkov based on archival sources was published by N. M. Rassudovskaia in 1960, most likely as a result of the cultural thaw taking place at the time. Rassudovskaia prefaces her work with the remark that the publishing activities of Pavlenkov were only partly illuminated by the memoirs of contemporaries such as Korolenko, Rubakin and Alchevskaia. She squarely situates his work within the series of 'great historical events' taking place from the middle of the nineteenth century to the beginning of the twentieth century. During the 1970s more articles began to appear about Pavlenkov, always with the epithets 'rebellious' (*miatezhnyi*), 'progressive' (*ideinei*), 'idealistic' (*ideal'nyi*), 'fanatical' (*fanatichnyi*) or 'enlightening' (*prosveshchenyi*), which all speak to the one-sidedness of his portrayal. During the Soviet era, other progressive publishers (such as I. D. Sytin, K. T. Soldatenkov, the Sabashnikov and Granat brothers) had an abundance of materials detailing their contributions to Russian publishing, although Pavlenkov was still side-lined.[65] Nevertheless book collectors and other avid fans of the pre-Revolutionary series sought out the booklets and began to delve deeper into the history of the publisher and his works. Perhaps not surprisingly, the revival of Pavlenkov's biographical library coincided with the resurgence of interest in Pavlenkov as a publisher.

In the aftermath of the collapse of the Soviet Union and the end of state-subsidized publishing, the original Pavlenkov series was republished by Ural Press in Cheliabinsk (from 1994 to 1999), and included a new biography of Pavlenkov by Iunii Gorbunov (1999) as its final volume.[66]

---

[64] S. V. Belov, A. P. Tolstiakov, *Russkie izdateli kontsa XIX–nachala XX veka*, Leningrad, 1976, especially pp. 36–63.

[65] In fact, Sytin and Soldatenkov were both featured in a ZhZL volume, *Moskovskie obyvateli*, which went through two editions before the Pavlenkov biography by Desiaterik was even published in the series that Pavlenkov founded. See M. I. Vostryshev, *Moskovskie obyvateli*, Moscow, 1999. A second edition followed in 2003, and a third in 2007. Works on Sytin, Soldatenkov, Soikin, Sabashnikov and the Granat brothers, all publishers who were taken up by the Soviets as ideologically correct, were published from the 1960s to the 1980s. See, for example, Aleksei Admiral'skii, *Rytsar' knigi*, Leningrad, 1970, on P. P. Soikin; S. V. Belov, *Brat'ia Granat*, Moscow, 1982 and *Knigoizdateli Sabashnikovy*, Moscow, 1974; E. A. Dinershtein, *I. D. Sytin*, Moscow, 1983 and *'Fabrikant' chitatelei A. F. Marks*, Moscow, 1986, and A. P. Tolstiakov, *Liudi mysli dobra: russkie izdateli K. T. Soldatenkov i N. P. Poliakov*, Moscow, 1984. Desiaterik also wrote a biography of Sytin in 2015 for the ZhZL series.

[66] Iu. A. Gorbunov, *Florentii Pavlenkov, ego zhizn' i izdatel'skaia deiatel'nost: Biograicheskii ocherk*, Cheliabinsk, 1999, was published as vol. 40 of the Cheliabinsk republication of the original series.

The main editor of the Chelyabinsk republication, N. F. Boldyrev, gave several reasons for the republication of the series, citing the multifaceted perspectives of the series' authors and the merits of the biographies' laconicism: 'Pavlenkov created a genre for *our* hectic times and *our* psyche, that refrains fairly well from rhetoric and wordiness.'[67] Boldyrev stressed the need for a less ideologically charged biography series than the Soviet ZhZL to provide models for individual personalities and to reinstate a collective identity for a post-Soviet age:

> The biographies once commissioned by F. Pavlenkov present a kaleidoscope of authorial points of view, but it is precisely this fragmentariness, the serial's tendency not to favour any one particular world-view, that grants today's reader the enticing chance to be an unbiased observer, to come and go according to his own desire.[68]

Boldyrev specifically rebukes the Soviet-era Molodaia gvardiia publishing house for letting the series 'enter into the ideologically monotone, Procrustean bed of the *Sots-realist* model'.[69] The Chelyabinsk press was only one of several that sought to capitalize on the upsurge of interest in the original series — which was out of copyright — and republish it.[70]

In response to other presses' co-optation of Pavlenkov's series, Molodaia gvardiia struck back with its own correction of the historical record in Vladimir Desiaterik's biography of Pavlenkov, published in 2006 in the ZhZL series. It appears that the primary reason Pavlenkov's name was only mentioned in passing in the history of Russian publishing came as the result of Lenin's assessment of Pavlenkov's contribution. Although at one point, Lenin looked to Pavlenkov's *Entsiklopedicheskii slovar'* as a model for a 'people's encyclopedia' after the establishment of the Soviet Union,[71] he ultimately denied Pavlenkov's inclusion into the Soviet canon because of his financial success as a publisher and his gentry origins. In Marxist-Leninist terms, Pavlenkov was considered a bourgeois capitalist

---

[67] N. Boldyrev, 'Chelovek v nepreryvno meniaiushchemsia landshafte', *Biograficheskaia biblioteka F. Pavlenkova, tom. 1*, Cheliabinsk, 1994, p. 7.

[68] Ibid., p. 10.

[69] Ibid., pp. 6–7.

[70] Ol'ma-Press (in 2001) and Ruppol Klassik (in 2014–15) have also republished Pavlenkov's biographical library.

[71] 'Iz vospominanii F. N. Petrova "Ob otnoshenii V. I. Lenina k Entsiklopedii"', cited in A. I. Drobinskii, *K. Marks, F. Engel's, V. I. Lenin i entsiklopedicheskaia literatura*, Moscow, 1958, p. 60, cited in Rassudovskaia, *Izdatel' F. F. Pavlenkov*, p. 77. In fact, the *Bol'shaia Sovetskaia entsiklopediia* neglects to mention that Pavlenkov founded ZhZL, cf. entry for F. F. Pavlenkov in *Bol'shaia Sovetskaia entsiklopediia*, vol. 31, 2nd edn, Moscow, 1955, p. 513.

exploiter, despite evidence to the contrary that he lived an austere life, published high-quality books with an educational slant and donated his company's profits to charitable causes that benefited the masses. Lenin claimed that Pavlenkov was insufficiently 'revolutionary' and thus his progressive publications, donations and the good he did was minimized and overlooked. Desiaterik imagines Lenin thinking: 'rich people shouldn't waste their money on opening libraries; it's a useless enterprise. It would be better instead to give means to the revolutionary cause directly.'[72] Desiaterik suggests that Lenin's comments effectively consigned Pavlenkov to the dark side of history in opposition to the Marxist-Leninist path. As a result of Lenin's characterization, Pavlenkov was not a forbidden figure, but he remained in historiographical limbo.

Desiaterik then goes on to list Pavlenkov's publishing (as opposed to financial) achievements:

> He won the reputation of an unyielding fighter for the freedom of the press with his publication of the collected works of the indomitable nihilist Dmitrii Pisarev. Along with the writer Vladimir Korolenko he shortened his days in Vyshnevolotsk political prison. He gave help to Nikolai Chernyshevskii, persecuted by the autocracy. He bought the rights to publish the collected works of Alexander Herzen, the disgraced exile from Russia. He published the biography of Lev Tolstoi in the *Zhizn' zamechatel'nykh liudei* series when the writer was excommunicated by the church. He gave Anton Chekhov books for distribution to prisoners on Sakhalin Island. He befriended the *narodnik* Nikolai Mikhailovskii. He published translations into Russian of Friedrich Engels and Karl Kautsky.[73]

Free of the Soviet version of publishing history, Desiaterik makes an argument for the reintegration of Pavlenkov by explaining his lack of centrality as the result of Lenin's interpretation. Desiaterik's biography returned Pavlenkov to the forefront of the history of the ZhZL series. V. F. Iurkin, the former, long-time director of Molodaia gvardiia press, specifically referred to Desiaterik's biography as 'a sign of gratitude' to Pavlenkov for creating the series.[74]

Also in 2006 Molodaia gvardiia staked its right to Pavlenkov's legacy by reinstituting him as the founder of ZhZL in the frontispiece in each volume of the series, beginning with Desiaterik's biography of Pavlenkov

---

[72] Desiaterik, *Pavlenkov*, p. 7.
[73] Ibid., p. 6.
[74] Iurkin, *Vremia i knigi*, p. 119.

and continuing to the present day. Thus Pavlenkov's name appeared in its proper place as the founder of the 'most famous series in the world [*samaia znamenitaia na svete*]'.[75] To highlight the symbolic significance of Pavlenkov's biography even further, Desiaterik's ZhZL biography was the 1,000th volume of the series (or, depending on the numeration of the combined series, original and Soviet and post-Soviet successors, the 1,200th volume). The reinstitution of Pavlenkov as founder was a savvy marketing ploy, a way for the press to distinguish it from other biography series, and to cite its historical importance not just as the first Russian biography series, but as the longest running series of any type anywhere, spanning three centuries and three regime changes.

The series has long been a barometer for changes in ideological trends, but only in the new millennium did the claims for ZhZL's importance gain mythic status. In the years preceding the Soviet collapse, ZhZL tapped into a sense of growing Russian nationalism, which has only increased with the current regime. Pressing Pavlenkov and his series into service to yet another ideological stance which does not reflect the founder's own social and political orientation, Vladimir Iurkin has called ZhZL a 'national treasure', a source of Russian patriotism and spirituality,[76] and sees helping today's youth as one of its most important goals:

> We cherish the hope that these books that we offer with our authors will bring readers political consciousness, enlightenment, a moral algorithm and strong feelings and ideas; without these things a nation is just a flock of sheep. Where can they be drawn from? Perhaps from the sum total of that experience that Russian and world history contains?[77]

Yet ZhZL is now far from both the original and Soviet precursors of the series. Iurkin has noted this change:

> The series, taking such a long journey, has transformed its fundamental form from the modest brochure of Pavlenkov to thousand-page volumes, absorbing the entire contemporary literary, scientific experience of this oldest of genres.[78]

---

[75] This phrase was used as the title of Sergei Semanov's aforementioned article on ZhZL in honor of the 75th anniversary of Molodaia Gvardiia press published in V. F. Iurkin (ed.), *Zhizn' zamechatel'nykh izdatel'stva* (cf. note 1).

[76] Iurkin, *Vremya*, p. 119.

[77] 'ZhZL — kniga na vse vremena', in ibid., p. 111.

[78] Ibid., p. 113.

The current strategies of the press demonstrate the diversity of media that need to be made available to cater to the variety of readers in Russia today. Although during the Soviet era, almost 75 per cent of the series' subjects were Russian, in the twenty-first century, the market has driven the series to expand again to include a greater variety of international figures, more foreign authors of biographies and more representatives of mass culture in such new off-shoot series as 'Biografiia prodolzhaetsia' (for still living figures), 'Malaia seriia' and new media products.[79] These days, anyone looking for new ZhZL biographies can find such diverse historical figures as Marilyn Monroe and Genghiz Khan appearing almost simultaneously, as they jockey for space on the shelves with more scholarly biographies written by leading historians and literary critics from Russia and abroad. The varied tastes of different generations of Russian readers are catered for by the range of biographies provided. The massive thousand-page tomes appeal to serious readers and bibliophiles; the less serious reader can turn to the celebrity biographies or shorter works. Even the non-reader now has audio book options as well as a YouTube channel with short ZhZL videos, organized in thematic playlists such as 'Famous Seducers' and 'Great Romances'. The degree to which the new biographies draw on the research of the international scholarly community varies widely, however, and the tension between being a national biography series or a post-national series is still unresolved.

---

[79] For example, see the playlists of ZhZL biography videos on YouTube at <https://www.youtube.com/user/LifeOfGreatPeople> [accessed 6 January 2016].

3

'Remembrances of a Distant Past': Generational Memory and the Collective Auto/Biography of Russian Populists in the Revolutionary Era

BEN EKLOF and TATIANA SABUROVA

'We are linked inseparably by the irretrievable past.'[1]
Egor Lazarev to Fanni Kravchinskaia, 29 October 1932

RECENT studies of Russian Populism, many of which are biographical in approach, have focused almost exclusively upon its engagement with terrorism.[2] In reality, while the terrorist People's Will did emerge out of the Populist movement, that organization was in fact a radical departure from the deeply-held beliefs of its founders, one driven by frustration rather than by temperament or core doctrine. The larger movement had its origins in the Chaikovskii Circle in the 1870s: a group of young men and women who, in reaction to the infamous Nechaev scandal,[3] set out to

---

Tatiana Saburova carried out research for this article as part of the Basic Research Program at the National Research University Higher School of Economics (HSE), which is supported by a subsidy from the Government of the Russian Federation for the implementation of the Global Competitiveness Program. Ben Eklof received a grant from the College Arts and Humanities Institute at Indiana University.

[1] Columbia University, Rare Book and Manuscript Library, Bakhmeteff Archive, the Sergei Mikhailovich Kravchinskii Papers, Box 1. (By 'we' Lazarev is referring to Ekaterina Breshko-Breshkovskaia.)

[2] Much recent work concentrates primarily on the links between Populism and either terror or religion. See Susan K. Morrissey, 'Terrorism, Modernity, and the Question of Origins', *Kritika: Explorations in Russian and Eurasian History*, 12, Winter 2011, 1, pp. 215–26, and Claudia Verhoeven, *The Odd Man Karakozov: Imperial Russia, Modernity and the Birth of Terrorism*, Ithaca, NY, 2009.

[3] Nechaev was an unscrupulous but charismatic Populist affiliated with Bakunin, author of 'The Catechism of a Revolutionary', in which youth were encouraged to reject all conventional moral values in the cause of the revolution. He convinced a small group that he was connected with a vast conspiratorial organization abroad; when one student became suspicious of these false claims, Nechaev had him murdered. The episode was the

establish a movement based upon high ethical standards, group solidarity and a dedication to serving the people by bringing about a social and political transformation of Russian life. Populism (the name came later — at the time this generation called themselves 'propagandists' or socialist revolutionaries) evolved into a huge, diversified and somewhat amorphous political constellation, one which (especially in its neo-Populist variant) espoused radical goals, but sought a pathway to these ends through gradualist means.[4] It developed a sophisticated and detailed programme of societal and political transformation, as well as economic theories (especially that of the Chaianov school), which later in the twentieth century caught the attention of global developmental economists. In 1917, Populists occupied prominent positions in the Provisional Government, both in Petrograd and in the provinces, but of course ultimately their cause lost out to the Bolsheviks, who offered, as William Rosenberg has pointed out, 'a capacity for organization, an ideological clarity, and a social positioning that facilitated affiliation with the radical relocation of power and authority'.[5]

In this article, we describe the construction of a collective remembrance by 'losers' in the events of 1917 and the subsequent Civil War; a concerted writing project which unfolded during the first decade or so of Soviet rule. In short, below we apply the tools of memory[6] and generational

---

subject of Dostoevskii's novel, *Besy* (*The Possessed*).

[4] There is an enormous literature on Russian Populism. Foundational works include Franco Venturi, *Roots of Revolution: A History of the Populist and Socialist Movements in Nineteenth Century Russia*, New York, 1966; Boris Itenberg, *Dvizhenie revoliutsionnogo narodnichestva*, Moscow, 1965; Nikolai Troitskii, *Pervye iz blestiaschei pleiady: Bol'shoe obshchestvo propagandy 1871–1874*, Saratov, 1991. For the wave of interest in Populism in the 1960s and '70s, see Philip Pomper, *The Russian Revolutionary Intelligentsia*, 2nd edn, Wheeling, IL, 1993, and especially on the Chaikovskii Circle: Reginald Zelnik, 'Populists and Workers: The First Encounter between Populist Students and Industrial Workers in St. Petersburg, 1871–1874', *Soviet Studies*, 24, October 1972, 2, pp. 251–69, and Martin A. Miller, 'Ideological Conflicts in Russian Populism: The Revolutionary Manifestoes of the Chaikovsky Circle', 1869–1875, *Slavic Review*, 29, March 1970, 1, pp. 1–21.

[5] Edward Acton, V. I. Cherniaev, and William G Rosenberg, *Critical Companion to the Russian Revolution 1914–1921*, Bloomington, IN, 1997, pp. 29–30.

[6] On the approaches of memory studies, see the recent article by Gregor Feindt, Félix Krawatzek, Daniela Mehler, Friedemann Pestel and Rieke Trimçev, 'Entangled Memory: Toward a Third Wave in Memory Studies', *History and Theory*, 53, February 2014, pp. 24–44. About the theoretical foundations and basic concepts, see Aleida Assmann, and Sarah Clift, *Shadows of Trauma: Memory and the Politics of Postwar Identity*, New York, 2016, and specifically, Astrid Erll, 'Travelling Memory: Whither Memory Studies', *Parallax*, 17, 2011, pp. 4–18.

studies[7] to show how networks of exiles in the imperial period came together in the Soviet era to defend and preserve the legacy of their movement through a collective project of autobiographical writing in which the genres of memoir, biography and autobiography merged, and individual voices combined. Specifically, we follow the stages by which one 'Old Revolutionary' (as members of this generation insisted on labelling themselves) Nikolai Charushin (1851–1937), turned reluctantly to writing his memoirs, *O dalekom proshlom* (Remembrances of a Distant Past), published in three volumes. First published in 1926, the volume was positively received. A second volume, *O dalekom proshlom. Na Kare* (Remembrances of a Distant Past: Kara), went through a tortuous route and was published in 1929 only with a critical introduction by (the prominent figure in early Soviet ideological affairs and fellow former exile) Felix Kon. The third segment, *O dalekom proshlom. Na poselenii* (Remembrances of a Distant Past: Penal) was delayed and published in a limited print run in 1931.[8] For our purposes, most revealing was the process by which the memoirs culminated in a collaborative effort by the 1870s generation of Populists to inscribe, preserve and defend their memory.

Others more prominent, especially the venerable 'icon of the revolution', Vera Figner (1852–1942), appear on these pages as significant contributors to this project. As for Charushin, despite having played an important role in the early Populist movement, his is hardly a household name even among historians of modern Russia.[9] Yet his memoirs appear frequently in

---

[7] Karl Mannheim, 'The Problem of Generations', in Karl Mannheim, *Essays on the Sociology of Knowledge*, London, 1952 (1923); Howard Schuman, Jacqueline Scott, 'Generations and Collective Memories', *The American Sociological Review*, 54, 1989, pp. 359–81; Alan B. Spitzer, 'The Historical Problem of Generations', *The American Historical Review*, 78, 1973, pp. 1353–85 (see also his book, *The French Generation of 1820*, Princeton, NJ, 1987); Harald Wydra, 'Dynamics of Generational Memory: Understanding the East and West Divide', in Eric Langenbacher, Bill Niven, and Ruth Wittlinger (eds), *Dynamics of Memory and Identity in Contemporary Europe*, New York, 2012.

[8] *O dalekom proshlom*, Moscow, 1926. A second edition was published in 1973 with annotations by Boris Itenberg; all references below are from the second edition. *O dalekom proshlom. Na Kare*, Moscow, 1929; *O dalekom proshlom. Na poselenii*, Moscow, 1931.

[9] See Tatiana Saburova and Ben Eklof, *Druzhba, sem'ia, revoliutsiia: Nikolai Charushin i pokolenie narodnikov 1870-ikh godov v Rossii*, Moscow, 2016; Ben Eklof and Tatiana Saburova, *A Generation of Revolutionaries: Nikolai Charushin and Russian Populism from the Great Reforms to Perestroika*, Bloomington, IN, 2017. A brief autobiographical sketch of his life can be found in *Deiateli SSSR i revoliutsionnogo dvizheniia Rossii. Entsiklopedicheskii slovar' Granat*, Moscow, 1989, pp. 539–63. See also, V. D. Sergeev, *Nikolai Apollonovich Charushin: narodnik, obshchestvennyi deiatel', izdatel', kraeved*, Kirov, 2001.

histories of the Russian revolutionary movement.[10] For that reason — the relative obscurity of the person and the prominence of the memoirs — we believe an examination of how they came into being forms a promising platform for studying the intersection of self (life)-writing, collective auto/biography, generational identity and social memory in modern Russia.

Below we analyse how the individualized effort at memoir writing became a process of consolidating social memory, resulting in an 'entangled' or 'travelling' narrative and, in effect, an autobiographical account which at the same time served to tell the life stories of Charushin's comrades of the 1870s generation — a collective auto/biography. In this account Charushin himself sometimes fades into the background; at many points in O dalekom proshlom in fact, the voice of the author of the text becomes problematic, so that memoir, autobiography and biography become scrambled. Writing in exile from Viatka in 1929, the anarchist and philosopher Aleksei Borovoi caught the essence both of Charushin's personality and the task that person had set for himself in writing his memoirs, which Borovoi had just completed reading. While praising the parsimony of language, the unadorned style of the narrative and the person of the author himself which emerges from the pages of O dalekom proshlom, Borovoi hits upon the collective nature of the Populist memory project in his assertion that the author 'always and in every way left himself in the shadows'.[11]

Social Memory and Generational Identity

Much has already been written about the Soviet state's efforts to mobilize and manipulate social memory through the device of commemorations, museums, memoirs — the *lieux de mémoire* (sites of memory) classically described in a different context by Pierre Nora.[12] In particular, the work of Frederic Corney deftly examines how Party institutions worked hard to create and polish an official narrative describing the October revolution of 1917 as a seminal event in history — something seemingly evident in retrospect but needing to be established at the time.[13] Sandra Pujals and

---

[10] In his monumental history of the Populist movement Franco Venturi refers often to Charushin's memoirs, but concludes that Sinegub's were even more valuable for the historian. Venturi, *Roots of Revolution*, p. 474. For a more recent work utilizing his narrative, see E. I. Shcherbakova, *Otshetpentsy: Put' k terrorizmu (60–80-gody XIX veka)*, Moscow, 2008, pp. 83–152.

[11] Russian State Archive of Literature and Art (hereafter, RGALI), f. 1023, op. 1, d. 173, l. 85.

[12] Pierre Nora, 'Between Memory and History: Les Lieux de Mémoire', *Representations*, 26, Spring 1989, pp. 7–24.

[13] Frederick C. Corney, *Telling October: Memory and the Making of the Bolshevik*

Marc Junge have both produced studies of the Society of Former Political Prisoners and Exiles (OPK) founded in 1921, which became a pivotal battleground in the 'memory wars' between the Bolsheviks and remnants of other leftist parties.[14] These struggles culminated in 1935 with the dismantling of this organization, the banning of all discussion of Populism and the arrest of many of its surviving members.

The terminology employed in memory studies remains a work in progress.[15] To use the terms of one of the founders of memory studies, Maurice Halbwachs, collective memory is shaped only within and by a distinctive 'social frame'. However, some scholars have challenged the very existence of collective memory, arguing instead that only individual memory endures, or that memory shapes social identity itself. Aleida Assmann seeks to bridge these differences by arguing that all individual remembrances do in fact have a societal component, since they are constructed within a web of societal engagement and are always connected with the recollections of others. But, she continues, as long as such multiple recollections remain unintegrated into a common narrative both situating and simultaneously providing them with meaning, they remain fragmentary and disconnected, subject to alteration or even loss.[16] Thus, 'social memory' (the term she prefers to collective memory) emerges from a conscious and collaborative effort to shape a distinct narrative.

One such variant of social memory is generational memory, which is especially stable, and also shaped by the social frame. As Assmann notes: 'generational memory is an important element in the constitution of personal memories, because [...] once formed, generational identity cannot change'.[17] In Assmann's lexicon, generational memory is distinct from both political and cultural memory, both of which have trans-generational potential. In this essay, we adhere to her conceptualization.

Revolution, Ithaca, NY, 2004.

[14] Marc Junge, *Revoliutsionery na pensii: Vsesoiuznoe Obshchestvo Politkatorzhan i Ssyl'noposelentsev, 1921–1935*, Moscow, 2015; Sandra Pujals, 'When Giants Walked the Earth: The Society of Former Political Prisoners and Exiles of the Soviet Union, 1921–1935', unpublished PhD dissertation, Georgetown University, 1999.

[15] On memory studies, see Jeffrey K. Olick and Joyce Robbins, 'Social Memory Studies: From "Collective Memory" to the Historical Sociology of Mnemonic Practices', *Annual Review of Sociology*, 24, 1998, pp. 105–40.

[16] Aleida Assmann, 'Re-framing Memory: Between Individual and Collective Forms of Constructing the Past', in Tilmans, Karin, Frank van Vree and J. M Winter (eds), *Performing the Past: Memory, History, and Identity in Modern Europe*, Amsterdam, 2010, pp. 35–50 (pp. 40–41).

[17] Ibid., p. 41.

We see then that in the theoretical literature discussions of social memory often overlap with attempts to conceptualize identity (or 'self-identification' as a process).[18] Stephen Lovell has aptly shown how, in the multi-layered society that was imperial Russia, generational 'thinking' was a crucial means of self-identification.[19] As for generation, we understand the term as Karl Mannheim used it — namely as an age cohort sharing a common societal experience — but also in the terms Pierre Nora used: as a specific 'site of memory'. One is a sociological frame, the other a discursive construct. Thus, the 'seventies generation' we describe was a self-selective group drawn from the larger age cohort, many of whom — including often siblings — though sitting on the same school benches became civil servants, military officers, or prominent entrepreneurs rather than revolutionaries.[20] Below we trace how a group thinking in generational terms ('the seventies generation') evolved from the early twentieth century into the Soviet era when 'old revolutionaries' were forced to defend themselves and the legacy of Populism against an increasingly hostile state, and sought to create a larger, historical memory.

Charushin: A Short Biography
Nikolai Charushin grew up in provincial Viatka, five hundred miles northeast of Moscow. Like many others of his generation, upon completion of his studies at a local gymnasium he enrolled in the Technological Institute at St Petersburg, but soon dropped out to join the small circle of young men and women, including more notable figures such as Nikolai Chaikovskii, Sofia Perovskaia and Petr Kropotkin, which sought to spread its influence among students and the intelligentsia, and then to reach out to the peasantry by recruiting factory workers with ties to the countryside. This Chaikovskii Circle was soon penetrated by the police and most of its members arrested. Charushin himself spent nearly four years mostly in solitary confinement before being tried and convicted in 1878 in the sensational 'Trial of the 193'. Sentenced to hard labour and exile, Charushin and his wife, Anna Kuvshinskaia, also a dedicated Populist, spent the next seventeen years in Siberian exile; first in Kara, then in Nerchinsk, and finally in Kiakhta-Troitskosavsk, the tea *entrepôt* on the

---

[18] Rogers Brubaker and Frederick Cooper, 'Beyond "Identity"', *Theory and Society*, 29, 2000, 1, pp. 1–47.

[19] Stephen Lovell, 'From Genealogy to Generation: The Birth of Cohort Thinking in Russia', *Kritika: Explorations in Russian and Eurasian History*, 9, 2008, 3, pp. 567–94.

[20] Alfred J. Rieber, 'The Sedimentary Society', in E. W. Clowes (ed.), *Between Tsar and People: Educated Society and the Quest for Public Identify in Late Imperial Russia*, Princeton, NJ, 1991, p. 351.

border with China. In this period of exile, the Charushins interacted with many prominent fellow populists, such as Ivan Popov, Dmitrii Klements, Felix Volkhovskii, Leonid Shishko and Sergei Sinegub, but also established a lasting friendship with the commandant of the Kara penal system, Vladimir Kononovich; befriended prominent figures such as the Kiakhta tea merchant and public philanthropist A. M. Lushnikov and worked and travelled about Mongolia with the renowned explorer Grigorii Potanin. In exile, Charushin became a professional photographer, whose works were collected by the Russian Geographic Society, and have gained entry into histories of Russian photography. Upon returning in 1895 to his native Viatka, Charushin soon was engaged by the zemstvo, which he served for twelve years before being purged in the aftermath of the 1905 Revolution. In late 1905 he founded a newspaper, *Viatskaia Zhizn'* (later renamed *Viatskaia Rech'*, 1907–17), which soon gained national recognition and was labelled by Prime Minister Stolypin 'the most radical provincial newspaper in Russia'. In these years, he was active in the Peasant Union and the People's Socialist (NS) Party.

With the arrival of the Provisional Government in 1917, Charushin renewed his civic activities on several fronts. He served in the reborn Peasant Union as well as on the Central Committee of the NS Party, now renamed the Trudovaia Narodno-Sotsialisticheskaia Partiia, which played a significant role in the Provisional Government. He was again active in zemstvo affairs and served on the crucial food provision committee.[21]

With the Bolshevik seizure of power in October in Petrograd, Charushin gave a passionate speech to an extraordinary session of the zemstvo assembly, in which he lamented that:

> Fellow citizens and delegates, that which we feared and awaited apprehensively, has happened — in Petrograd a civil war has begun. A host of new calamities has now been added to general internal collapse at the front and in the rear lines. I believe that we, and not only the old regime, are to blame for the current situation. We worked relentlessly to deepen the revolution, and in the end deepened it to the point of Bolshevism.[22]

He was elected to serve on a Supreme Council formed by the provincial zemstvo assembly, which proclaimed Viatka an independent republic and

---

[21] A full listing of his affiliations can be found in a biographical entry in *Trudovaia Narodno-Sotsialisticheskaia Partiia: Dokumenty i materialy*, Moscow, 2003, pp. 583–84.

[22] Gosudarstvennyi Arkhiv Kirovskoi Oblasti (hereafter, GAKO), f. 616, op. 1, d. 267, l. 66; *Viatskaia rech'*, 28 October 1917, p. 3.

sought to organize resistance to the Bolsheviks. Charushin was arrested in late December, came before a revolutionary tribunal in January 1918, was released because of his 'irreproachable past service to the revolution', but incarcerated three more times during the subsequent civil war. Undeterred, he wrote to the Revolutionary Tribunal judging his case a bitter note:

> At the very time that the new Soviet regime is memorializing those who gave their lives in the cause of freedom, paying them every manner of tribute — plans are underway to build monuments to [Sofia] Perovskaia, [Andrei] Zheliabov and others of my comrades in the revolutionary struggle — at the same time, I repeat, those among their comrades who survive today and can boast of an 'irreproachable political past' which one would think this regime would also respect, can find no place in the Soviet Socialist Republic other than in prison![23]

These words foreshadowed the situation he would face in the following decade as he was writing his memoirs: a complex official martyrology in which the sacrifices of earlier Populists were commemorated at the same time that survivors of that cohort were being marginalized or worse in the new Soviet reality. When released for good in 1919 at the age of sixty-seven, it was on the condition he stay out of politics. Charushin, unlike some of his friends, chose to remain in the country seeking meaningful activity in what was becoming an increasingly constraining political environment. He worked briefly in the cooperative movement, and then, between 1921 and 1930 was employed at the Herzen Regional Library in Viatka. From 1922 he was a member of the OPK, a year after its founding. Resigning from the library in 1930 in despair over the ripples of the Cultural Revolution there, he lived a solitary and hungry last few years, before dying a natural death at the age of eighty-five in 1937.

Charushin's life was certainly a tragic one. Arrest and exile, physical hardship, personal loss, and having to witness the social and political transformation he had worked for all his life going so terribly awry in the years after the Revolution left its imprint on him. But it was also a rich and meaningful life, in both private and public terms. In fact, Charushin's engagement with civil society after returning from exile in 1895, his work for the zemstvo as a fire insurance and famine relief agent, his years with

---

[23] Gosudarstvennyi Arkhiv Sotsial'no-Politicheskoi Istorii Kirovskoi Oblasti, f. SU 6799, op. 4, d. 4577, l. 22–23 ob. The reference to 'irreproachable service' is a reference to the conclusions of the Revolutionary Tribunal's conclusions following his first arrest and trial by the Bolsheviks in January 1918.

Viatskaia Rech', his affiliation with liberal democratic and neo-Populist political organizations, and even with prominent local entrepreneurs in the world of business, might lead us to question his revolutionary credentials later in life.

However, as he aged he never wavered from his self-description as 'an old revolutionary' who, along with his friends, had given their best years of their life to the cause of socialism. The friendships which had coalesced in Viatka circles during his student years and the bonds of the Chaikovskii Circle remained tight to the end of his life. He participated in a large and diverse network of fellow former exiles circulating between Kazan', Nizhnii Novgorod, Viatka, Perm', St Petersburg and Moscow, and pursuing life trajectories similar to his. It is no wonder that in his later years when, determined to protect and memorialize the meaningful legacy of his own life, he sought to include his peers and comrades, both in the writing and in the text itself of his memoirs. To that production of a hybrid genre of life writing in the 1920s we now turn.

Inscribing the Populist Legacy
In the 1920s there was both official and societal demand for memoirs dealing with the revolutionary movement. At this time in Soviet Russia, official prominence was given to recollections of tsarist prisons, hard labour and exile, creating a narrative of martyrdom or heroism, articulated through repression and 'suffering'. Those who experienced incarceration under the tsarist regime genuinely underwent much hardship, and some had not been able to endure the sufferings and indignities heaped upon them; they went insane, or even committed suicide when the accumulated physical and moral trauma proved to be too much. But as we see below, suffering — a trope much repeated by Western historians in their analysis of the memoirs forthcoming in this generation, was by no means the only motif emphasized.[24]

Scholars have accordingly labelled the decade after the Revolution one of an 'explosion' of memoirs; an outpouring generated both by Soviet policies and by the activities of the OPK. The notion of a 'memoir explosion' is supported by the abundance of publications of that society, many of which were issued by its house journal, *Katorga i Ssylka* (Hard Labour and Exile). The majority of such memoirs received positive reviews in the 1920s; their

[24] The trope of suffering, in terms both of experience and of self-presentation, is central to the biography of Figner written by Lynne A. Hartnett, *The Defiant Life of Vera Figner: Surviving the Russian Revolution*, Bloomington, IN, 2014. See Tatiana Saburova's review of this book in *The American Historical Review*, 120, 2015, 1, pp. 357–58.

educational value was emphasized by Dmitrii Furmanov, the popular Soviet author and former political commissar (author of *Chapaev*), who wrote 'the will to struggle is reinforced by such vibrant and convincing material'.[25] The most illustrious example of such memoir literature was the work of Vera Figner, *The Imprint of Life's Endeavours* (*Zapechatlennyi trud*). Bringing up the next generation on tales of the heroic exploits of opposition to autocracy, of sacrificing one's personal interests and needs on the altar of the common good and dedication, of one's life to the cause of revolution — all of this was called for and met a positive response in society, as is demonstrated by the abundance of letters addressed to Figner personally after publication of these memoirs. Here we have an obvious case where individual, societal and political memories are inseparable since, as Assmann points out, 'political memory is not fragmentary and diverse but emplotted in a narrative that is emotionally charged, and conveying a clear and invigorating message'.[26] Assmann further argues that political memory, reinforced by a plethora of visual, material objects as well as commemorative practices, achieves a definitive stability and (unlike generational memory) can be passed from generation to generation.

Figner was also instrumental in recruiting a series of autobiographical essays for publication by Granat in 1926. The more than forty autobiographical essays collected for that oft-utilized volume were written at her request, and after she had sent out guidelines asking them to answer the question 'why they had become revolutionaries'.[27] As Hilda Hoogenboom has shown, Figner energetically corresponded with the participants to help them shape their narratives, emphasizing the need to search for formative emotional experiences or readings in their childhood. Some of the published autobiographies in the Granat volume include Figner's annotations.[28]

Another compilation of revolutionary life stories put together at roughly the same time was the never completed (for political reasons) multi-

---

[25] *Pechat' i revoliutsiia*. 1, 1926, p. 189.

[26] Assmann, 'Re-framing memory', p. 43.

[27] The line originated in a notorious open letter, 'Why I Ceased Being a Revolutionary', written by the renegade Populist, Lev Tikhomirov, who had forsaken his comrades and the movement to become a conservative (Figner at this time was engaged in writing an introduction to Tikhomirov's memoirs), explaining his apostasy. Furthermore, it was noted, the memoirs tended to concentrate on the experience of prison and exile rather than on revolutionary events.

[28] Hilde Hoogenboom, 'Vera Figner and Revolutionary Autobiographies: The Influence of Gender on Genre', in Rosalind Marsh, *Women in Russia and Ukraine*, Cambridge, 1996, pp. 78–93 (pp. 82–83).

volume bio-bibliographical dictionary entitled *Figures of the Revolutionary Movement in Russia: From the Predecessors of the Decembrists to the Collapse of Tsarism* (1927–33). An entire volume in this project was devoted to the revolutionaries of the 1870s; for this volume the compilers utilized archives and published sources as well as interviews with surviving participants, and then turned to members of the OPK to review the finished manuscript. As for their memoirs, largely published around the turn of the century, the editors of the series note in the foreword to that volume that they had been valuable primarily in describing the personalities of the memoirists themselves, less so in terms of clarifying events or describing the rank-and-file members of the movement, which in any case, they added, might not be recalled with any accuracy: 'Thirty to fifty years are a long enough interval to cause memoirists to err in the precise dating of events.' The authors of the foreword also disputed the pessimistic appraisal that memoirists had given to the outcome of their efforts: 'in the light of the present [i.e., the establishment of Soviet power], the movement of that time was by no means as fruitless as the propagandists of the era themselves judged it to be.'[29] This was a mild version of the criticism that Populist efforts to memorialize the past were later to encounter.

'I confronted the emptiness of my situation'
We can discern several specific reasons this generation as a whole turned to the writing of memoirs, to biography and autobiography, including: to share their experience at revolutionary struggle with future generations; to compensate for their long isolation from society while in exile by leaving behind a 'trace' in the memories of their descendants, and to demonstrate the significance of their own contribution to the country's liberation movement. For those who survived imprisonment and exile, the memories remained vivid and central to their being, often shaping the rest of their lives. Thus, after experiencing more than twenty years of solitary confinement in Shlisselburg, Vera Figner wrote: 'You can't erase twenty years of your own life, years in which you experienced more than during all the rest of your life; for me the years in Shlisselburg are always with me, I won't reject them, I don't want to, nor am I able to shake them off.'[30]

---

[29] F. Kon, A. Shilov, B. Koz'min, V. Nevskii (eds), *Deiateli revoliutsionnogo dvizheniia v Rossii. Bio-bibliograficheskii slovar': Ot predshestvennikov dekabristov do padeniia tsarizma*, Moscow, 1929, vol. 2, part 1, p. xi.

[30] Figner to Novorusskii, 19/6 November 1912. Clarens in Vera Figner, *Sobranie sochinenii*, 7 vols, Moscow, 1933, 7, p. 197.

Psychologically, memoir writing was also an individual tool to overcome the traumatic experience of prison and hard labour as well as to facilitate the adaptation to life under difficult new conditions. Even in the late tsarist era, after being released, former revolutionaries had trouble orienting themselves in life; perhaps the only way to do so was to put down one's experiences on paper. In search of new meaning in life, and given the impossibility of renewing their societal activities where they had left off, a commitment to this endeavour provided an exit from political and societal isolation. This was true in the aftermath of the 1905 revolution, but even more so after the far more cataclysmic events of 1917–21. Figner described her own path in this way: 'In 1913 I confronted the emptiness of my situation: there were no revolutionary tasks I could apply myself to, indeed nothing that could serve the common cause. So instead I turned to a task my friends had long urged upon me and about which I had myself been thinking for some time. I began to write.'[31]

To be sure, her correspondence suggests she had actually started writing earlier, given lectures on the conditions experienced by political prisoners, written articles, all of this with such frequency that she finally had to make a conscious choice whether to concentrate on her memoirs alone or continue to give lectures. In a letter to Sophia Kropotkina (July 1909), Figner had described her decision to focus on her memoirs alone as an obligation to society:

> In August I arrived in Switzerland and since then have started working on my memoirs. If I can proceed with the kind of energy that I occasionally experience I should be able to finish a book 5 or 6 printer's lists in length. If I can do so then I will be fulfilling an obligation I have felt ever since the moment I was released [from incarceration] and at the same time satisfying a deeply felt personal need [*i vysshim udovletvorenim moego vnutrennego ia*].[32]

Her accounts of the writing process are very purposeful and goal-oriented. At the same time, the reader will note her repeated attempts to begin with her memoirs. In one case she is too busy, but feels a moral obligation. In the second and later statement she is confronting a spiritual void. All of this is indicative of a post-traumatic experience and of a loss of meaning in life after a decade of concerted and collective

---

[31] Vera Figner, *Zapechatlennyi trud*, 2 vols, Moscow, 1964, 1, p. 42.

[32] Figner to Kropotkina, July 1909. Vera Figner, *Polnoe sobranie sochinenii*, 6 vols, Moscow, 1930, vol. 6, p. 510.

revolutionary activity followed by two decades of solitary confinement, which she survived only because of the determination and resolve of her revolutionary convictions. Indeed, if one reads closely the memoirs themselves, what leaps out is just how fractured and fragile had been her orientation and sense of self upon initially returning to society, and how arduous was the process of restoring sustained contact with humanity, never mind society, itself in turmoil in 1905. Thus, we can recognize her turn to writing memoirs as proceeding in stages, as part and parcel of overcoming isolation and recovering a search for purposefulness in life.[33]

In different combinations we find the same mix of psychological and societal episodes in the path taken by Populists of the seventies generation to writing their memoirs. The majority of Populists rejected the October Revolution, viewing it as a political *coup d'état* rather than a social revolution. Echoing Charushin's own response to events, Egor Lazarev lamented:

Fifty-five years of struggle for political freedom! I sat in solitary confinement for 5–6 years, and on three occasions was subjected to administrative [rather than judicial] exile in Siberia. Oh how many years spent abroad, in emigration and in flight. Finally — an end to autocracy! Russia undergoes the greatest of revolutions and in March 1917 the ossified tsarist order is overthrown! Yet what kind of absurdity do we see then, when thousands of socialists, having paid for their free-thinking with years of confinement and hard labour, are now once again scattered over the endless tundra of Siberia and exile only to experience conditions immeasurably harsher than under tsarism.[34]

For Lazarev and other former Populists, a growing disillusionment with the outcome of this decades-long revolutionary struggle, as well as a perception of individual and collective superfluity in the new political environment combined to cause them to reflect upon earlier times, which they now often described as 'that distant past' (indeed, several of their memoirs, as well as Charushin's, included in the title a variant of that

---

[33] Despite all of these hardships, Figner did in fact recover a capacity not only to write, but also to enjoy life; she took pleasure in her travels in Europe, visits to museums, and recorded joyous impressions of Europe's cultural heritage and beautiful landscapes. The depiction of Figner's psychological devastation and deep desperation during and after exile, while certainly identifying one strand in her life, makes for a monochromatic portrait.

[34] Columbia University, Rare Book and Manuscript Library, Bakhmeteff Archive, The Sergei Mikhailovich Kravchinskii Papers, Box 1.

phrase). Here one can also detect a strong note of nostalgia for a past which had swallowed up their youth, consumed their energies and given them hope for the future. And let us not forget that this ageing generation was literally dying out; few remained on earth to defend its legacy, and those who did felt a moral obligation to preserve the memory of those who had fallen by the wayside.

Finally, as time passed, Populists sought to ward off 'erasure' brought on not only by the passage of time, but increasingly by a hostile environment. The endeavours by Populists to leave behind their recollections at first fit well with the needs of the new Soviet state, but over time increasingly diverged from them. Vera Figner played a key role in convincing Charushin, among others, to join together in a collective effort to defend the Populist legacy against a mounting threat. In 1921 Figner had encountered what was for her an entirely unexpected and shocking challenge to her sense of place in history — to her identity. In a letter to a colleague she described what had happened:

> Yesterday I was at the Petrovsko-Razumovskaia [Academy] at the invitation of students who sent along fifteen or twenty queries in advance. But it was late and I didn't get around to reading them; and I knew there would be some unwelcome questions which I had no wish to address. I had already had the occasion to respond to the likes of 'what is your stance towards the current political order?' or 'why don't you belong to the party in power today?'. But I certainly didn't anticipate what I read in one of the notes I perused *after* returning home from my presentation; concerning the historical significance of the People's Will it read: '*your efforts were all in vain, your energies were expended heedlessly and produced no results.*'[35]

'*I urge you to write down your recollections*'

It was at this point that memoir writing and autobiographical essay merged with collective autobiography, especially through the process of 'travelling narratives'. In order to combat the notion that their lives had been spent in vain and fruitlessly, the seventies generation set about determinedly to create a 'collective remembrance' supporting another's efforts, verifying the accuracy and veracity of their judgements, and analysing each other's testimonies. They felt it incumbent upon themselves to preserve the historical memory of the times they had lived and to recount the lives of

---

[35] Figner to Novorusskii, 23 October 1921. RGALI, f. 1185, op. 1, d. 239, l. 185. Emphasis added.

their fallen comrades, a task made all the more pressing in that so few witnesses of the era were still alive.

In 1922, Vera Figner convinced Charushin to register with the OPK. By the middle of the decade he had been drawn into the collective efforts of members of that society to defend the legacy of Populism against increasingly shrill attacks mounted by young Bolsheviks and historians. But the process was gradual and his reluctance evident. Early in January, 1924 Figner wrote in a note to Charushin:

> I urge you to write down your recollections about the origins, activities and organizations of the Chaikovtsy in several cities. Such a history of the circle, remarkable in all ways, is lacking, and *you must write down what you know, what you did and what you learned from others*.[36]

Note here and below the oft-repeated accent in the correspondence of the old revolutionaries on the need to give as full and reliable a version of the activities of the Chaikovskii Circle as possible ('what you know...') The claim to authenticity would be legitimized by the fact of direct participation in the affairs of the circle itself. In reply, Charushin pointed out that:

> I've been waiting all along for one of the better informed members of my circle to fulfil this task, but up to now have been disappointed in that expectation. Yours is not the first time I have heard such a request, but I confess that with all the unremitting cares of daily life, when matters of the present can swallow up one's attention, there has simply been no time to think about the past. Now however, with almost none of the Chaikovtsy still alive, the feeling is much more acute that I am *obliged* to the best of my abilities to fill the gaps in that area.[37]

But he was slow to move, and two weeks later, on 29 January 1924, Figner again urged Charushin to take up writing his memoirs, describing the act as a moral debt to those who were no longer among the living; otherwise much would be forgotten, and then irretrievably lost. She wrote:

> So, for all these reasons you must get down to business, and please, no more delays. Otherwise, what if you are taken ill and won't be able to recall the details; after all this is a debt owed to the public by those of us who have outlived our comrades. I am so happy I have already made my own

---

[36] RGALI, f. 1642, op. 1, d. 77, l. 1. Emphasis added.
[37] RGALI, f. 1185, op. 1, d. 817, l. 5.

contribution — if I had to start today and write the way I did then — I just couldn't do it.[38]

Figner was not alone in entreating Charushin; fellow member of the Chaikovskii Circle and lifelong friend of Charushin, Aleksandra Kornilova-Moroz added her own voice to the choir:

> All of us, the last among the living, have the obligation to finally clarify in a truthful and comprehensive way the many activities of that circle which made such a profound and vivid imprint upon the memories of contemporaries, set it apart from all others and put it at the forefront of the movement.[39]

In their letters to Charushin we again see the emphasis upon a debt to one's departed comrades of the Chaikovskii Circle as well as the striving to fix in the memory of generations to come the prominent role that that circle had played in the history of the revolutionary movement as a whole. This idea had arisen much earlier, during their collective imprisonment awaiting trial in the middle of the 1870s, and again after release at the turn of the century, but now was posed with far more urgency.[40]

Later, in December 1924, Kornilova-Moroz (who was herself writing a biography of Sofia Perovskaia, the legendary terrorist and member of the Chaikovskii Circle), prepared to send Charushin the memoirs of Leonid Shishko for use in his own account of events. She added a note: had he actually begun writing yet? Once more, in February 1925 she wrote to let him know that Vera Figner had confirmed the accuracy of his own replies to queries she, Kornilova-Moroz had made for her book concerning the early activities of their circle, as well as his commentary on Shishko's memoirs. Hence they were all on the same page on such matters — all the more reason for him to finally begin.

It seems that at this time Charushin was genuinely turning to the task of writing, for he sent Kornilova-Moroz a letter with a list of queries about the political stances of members of the circle, the details of the programme of the Chaikovtsy and their understanding of the practical tasks confronting them. But she was taking no chances. He received a detailed response from her in which she passionately reminded him once again of the importance

---

[38] RGALI, f. 1642, op. 1, d. 77, l. 30b.
[39] RGALI, f. 1642, op. 1, d. 51, l. 1.
[40] Gosudastvennyi Arkhiv Rossiiskoi Federatsii (hereafter, GARF). f. 112, op. 2, d. 2468.

of contributing his remembrances: 'Your recollections are extremely valuable [...] please get down to this soon.'[41]

When he finally set about the task of writing its memoirs, it was not only because of the persistent entreaties of Vera Figner, who enjoyed enormous authority among the older revolutionaries, or of a lifelong fellow member of the Chaikovskii Circle and family friend, Kornilova-Moroz, or even his own sense of moral obligation to his generation. Also weighing in to convince him to write about his past were the core of old revolutionaries in the OPK. Evidence of this can be found in a later letter Charushin sent after the fact in 1927 to one of its members, Maria Shebalina: 'Please give my warmest greetings [...] to the circle, *whose assignment I received last summer and now have carried out*, for better or worse'.[42] In short, when Charushin set about the task of putting in words his recollections it was only after prolonged procrastination and despite deep reservations, at the urging of his friends and insistence on their importance as a collective project of reconstruction and authentication.

The Writing of 'Remembrances'
Perhaps Charushin's lengthy hesitation also stemmed from his awareness of the perils of relying upon individual recollection alone. Writing in 1926 he commented upon the doubts that had beset him when he first took up this project:

> Over the years the memories had faded, much had been entirely lost. Most importantly, I was apprehensive that my efforts to reproduce and evaluate the events of the past would be involuntarily coloured by the atmosphere of subsequent times and that the result would convey a distorted picture of what I was describing.[43]

From the start, in order to avoid that from happening, Charushin's memoirs were written with a keen eye to the accounts of other members of the Chaikovskii Circle; citing these accounts, and utilizing a voluminous correspondence with these others in the movement. Earlier, as his correspondence shows, he had paid close attention to the memoirs written by his peers: in 1906 he had written to his wife Kuvshinskaia, who had been exiled to Perm′, describing his excitement at reading for the first

---

[41] RGALI, f. 1642, op. 1, d. 51, l. 12 ob.
[42] Charushin to Shebalina, 3 March 1927, Viatka. Tsentral′nyi Istoricheskii Arkhiv Moskvy (hereafter, TsIAM), f. 2241, op. 1, d. 138, l. 1a. Emphasis added.
[43] Nikolai Charushin, *O dalekom proshlom*, Moscow, 1973, p. 17.

time the memoirs of Sinegub and Shishko: 'The mail has arrived, bringing new issues of *Byloe* and *Russkoe Bogatstvo* and I was absorbed reading [...] about those "old" times.'[44] Those two journals with a Populist orientation had begun publishing memoirs of the seventies generation, many of whom had only recently been released from exile. Charushin discussed these memoirs with Kuvshinskaia, encouraging her to write down her own remembrances, since he felt that those of their good friend Sinegub were incomplete and excessively subjective. Even more, they were 'simplistic and imprecise to the degree that he even makes me out to be a died-in-the wool anarchist'.[45] In contrast, later, when contemplating writing his own memoirs, Charushin read carefully those of Ivan Popov, and confessed to the latter that in doing so: 'I was pleased and even surprised at how luminous were your recollections of that relatively distant past — so much so that I am now intimidated at the thought of launching such a project.'[46]

Once he did start writing he discussed his recollections regularly with Kornilova-Moroz. In April, 1926 she wrote to him:

> If you find it more opportune to meet with me in Moscow to go over your memoirs, I will be able to travel there in May. There I hope we will be able to get permission to work in Petr Alekseevich's [Kropotkin's] room in the museum [of that name], where nobody will disturb us, since the museum is open only two days a week.[47]

Moreover, in the introduction to his memoirs Charushin underscores the fact that Kornilova-Moroz had given her seal of approval to the manuscript as a whole. In his view this served as testimony to the veracity and authenticity of his account. Once *O dalekom proshlom* had been published Charushin welcomed the proposal made by members of the OPK that it was she and nobody else who should write a review for the organization's own journal, *Katorga i Ssylka*. In his view, she would be best, for as a veteran of the Chaikovskii Circle she could testify that 'what I had written did not

---

[44] Charushin to Kuvshinskaia, 3 November 1906. RGALI, f. 1642, d. 108, l. 11 ob.–12.

[45] Charushin to Kuvshinskaia, 17 November 1906. RGALI, f. 1642, d. 108, l. 16 ob. The assertion that Charushin had anarchist leanings in earlier years was one he vehemently denied. It should be added that despite this criticism, Charushin had tried to convince his acquaintance, the noted Moscow bookman and sponsor of Charushin's newspaper, Aleksandr Charushnikov, to publish Sinegub's memoirs as a book, in order to help out his friend 'Silych' (as he affectionately called him) financially. Charushin to Kuvshinskaia, 10 February 1907. RGALI, f. 1642, d. 108, l. 41 ob.

[46] Charushin to Popov, 24 April 1924. RGALI, f. 408, op. 1, d. 114, l. 1.

[47] RGALI, f. 1642, op. 1, d. 51, l. 18 ob.

doctor up the facts or include any outright inventions... When she does write the review, she can also make up for any omissions on my part'.[48]

In addition, in 1926, after the first volume of *O dalekom proshlom* had been published and, at the urging of the editors of *Katorga i Ssylka*, a circle of 'elders' at the OPK was established (it was this group whose 'assignment' Charushin above mentioned having completed). As Kornilova-Moroz wrote: 'they met weekly, during which one of them would relate his own life story, which was then taken down by a stenographer, and later turned into an article for the journal.'[49] Charushin continued to work on his own memoirs, now focusing on the period of exile, and in so doing continued to turn to his peers in this group to verify dates and to clarify the historical context.

In his third and final volume, covering the period of resettlement in the region of the notorious Nerchinsk gold mines, and later in Kiakhta on the border with China, Charushin continued to rely upon others to clarify and validate his own description of people, sites and events. For example, when engaged in writing about the visit of the Stakhevich family (Vera Figner's sister Lydia was married to Sergei Stakhevich) to Troitskosavsk in 1894–95, Charushin wrote to their daughter Tatiana Stakhevich to clarify a misunderstanding about that date. Another connected figure, Mikhail Sazhin (married to Vera Figner's sister Evgeniia), had insisted that the Stakhevich family had actually been there at an earlier point; in response Stakhevich's daughter sent him an exhaustive description of the visit drawn from her family's archive.[50] In the volume itself, Charushin refrains from a detailed description of the colourful and diverse tea *entrepôt* Kiakhta, noting that he deferred to the memoirs of Popov, which had done just that. Throughout this interval he was also re-reading 'with enormous pleasure' the five volumes of Figner's memoirs, something he noted to Popov himself in December 1929.[51]

It was not always smooth going, and however important achieving factual accuracy was for the group, other conditions also sometimes weighed in, for leaving behind the legacy of a group which had always observed a high standard of ethics was also crucial. For example, after reading Mikhail Chernavskii's Kara memoirs, which he found highly interesting and well written, Charushin noted that they had also helped

---

[48] TsIAM, f. 2241, op. 1, d. 138, l. 2 ob.
[49] RGALI, f. 1642, op. 1, d. 51, l. 15 ob.
[50] RGALI, f. 1185, op. 4, d. 29, ll. 1–2.
[51] Charushin to Popov, 26 December 1929. RGALI, f. 408, op. 1, d. 114, l. 15.

him substantially in his description of the ignominious Uspenskii episode, which he himself was grappling with in his own volume, *Na Kare*.

In this episode, Petr Uspenskii, a member of Nechaev's organization, had been sent to the Kara mines in 1875, where he intermingled with Chaikovtsy until 1881. In that year he was transferred to the prison in the Lower Kara region along with others who had been consigned to hard labour. There, because he was suspected of betraying his comrades, who had been digging an escape tunnel, he was murdered. In his memoirs Charushin depicts Uspenskii's psychological condition, his conflict with other prisoners, and searches to explain what led his comrades to falsely suspect Uspenskii of treason, something which led to that tragic outcome. At the time this had happened, Charushin was no longer imprisoned or in the locality, so he had of necessity relied heavily upon Chernavskii's account, citing his contribution to *Katorga i Ssylka*.[52]

At the same time, long before that he had known of Uspenskii's innocence, having been told crucial information shortly after the event by the Kara camp commandant Kononovich, with whom he had a cordial relationship. In a letter to Shebalina written in 1927, Charushin confided:

> I had the distinct impression that the suspicion of Uspenskii originated in the collapse of the first tunnel and that Kononovich had learned about it quite accidentally from somebody close to the prison who had had no intention of divulging the fact. Anna Dmitrievna [Kuvshinskaia] and I heard this directly from Kononovich when we were living in Nerchinsk. Unfortunately, I still can't make that fact public; all I can do is, based upon what I do know, categorically deny that Uspenskii had anything to do with the matter — whether directly or indirectly. Even with that knowledge, however, I would prefer to address a number of questions to Mikhail Mikhailovich [Chernavskii] about the matter.[53]

It was doubly uncomfortable for Charushin to write about this episode because, on the one hand he could not believe that Uspenskii was a traitor, given that he of all people was the least likely to have had any contact with Kononovich. In fact Charushin believed that the accusations had been inept and shameful. Yet on the other hand, the wrongful execution of Uspenskii cast the community of political prisoners in an odious light. All he could do by means of exoneration was to emphasize how the prison experience

---

[52] Mikhail Chernavskii, 'Ippolit Nikitich Myshkin (Po vospominaniiam katorzhanina 70-80-kh g.g.)', *Katorga i Ssylka*, 7–8 (28–29), 1926, pp. 104–24.

[53] TsIAM, f. 2241, op. 1, d. 138, l. 1a.

shaped people, creating unfounded suspicions of one another, with tragic outcomes of this sort. For Charushin this had certainly been a catastrophe, since it seemed to imply that the Chaikovtsy were not above the amoral methods of Nechaev — rejection of which had been the alpha and omega of their own group and was at the centre of their generational identity.

We note in this story Charushin's determination not to distort the facts or err in the depiction of events, but also see the moral constraints framing his recollections of those of his comrades who were no longer among the living, or even those still with him. It was no accident that Charushin was circumspect in describing Kononovich's revelations even in his private correspondence. It might well also be the case that Kononovich had actually shared with him the name of the person who had inadvertently spilled the news about the tunnel and escape plans of the prisoners, and that Charushin had no wish to expose that unfortunate person.

Others in the group shared the concern not to wash their dirty linen in public. In a letter to Vera Figner, Aleksandra Kornilova-Moroz vented her anger against Mikhail Sazhin for wanting to include in his memoirs examples of the interpersonal discord in their earlier years. As she put it, writing his memoirs was all well and good:

> But it is repulsive that Sazhin wants to bring up all the garbage [...]. Instead of giving our young people something uplifting to bolster their downtrodden spirits, here you are: he and Svetlovskii beat up an ailing Smirnov; an aggrieved Zavadskaia slaps [illegible] in the cheek, who in turn rips up her clothing and pulls a revolver on her; it's only due to the actions of Zavadskaia's companion Frits, who knocks the gun out of [that person's] hand that a murder is avoided. What a great scene, how worthy of our intelligentsia and right-thinking [*ideinye*] people!! Mucking around in the garbage heap! It's bad enough that it actually happened in the past; bringing it all up again is really awkward [...]. And he wants to commemorate these inspiring episodes!!![54]

The Uspenskii and Sazhin incidents serve as a useful reminder that interpersonal relations were not always stable and the actions of these revolutionaries sometimes felt short of their ethical ideals — whether it concerned private or public matters. Indeed, in their efforts to create a collective biography of their generation they were not averse to leaving out such episodes. Nevertheless, a close reading of their abundant

---

[54] Aleksandra Kornilova-Moroz to Vera Figner, 31 August n/d. RGALI, f. 1185, op. 1, d. 602, ll. 66–66 ob.

correspondence also tells us that these were the exception rather than the rule — their close friendships and aspirations to live lives governed by high moral standards prevailed.

Travelling (Entangled) Narratives
Turning frequently to the memoirs and biographies of other revolutionaries, and consulting over and over again by mail or in person led ineluctably to something resembling a 'collective' remembrance. On occasion one or another former Chaikovets might even directly borrow a passage from the works of another without acknowledging its origins, simply merging the words written by another into one's own text — something only a close word-by-word analysis of these memoirs has revealed. For instance, Kornilova-Moroz borrowed freely from the memoirs of Kropotkin and Figner. She made it clear that doing so was part of the normal creative process of writing. She wrote:

> Thanks to books I obtained from the library [...] I was able to insert into my own account some really interesting passages, such as the one of the colourful scene from the Trial of the 193 when [Hyppolite] Myshkin finished his speech and the gendarmes dragged him by force out of the courtroom. [Vasily] Bogucharskii himself borrowed this from the newspaper *Obshchina* published in Geneva in 1877–78. I also took the obituaries of [Anatoly] Serdiukov and [Mikhail] Kupreianov from Lavrov, which I found there. As for the depiction of the Chaikovskii Circle, I borrowed that from Kropotkin, and pulled a couple of passages from [Figner's] *The Imprint of Life's Endeavours*.[55]

One such example of the kind of 'travelling narrative' that such endeavours produced in *O dalekom proshlom* is the description of Kara, the notorious prison and hard-labour site in Siberia. In his description of his stay at Kara, Charushin made use of both Shishko's and Sinegub's own memoirs. As he put it in the foreword to his second volume published in 1929: 'Life at Kara at that time has already been described in part by Sinegub and, less so, Shishko; for that reason there is some inevitable repetition in my own narration, something unavoidable if I wanted to give a full picture of what life was like there.'[56]

---

[55] RGALI, f. 1642, op. 1, d. 51, ll. 14–14 ob.
[56] Charushin, *Na Kare*, Moscow, 1929, p. 8.

Before 1882, the prisons at Kara were the only place to which those convicted of crimes against the state were sent. Stories circulated of gross and arbitrary treatment there by the authorities, of the lack of rights, the desolate taiga, which provided no opportunity for flight. At the same time, according to a former prisoner, Naum Gekker, 'being sent to Kara was considered a great privilege, for it was regarded as a site of freedom, even a republic, and for that reason was in bad repute among the higher authorities'.[57] Judging by the memoirs of Sinegub and Charushin, life at Kara was not difficult for them, and in contrast to later recollections, the Chaikovtsy were free to dispose of their time, to study foreign languages and crafts, and read widely and interact freely, more of a club than penal servitude. Recalling his stay at Kara almost fifty years earlier, Charushin admitted that after almost four years of solitary confinement in the Peter-Paul fortress and elsewhere, Kara was almost like a resort, providing for the restoration of one's physical and mental capacities.

Such descriptions of the tsarist penal system, published in the 1920s, ran contrary to the prevailing narrative. At this very time *Katorga i Ssylka* was frequently printing the accounts of other former political prisoners, depicting cruel conditions, suffering and abuse. These other accounts came largely from those who arrived at Kara later, during the 1880s, when there was a vast expansion in numbers, a specially built prison and new rules. But even among these later prisoners there were many whose account of their time at Kara fit poorly with the general narrative of suffering. They recalled their life together at Kara in warm language, as a period rich and complex in its social interaction, one observing an unwritten constitution, rules and customs, an important source of education and socialization. 'An entire generation of revolutionary youth passed through the Kara political prison, and for scores of young people just coming into maturity it was a welcoming alma mater, a university and a public arena.'[58] Why, then, this type of narrative, despite the undoubted instances of violence on the part of the authorities, protests by prisoners extending even to hunger strikes and suicide, as well as internal conflicts? First of all, conditions were truly better than those prevailing in Shlisselburg or the Peter-Paul Fortress. Second, the period of incarceration came during the 'best years of their lives' (as they wrote), when youth, close friendships in the revolutionary movement, and belief in a bright future provided the strength to endure the hardships of imprisonment. Many explained the

---

[57] Naum Gekker, 'Politicheskaia katorga na Kare (vospominaniia)', *Byloe*, 1906, 9, p. 71.
[58] Ibid.

existence of a society of equals, a prison 'parliament' and 'constitution' by the high level of consciousness, the intellectual and moral qualities setting the revolutionaries apart from the world outside. Because of these qualities they were able to create an almost ideal community and full equality, that which they had failed at doing earlier because of, so they believed, the low level of development of the peasantry. The 'Kara Republic', as they called it, could serve as a social experiment of sorts, displaying both the successes and difficulties of building a new society.

The search for a common narrative when it came to the Kara experience often led the memoirists to a striking correspondence in phrasing. One example can be found in the depictions of the camp commandant, Kononovich, who treated the prisoners with respect and did everything in his power to ameliorate their conditions. Sinegub describes Kononovich as follows: 'He was a man not yet old, well built, with a wise, intelligent face, dressed in a military uniform.'[59] In Charushin's account, we read: 'This was a tall man, around 40–50, with a military demeanour, a wise and intelligent face, dressed military style.'[60] Again, Sinegub: 'Kononovich was both a smart and intelligent man, well able to defend his turf as long as it was even possible.'[61] And, Charushin: 'Kononovich was a smart man, no coward, and able to defend his turf.'[62]

In order to add weight to the veracity of his portrait of Kononovich, Charushin refers to George Kennan's famous book on the exile system,[63] translated into Russian in 1906, well known there, and often cited in other memoirs.[64] For all practical purposes, Kennan's text became a part of historical memory and a means of legitimating the revolutionaries' recollections about their experience of exile, but was also inseparably interwoven with their own collective narrative. Charushin introduces a lengthy quotation from Kennan, in which he writes: 'Political prisoners, local bureaucrats, and decent people in general, always spoke to me in one voice, that this was a humane, attractive, courageous, intelligent and complete incorruptible civil servant.'[65] Strikingly, Kennan himself, referring to the views of the political prisoners as a whole, directly cited

[59] Sergei Sinegub, *Zapiski chaikovtsa*, Moscow, 1929, p. 253.
[60] Charushin, *Na Kare*, pp. 18–19.
[61] Sinegub, *Zapiski chaikovtsa*, p. 256.
[62] Charushin, *Na Kare*, p. 38.
[63] George Kennan, *Siberia and the Exile System*, vols 1 & 2, New York, 1970, 2, pp. 206–10; 216–20. The volumes were first published in 1891.
[64] For the history of the translation and publication of this work, see E. I. Melamed, *Dzhordzh Kenan protiv tsarizma*, Moscow, 1981, pp. 60–72.
[65] Charushin, *Na Kare*, p. 102.

the opinions of Charushin, whom he had met while in Siberia, on the topic.[66] As a result, on more than one occasion, in the descriptions of Kononovich in the memoirs of Sinegub, Charushin, Kennan, and later, the monumental history of tsarist prisons by Gernet, we find a word-for-word correspondence.[67] They all quote each other — a hall of mirrors of sorts.

This gives rise to the thorny question of who in fact originated the description which, repeated over and over again, turned into a 'travelling' or 'entangled' narrative. At times it was a conscious endeavour; at others, as Figner wryly pointed out, their connection was so close that this occurred *unintentionally* even when they were writing largely in isolation from one another. After reading Mikhail Novorusskii's remembrances of their time at Shlisselburg Vera Figner wrote to him:

> Despite all the differences in tone and construction [...] I found so much agreement on so many occasions, and *to such a degree that you might even think we copied from one another* — which given the time of writing could not have been the case. I got a good laugh reading the first part of your foreword: the draft of my own foreword, written while I was in Lugan' [in Orel province] is virtually the same, word-for-word! In general your book and mine will complement each other.[68]

Thus we find considerable evidence of the 'intertextuality' — to use the term freely — of Populist memoirs.[69] The former Chaikovtsy sought to speak in unison. The process of constructing memoirs involved relying upon individual memory, turning to the already formulated recollections of other participants in the revolutionary movement, and discussion when possible of key moments, all of which in the end led to the creation of a 'collective autobiography'. At the same time the commonality of views, the collective experience and even — one might say — identity, also led on its own to the construction of almost identical narratives.

---

[66] Kennan, *Siberia and the Exile System*, 2, pp. 118, 209, 210, 216, 324, 325, 450.

[67] Mikhail Gernet, *Istoriia tsarskoi tiur'my*, 5 vols, Moscow, 1960, 3, pp. 317–18, 320–21. Gernet calls him Kananovich.

[68] Figner to Novorusskii, 17 May 1920. RGALI, f. 1185, op. 1, d. 239, l. 145. Emphasis added.

[69] It was common practice for these former revolutionaries to utilize other memoirs, biographies, histories of the movement in their own autobiographical writings. The result was a 'collective remembrance' in which passages pulled from elsewhere were inserted into the new text without what we would call the proper attribution. Only a line by line comparison of memoirs made it possible to identify this practice among the Populist memoirists.

Conclusions

In sum, the memoirs of Nikolai Charushin, as well as of Sergei Sinegub, Aleksandra Kornilova-Moroz, Leonid Shishko, Ivan Popov, Sergei Kovalik and others can be viewed as an element of *generational memory*. As Lazarev wrote: 'We are linked inseparably by the irretrievable past.'[70] As Assmann pointed out, of all the variants of social memory, generational memory is the most stable, and indeed the seventies generation of Chaikovtsy retained their identity through thick and thin until the end of their lives.

It was of course nothing out of the ordinary for these former revolutionaries, when sitting down to write their memoirs, to turn to one another to corroborate facts and compare notes. Yet we believe that something else was afoot here; the determination to speak in one voice was a political statement but not only. It was also a collective effort at life writing as an attempt to fix the image of their generational cohort, along with its ideals and activities, in *historical memory*. Because of this, Charushin's' contemporary, Shmuel Levin, was surely right when he observed, in his review of *O dalekom proshlom*:

> Charushin put his pen to paper later than all his other comrades and contemporaries and had their accounts in front of him when writing, as well as much only recently published materials from the archives. *For this reason his account can be viewed as a dialogue with, but also summation of, all others.*[71]

In her book on the legacy of the Decembrist movement, Ludmilla A. Trigos astutely emphasizes the strivings of the Decembrists themselves to mythologize their own history; she depicts the later reshaping and mobilization of this mythology in order to establish a genealogy of the revolutionary movement in the Soviet era.[72] As we have seen, the portrait of the seventies generation was likewise actualized in the Soviet Russia of the 1920s in the context of the effort to create and instil a new values orientation, to raise the younger generation with a diet of heroic images of the past, to establish a pantheon of heroes and sites of memory.

But the catcalls Vera Figner had heard earlier in the decade ('*your efforts were all in vain, your energies were expended heedlessly and produced no*

---

[70] Columbia University, Rare Book and Manuscript Library, Bakhmeteff Archive, Sergei Mikhailovich Kravchinskii Papers, Box 1.

[71] Levin Sh., 'N. A. Charushin. O dalekom proshlom', *Istorik-Marksist*, 1927, 4, p. 242. Emphasis added.

[72] Ludmilla A. Trigos, *The Decembrist Myth in Russian Culture*, New York, 2009. See, especially, chapter 2.

results') now threatened to drown out the voice of the Populists entirely. The social memory of that cohort contradicted the new and official political memory under construction at the time; it was destined to be altered or entirely obliterated without become a trans-generational memory. As Trigos shows, discussion of the Decembrist myth temporarily faded in the decade after the 1925 centennial just as the struggle over the legacy of Populism intensified. By the 1930s, during the Cultural Revolution and with the rise of the Stalinist cult of personality, Populist heroes, and therefore the seventies generation, were no longer needed by the authorities and relegated to the dustbin of history. The stream of memoirs dried up and representatives of this generation, bearers of this collective memoir, gradually left the scene. Finally, in 1935, in a fate perhaps worse than oblivion, the Populists were dressed up in history textbooks as the most treacherous enemies of Marxism.[73] Under Stalinism, the 'Decembrist myth' continued to be reshaped, while the nightmare of oblivion feared by the Populists seemed to have come true.

Returning to the theoretical framework of memory studies, we have seen how *generational memory* shaped by the shared political experiences of the 1870s and inscribed over time by a collective autobiographical project, briefly became institutionalized as part of *political memory* in early Soviet Russia, and then was erased. But in the post-Stalin era it was to re-emerge as *historical memory*.[74] The revolutionary cohort of the 1870s had been cast out of the new triumphal historical narrative of the Stalin era, but remained an integral part of the social memory of the Russian intelligentsia. The two strands — Decembrists and Populists — were joined again in the Thaw and Perestroika eras, as the intelligentsia, including some historians, sought to recover the interwoven, but occluded connections between revolution and freedom, along with notions of personal honour and ethical behaviour that many felt had been erased in the Soviet era.

---

[73] Nikolai Troitskii, *Russkoe revoliutsionnoe narodnichestvo 1870-kh godov (Istoriia temy)*, Saratov, 2003, pp. 16–31.
[74] See Tatiana Saburova and Ben Eklof, *Druzhba, sem'ia, revoliutsiia: Nikolai Charushin i pokolenie narodnikov 1870-ikh godov v Rossii*, Moscow, 2016 (chapter 10).

4

Lives and Facts:
Biography in Russia in the 1920s

ANGELA BRINTLINGER

'It is terrifying to think that our life is a tale without plot or hero…'
Osip Mandel′shtam, *The Egyptian Stamp* (1928)

IN the 1920s in Soviet Russia, biography seemed an urgent topic, and theorists and practitioners of the art of biography proliferated. The current article examines the 1920s debates about biography, looking at examples of the variety of biographical narratives produced in the post-Revolutionary, pre-Stalinist period in Soviet Russia. As the decade began, the Bolshevik Revolution and the subsequent Civil War continued to resonate, engendering chaos and confusion in literary and academic circles, in publishing and in public disputations. The difficulty of finding a path forward and sustaining a school or programme of publishing did not stop efforts by writers, especially in Petrograd/Leningrad at the Institute of the History of the Arts and among the scholars and theorists who were called Formalists, and in Moscow among academics and writers of the Moscow Linguistic Circle (MLK). Movement of scholars between cities and abroad, along with the stop-and-start publishing ventures and academic institutes of this complex time, did not stand in the way of sustained meditation on the question of biography, the meaning of an individual life, the place of the poet or other outstanding person in history, and so on. In the end, much biography, biographical theory and biographical experimentation happened on and around the name of Aleksandr Pushkin, whose anniversary date (125 years after the poet's birth) in 1924 prompted numerous publications, including biographical ones.

Versions of this article were presented at the Midwest Slavic Conference in Columbus, Ohio, in April 2016 and at the University of Genoa in April 2017. I would like to thank Steve Conn, Sara Dickinson, Polly Jones and the *SEER* anonymous reviewers for their insights along the way.

LIVES AND FACTS: BIOGRAPHY IN THE 1920s 95

This article will be divided into two sections, each featuring three main characters. In the first section I seek to explain why biography was an important area of research, classification and self-conception for figures in the 1920s, using three heroes: Semen Vengerov (the 'old guard'), Boris Tomashevskii (the 'taxonomist') and Grigorii Vinokur (the 'linguist'). In the second section, I give a sense of what biographies or kinds of biographical writing were being produced during this era, with the three heroes of Iurii Tynianov (the novelist), Boris Eikhenbaum (the experimenter) and Valeria Feider (the compiler). In the short final section I offer some suggestions as to what 'worked' and what did not, and show where biography was headed in Russia in the coming era.

1. Theories of Biography
Vengerov: The 'Old Guard'

In order to understand what kinds of conversations and projects were happening in the 1920s about biography, we have to look back to the previous decade and even earlier, when Semen Vengerov (1855–1920) was running his famous Pushkinskii seminarii (Pushkin Seminar) in the philological department of St Petersburg/Petrograd University. Vengerov was an empiricist whose method of study involved compiling vast amounts of material on individual authors and books. His own scholarly projects included *Russkie knigi. S biograficheskimi dannymi ob avtorakh i perevodchikakh (1708–1893)* (Russian Books: With Biographical Data about Authors and Translators, 1708–1893), projected to be twenty-five volumes (though he published only three) and *Kritiko-biograficheskii slovar' russkikh pisatelei i uchenykh (ot nachala russkoi obrazovannosti do nashikh dnei)* (A Critical-Biographical Dictionary of Russian Writers and Scholars from the Beginnings of Russian Education to Our Days), of which he completed six volumes, reaching only the third letter of the Cyrillic alphabet.[1] His next work, *Istochniki slovaria russkikh pisatelei* (Sources for a Dictionary of Russian Writers), also ran to four volumes and exemplified the logical development of his obsessive method of fact-collecting, given that he was now presenting raw material rather than

---

[1] S. A. Vengerov, *Russkie knigi. S biograficheskimi dannymi ob avtorakh i perevodchikakh (1708–1893)*, 3 vols, St Petersburg, 1895–1899, and *Kritiko-biograficheskii slovar' russkikh pisatelei i uchenykh (ot nachala russkoi obrazovannosti do nashikh dnei)*, 6 vols, St Petersburg, 1886–1904. See also Mark Gamsa, 'Two Million Filing Cards: The Empirical-Biographical Method of Semen Vengerov', *History of Humanities*, 1, Spring 2016, 1, pp. 129–53 (pp. 133–38).

trying to write the dictionary itself.² Though his scholarly investigations aimed to understand lives, particularly those of people who stood at the source of Russian literature and the literary language, Vengerov was unable to cull and organize the materials he gathered into true biographies. He was overwhelmed by the process and by the facts themselves.

A prime Russian representative of what Ira Bruce Nadel has called the 'age of evidence', Vengerov strove for maximal coverage; however, as Mark Gamsa has shown, Vengerov's approach to biography suffered from a very particular problem: wanting to include everything, he never finished anything.³ Nevertheless, if his scholarly work had less of an impact than might have been hoped, Vengerov still had a significant effect on the development of biography in Russia, largely through the students in his seminar, which he started in 1906, who included S. M. Bondi, Iu. N. Tynianov, N. V. Izmailov, Iu. G. Oksman, V. M. Zhirmunskii, S. D. Balukhatyi and B. M. Eikhenbaum, among others.

This was quite a collection of students, and their names ensured the legendary status of Vengerov's seminar. For example, S. M. Bondi became a respected textological expert on Pushkin, and his early paper from the seminar analysing *Evgenii Onegin*, though never published, was cited by other Pushkinists.⁴ Bondi's explanation of his own scholarly dogma went like this: 'Historico-literary scholarship must give exact, objective, true positions, and not just the more-or-less clever notions of one or another talented scholar.'⁵ These words sound like they might have come from the lips of his professor, Vengerov, and demonstrate the particularly data-based attitude toward the material which was to become characteristic of the Leningrad school of textologists.

The list goes on, and almost all the students continued their work on Pushkin once they left the seminar. To summarize briefly: Iu. G. Oksman

---

[2] S. A. Vengerov, *Istochniki slovaria russkikh pisatelei*, St Petersburg, 1900–1917, vols 1–4.

[3] Ira Bruce Nadel, *Biography: Fiction, Fact and Form*, New York, 1984, p. 185. See also Gamsa, 'Two Million Filing Cards'. It was N. V. Izmailov who called Vengerov's approach the 'historical-cultural method'. See N. V. Izmailov, 'B. V. Tomashevskii kak issledovatel′ Pushkina', in *Pushkin: Issledovaniia i materialy*, Moscow and Leningrad, 1960, vol. 3, pp. 5–24 (p. 5).

[4] Among these was M. L. Gofman (1887–1959), who before leaving Russia for Paris published *Pushkin. Pervaia glava nauki o Pushkine* (Petrograd, 1922). Though he became primarily a Pushkinist, in the introduction to this work he made the point that only by coming to terms with the relationship between Pushkin's life and work could Russian/Soviet literary scholarship create a model for biographies of writers generally.

[5] S. M. Bondi, 'M. A. Tsiavlovskii i ego stat′i o Pushkine', in M. A. Tsiavlovskii, *Stat′i o Pushkine*, Moscow, 1962, p. 5.

and N. V. Izmailov also became Pushkinists, the former eventually heading the Pushkin Commission to prepare the first academy edition of the author's works, while the latter directed the Manuscript Department of the Institute of Russian Literature (Pushkin House).[6] B. M. Zhirmunskii, a linguist, is still renowned for his book on Pushkin and Byron, published in 1924; while S. D. Balukhatyi worked in a later period, studying the late nineteenth and early twentieth centuries with a focus on Anton Chekhov; Maksim Gor'kii, Boris Eikhenbaum and Iurii Tynianov made major contributions to both biographical theory and practice and Pushkin studies and will receive further treatment below. Thus Vengerov's influence on the young students of Petersburg/Petrograd University was significant, and his legacy continued through the 1920s and well into the Soviet period.

Tomashevskii: The 'Taxonomist'

Boris Tomashevskii (1890–1957) spent much of his life working on Aleksandr Pushkin, finally publishing one volume of his biography in 1956 (the second was published only posthumously). But in 1924 he boldly asserted in his brief biographical essay about the poet, which served as an introduction to a collection of Pushkin's works, that 'a general biography of Pushkin does not yet exist'. In that same anniversary year — 125 years after the poet's birth — Tomashevskii participated in polemical back-and-forth reviews of other books about Pushkin.[7] These publications, Tomashevskii's *curriculum vitae* as a whole, and the essay which served as an outline for the incomplete second volume of *Pushkin*, were all part of Tomashevskii's life work on the major biography which in the end he was unable to complete.[8] For his part, Tomashevskii conceived of Pushkin's

---

[6] Oksman was arrested in 1936 and accused of slowing down the publication of Pushkin's *Polnoe sobranie sochinenii*, and thus inhibiting the 1937 commemoration of the centennial of the poet's death. He served a number of terms in Gulag prisons. Izmailov was arrested in 1929 in the 'Academy of Sciences case' and received a five-year sentence.

[7] See 'Pushkin: Biograficheskii ocherk', 14, in *Sochineniia*, Leningrad, 1924, pp. iii–xv. In 1924 Tomashevskii published three reviews: of P. Guber's *Don-Zhuanskii spisok Pushkina*; of Zhirmunskii's *Bairon i Pushkin*; Vladislav Khodasevich's *Poeticheskoe khoziaistvo Pushkina*; and a review essay touching on Leonid Grossman's *Etiudy o Pushkine*, Guber's book, and Ivan Ermakov's *Etiudy po psikhologii tvorchestva Pushkina*. When Khodasevich published a letter complaining about Tomashevskii's review, Tomashevskii felt compelled to respond in print. See V. B. Tomashevskii, *Pushkin. Kniga vtoraia: Materialy k monografii (1824–1837)*, Moscow and Leningrad, 1961, p. 545. The next year Tomashevskii included a 'biography' in his larger work, *Pushkin. Sovremennye problemy istoriko-literaturnogo izucheniia*, Leningrad, 1925.

[8] 'Pushkin (Monograficheskii ocherk)' was the closest Tomashevskii came to a full biography of the poet. See *Pushkin. Kniga vtoraia*, pp. 479–541. There is evidence that

biography as a combination of the work — including source materials, manuscript variants, foreign literary influences, etc. — and the life — political circumstances, personal history, family life.[9] And although he did not study with Vengerov at the Pushkin seminar, he was friendly with many scholars who had and was certainly aware of Vengerov's methods.[10]

But Tomashevskii's contribution to the 1920s conversation about biography went beyond his *Pushkinistika* and his own biographical writings. Indeed, it was his theoretical essay, 'Literature and Biography', that has had the most substantial long term resonance. In it, Tomashevskii asked a simple question: in the case of poets or other creative people, just what constitutes biography? Published in 1923, the article lays out one theoretical answer to this question.[11] As a scholar of literature, Tomashevskii had already by this time become concerned with the development of biography as a form and in particular with the way in which literary scholars seemed to be embracing it. Though he acknowledged that 'documentary biographies' of writers had just as much right to exist as similar biographies of 'generals and inventors', he argued that this was merely 'cultural history', not literary history.[12]

Such careful parsing of fields of scholarly inquiry enabled Tomashevskii to present a theoretical argument about a practice he found abhorrent: too much unmotivated digging around in the dirty laundry of deceased poets, what he called 'curiosity', an 'unhealthy sharpening of interest in documentary literary history'.[13] This practice, which would generate

Zhizn' zamechatel'nykh liudei tried to get Tomashevskii to write Pushkin's biography for that series, but he never delivered the manuscript. See Brintlinger, 'The *Remarkable Pushkin*', *Slavic & East European Journal*, 60, 2016, 2, p. 233.

[9] In Tomashevskii, *Pushkin. Kniga vtoraia*, from the editors, p. 4.

[10] Tomashevskii studied mathematics and engineering at the University of Liège in Belgium as well as French classical literature at the Sorbonne in Paris. Izmailov, 'Tomashevskii kak issledovatel'', p. 6. According to sources at Pushkinskii dom, Tomashevskii began working in the PD archive when he returned from Europe in 1913 and even wrote a paper for Vengerov's Pushkin seminar entitled 'Pushkin and French humorous poetry of the XVIII century'. Ia. Levkovich, 'Tomashevskii Boris Viktorovich (1890–1957)' <http://www.pushkinskijdom.ru/Default.aspx?PageContentID=17&tabid=131> [accessed 8 August 2017], paragraph 3 of 37. Tomashevskii devoted a significant section of his 'Stages of the Study of Pushkin' to Vengerov and his seminar, noting that about a quarter of the work of Vengerov's students was biographical in nature. See 'Etapy izucheniia Pushkina', *Pushkin. Kniga vtoraia*, p. 468.

[11] B. Tomashevskii, 'Literatura i biografiia', *Kniga i revoliutsiia*, 4, 1923, 28, pp. 6–9. Translation published as 'Literature and Biography', trans. Herbert Eagle, in Ladislav Matejka and Krystyna Pomorska (eds), *Readings in Russian Poetics: Formalist and Structuralist Views*, Cambridge, MA, 1962, pp. 47–55.

[12] Ibid., p. 55.

[13] Ibid., p. 47.

such explicit tell-all biographical works as P. K. Guber's *Don-Zhuanskii spisok Pushkina* (Pushkin's Don Juan List, 1923) and Vikentii Veresaev's compilation, *Pushkin v zhizni* (Pushkin in Life, 1933), appealed to a broader audience. Tomashevskii strove to separate what he saw as irrelevant gossip-mongering from truly productive inquiries into the lives of writers.

In short, Tomashevskii suggested looking at the *biographical legend* of those authors whose work used — or seemed to use — details from their personal lives. The biography presented to the audience by the creative figure was the only relevant one:

> For a writer with a biography, the facts of the author's life must be taken into consideration. Indeed, in the works themselves the juxtaposition of the texts and the author's biography plays a structural role. The literary work plays on the potential reality of the author's subjective outpourings and confessions. Thus the biography that is useful to the literary historian is not the author's *curriculum vitae* or the investigator's account of his life. What the literary historian really needs is the biographical legend created by the author himself. Only such a legend is a literary fact.

'Only such a legend was a literary fact.'[14] Here, too, facts and lives are key to understanding figures from the past.

Using the example of Pushkin's southern exile and supposed 'hidden love', Tomashevskii divides writers into poets *with biographies* and poets *without biographies*, a taxonomy he recommended when considering whether delving into biography gives scholarly insight or resembles nothing more than stuff found in tabloid investigations and gossip rags.[15]

It is fair to say that for literary scholars, in particular, this division was difficult to parse, and the masses of speculative biographies published about Pushkin and many other Russian historical personages suggest that this theoretical approach was almost impossible to apply, certainly so in a marketplace where readers clamoured for detailed stories about figures from the past. Although Tomashevskii's essay remains a cornerstone of Russian biographical theory and continues to be reprinted in collections on Russian formalism across the world today, in practice in the 1920s it did not generate significant followers.[16]

---

[14] Ibid.

[15] Ibid. This distinction, between writers *with biographies* and writers without, has been embraced by many in the field. See, for example, David Bethea, *Realizing Metaphors: Alexander Pushkin and the Life of the Poet*, Madison, WI, 1998.

[16] Tomashevskii contributed to Pushkin studies throughout his life, including

Vinokur: The 'Linguist'

It is no coincidence that the third theoretical approach to biography also emerged from a trip to Leningrad and from conversations with the members of OPOIAZ (Obshchestvo izuheniia poeticheskogo iazyka). In May 1924 Grigory Vinokur (1896–1947) travelled from Moscow to the State Institute of the History of the Arts (Gosudarstvennyi institut istorii iskusstv) where Eikhenbaum, Tynianov, Zhirmunskii and others worked. While there he gave a short lecture that became the basis for his eighty-plus-page book on biography, *Biografiia i kul'tura* (Biography and Culture), published in 1927. Vinokur conceived of this lecture as a polemic with OPOIAZ and the so-called 'formalist school', which included Tynianov, Eikhenbaum and Tomashevskii.

In *Biography and Culture*, Vinokur tried to ascertain first of all the difference between biography as a lived life and the genre of writing about someone's life, which also goes by the term biography. In this he demonstrated his psycholinguistic approach. Trying to understand what constitutes the individual's life, approach to living, behavioural choices, etc., Vinokur used terminology borrowed from contemporary psychology about identity formation as well as sociolinguistic terminology. 'What is a person's life,' Vinokur asked, 'if not the gradually changing landscape of impressions and memories, satisfactions and suffering, hopes and actions?'[17] Vinokur saw writing biography as a process of projecting the subject's internal and external experiences onto the screen of historical events meaningful for that individual. The biographer, he argued, has to sift through 'the entire context of social reality in its profound fullness — that is the material out of which history crafts biography'.[18] Beyond history, though, the individual biographer must make choices as to what facts and context to include when writing the life.

As R. M. Tseitlin explains, it was Vinokur who introduced the ideas of Ferdinand de Saussure into Russia, and in doing so he focused explicitly on what he termed *style* and *stylization*. Translating the concept of *langue* versus *parole*, Vinokur said: 'the difference between language itself and speech acts is nothing less than the difference between *language per se*

---

apparently co-writing a version of Tynianov's article 'Mnimyi Pushkin' ('The Imagined Pushkin') in 1924. See *Poetika. Istoriia literatury. Kino*, Moscow, 1977, pp. 422–23. The fact that Grigorii Vinokur also contributed to this article, possibly rewriting the conclusion, further demonstrates that many of these authors shared literary and biographical goals and methods.

[17] Vinokur, *Biografiia i kul'tura*, Moscow, 1927, p. 14.
[18] Ibid., p. 25.

and style.'¹⁹ Once an individual looks at his or her own life in any way at all, engages in self-reflection, that is already *stylization*, he argued. In terms of biography, what this means is that the materials upon which a biographer draws are necessarily in some ways tainted, already filtered through the consciousness and identity of the subject. At the same time, in his book Vinokur was concerned that contemporary biographers (i.e. biographers in the mid-1920s), were not doing enough to interpret the materials they found. 'Raw materials,' he wrote, 'take too significant a place in contemporary biographical work.'²⁰

In one way, then, Vinokur argued for further contextualization. Historical events must be a part of writing biography, but only to the extent that they actually influenced the individual being described. A 'connected narrative', a throughline, is what he sought in literary representations of the lives of individuals, but what he found instead was too much dependence on 'fate'.²¹ At the same time Vinokur noted that every individual lives life in a specific linguistic way, and drawing on, understanding and interpreting those specificities is the way to represent a particular life:

> The intonation and timbre of voice, accent and word order, syntactical construction and lexical uniqueness, thematic preferences and characteristic ways of narrating plot, this is all generally speaking *the stylistic mode* of speech, that is to say everything which distinguishes in it specifically *this speaker* among others, — these are, after all, the very facts in which we seek the traces of an individual manner of living and which permit us to look at the word not only as a symbol of an idea, but also as an action in the history of a private life.²²

Fate (*sud'ba*), in the end, for Vinokur was equivalent to a single life conceived of as a unity, to the final meaning of everything experienced and fashioned by the hero of a biography.²³ That self-fashioning by an individual — as seen through his or her speech acts and stylization —

---

[19] R. M. Tseitlin, *Grigorii Osipovich Vinokur (1896–1947)*, Moscow, 1965, p. 16; L. P. Krysin, 'Voprosy sotsiologii iazyka v rabotakh G. O. Vinokura', in S. N. Gindin and N. N. Rozanova (eds), *Iazyk, kul'tura, gumanitarnoe znanie: Nauchnoe nasledie G. O. Vinokura i sovremennost'*, Moscow, 1999, pp. 208–11 (pp. 208–09).

[20] Vinokur, *Biografiia i kul'tura*, p. 56.

[21] Ibid., pp. 57, 62.

[22] Vinokur, quoted in L. L. Fedorova, 'Nekotorye osobennosti rechevogo povedeniia predstavitelei gumanitarnoi i tekhnicheskoi intelligentsii', in Gindin and Rozanova, *Iazyk, kul'tura*, pp. 230–36 (p. 231).

[23] Vinokur, *Biografiia i kul'tura*, p. 61.

according to Vinokur's theory had to then be filtered once more through the biographer who presented the individual's life. In this, Vinokur's linguistic approach was quite similar to that of his colleague Iurii Tynianov — one of those who was present at the original lecture on the topic of 'Biography and Culture'. Tynianov too would come to believe, as Stephen Lovell summarizes it, that 'everyday life [*byt*] relates to literature primarily through its speech aspect'.[24]

Each of these three — professor, literary scholar, linguistic and cultural theorist — offered ways to imagine biography in the Russian setting, and each had an effect on biographers themselves, if sometimes indirectly. Vengerov's detail-oriented approach was in some ways rejected by Tomashevskii, who wanted to look at the work through the life without getting bogged down in irrelevant and potentially spurious information, while Vinokur tried to look at the individual life as a speech act, where any degree of self-awareness became a stylization. Vinokur's 'stylization' — if slightly more broadly conceived — does not differ drastically from Tomashevskii's 'biographical legend', and although Vinokur spoke out against Tomashevskii's belief that a poet's biography differs from a general's only in its material, he still advocated a historically grounded representation of lives.[25] In addition, as mentioned above, Tynianov was among those who strove to understand the relationship between the literary and 'extra-literary "series"', or in other words *byt*.[26] In the next section, we will look more closely at him and at two other authors who tried their hands at biography, with significantly distinctive results.

2. Published Biographies
Tynianov: The 'Scientific Novelist'

Iurii Nikolaevich Tynianov (1894–1943), along with his friend and comrade Boris Mikhailovich Eikhenbaum (1886–1959), studied in Vengerov's seminar at Petrograd University. Upon graduation he moved to the Institute of the History of the Arts, where he lectured students and continued to write literary scholarship and theory. As is well known, Tynianov then turned to fiction at the urging of another friend, Kornei Chukovskii, who assured him that his audiences were more interested in life stories than they were

---

[24] See Tynianov, *Poetika. Istoriia literatury. Kino*, Moscow, 1977, p. 278, quoted in Lovell, 'Tynianov as Sociologist of Literature', *Slavonic and East European Review*, 79, 2001, 3, pp. 415–33 (p. 420). On the relationship between Tynianov and Vinokur see Vinokur, 'Neskol´ko slov pamiati Iu. N. Tynianova', in V. A. Kaverin (ed.), *Vospominaniia o Iu. Tynianove: Portrety i vstrechi*, Moscow, 1983, pp. 65–68.

[25] Vinokur, *Biografiia i kul´tura*, pp. 69, 71.

[26] Lovell, 'Tynianov as Sociologist of Literature', p. 416.

in the dry analysis of poetic technique, rhyme and metre.²⁷ Even before this foray into storytelling, though, Tynianov began his investigations into the difference between fiction and biography with his essay 'The Imagined Pushkin', a co-authored effort with Boris Tomashevskii written in 1922, although not published until 1977.²⁸

With his first novel, *Kiukhlia* (1925), Tynianov launched himself on a hybrid career, one in which he continued to write about the external forms of literature while also drawing vivid biographical sketches in three novels of Golden Age poets: Vil'gel'm Kiukhel'beker, Aleksandr Griboedov and Aleksandr Pushkin. In *Kiukhlia*, Tynianov wrote a straight biographical novel, while the 1927 *Smert' Vazir-Mukhtara* (Death of the Wazir-Mukhtar) was experimental, modernist and influenced by the cinema, with its sudden cuts in narrative and visually arresting metaphors. *Pushkin*, which Tynianov wrote throughout the 1930s and 1940s, never came to full fruition before the author's death.²⁹

Though trained by Vengerov, Tynianov struck out in a direction his professor would have hated, famously quipping: 'Where the document ends, that's where I begin.'³⁰ In this, Tynianov found common ground with Vinokur: in order to represent an individual in a narrative, it was necessary to understand what was behind the extant files and data. As Tynianov put it, 'if you have entered into the life of your hero, your person, you can sometimes guess about many things yourself'.³¹ Lives, not merely facts, ruled his pen.

Tynianov, then, explored his historical characters through scholarly research — reading letters, notes, diaries, exploring archival folders of bills, menus, hotel registrations. But he also tried to remember that biography could not be based entirely on documentary evidence. Some days, he reminded readers, go by with no documentation being generated at all, and some documents 'are for show, and they lie like people'.³² Rather than

---

²⁷ Kornei Chukovskii, 'Pervyi roman', in *Vospominaniia o Iu. Tynianove: Portrety i vstrechi*, Moscow, 1983, pp. 138–46 (pp. 141–42).
²⁸ See 'Mnimyi Pushkin', in *Poetika. Istoriia literatury. Kino*, pp. 78–92, and commentaries pp. 420–22.
²⁹ On these novels, see my *Writing a Usable Past: Russian Literary Culture, 1917–1937*, Evanston, IL, 2000. See also Ludmilla Trigos, 'An Exploration of the Dynamics of Mythmaking: Tynianov's *Kiukhlia*', *Slavic & East European Journal*, 46, Summer 2002, 2, pp. 283–300.
³⁰ *Kak my pishem*, Leningrad, 1930, pp. 163. Also see Avril Pyman, 'Tynyanov and the "Literary Fact"', in Peter France and William St Clair (eds), *Mapping Lives: The Uses of Biography*, Oxford and New York, 2002, pp. 162–69.
³¹ Ibid., p. 163.
³² Ibid., pp. 161, 163.

searching out proof for everything, Tynianov came to a compromise: he tried to imagine the lives of the people he was writing about, and if he found evidence, then so much the better. Sometimes, as he lamented, he did not go far enough. One vivid example from *The Life of the Wazir-Mukhtar* is Griboedov's servant, whose name was Aleksandr Gribov. Tynianov came to believe — thanks to a friend who pointed out the noble tradition of giving illegitimate sons the slightly transformed surnames of their biological fathers — that Gribov was probably Griboedov's half-brother: 'Brother serving brother, Griboedov's brother — a lackey with a shortened surname, a person the poet and ambassador sometimes was friendly with and sometimes beat. Ekh, too bad that I was waiting for a [confirming] document.'[33] Despite the linguistic hints evident in the servant's name, Tynianov did not 'think his way' to this plot detail.

This case notwithstanding, it was Tynianov, ironic though it may seem, the one who was so dedicated to 'scientific' analysis, who was also most willing to move beyond his materials. Fully confident that he knew the 1810s and 1820s even better than he did his own era, Tynianov made bold assumptions and indulged in inventive explanations. Although his version, for example, of the British machinations behind the tragic death of poet/ambassador Griboedov has yet to be verified by historical data, it remains in the realm of possibility that his creative approach using psychological analysis yielded a truer picture of his subject's demise. Regardless, as far as constructing a life narrative that offered verisimilitude, Tynianov's portraits of Kiukhel'beker and Griboedov, and even the character of Pushkin which he drew for those two novels of the 1920s, rang 'true' to readers of that time and beyond.

The power of Tynianov's literary skill was famously highlighted by Soviet writer Maksim Gor'kii, who responded to *Death of the Wazir-Mukhtar* by saying, 'Griboedov is wonderful, although I did not expect to find him quite like that. But you showed him so convincingly that he must have been that way, and if not, he will be now'.[34] Biographers of Griboedov in years since have found this to be frustrating: Tynianov's portrait of this enigmatic figure is so powerful that it stays in the reader's mind, creating

---

[33] Ibid., p. 165. B. V. Kazanskii (1889–1962), who pointed out this possibility, was a 1913 graduate of Petersburg University and returned there to teach in 1920. His specialties included Roman biographies.

[34] 24 March, 1929, quoted in B. Kostelianets, introduction to Iu. Tynianov, *Sochineniia v dvukh tomakh, tom. 1*, Leningrad, 1985, pp. 5–30 (p. 25). Nadel writes that 'readers [prefer to believe] that what they read is the only way to present the facts' (p. 156); Gor'kii was just such a reader.

barriers that new literary and archival discoveries cannot overcome. But this is in part precisely why Tynianov turned to fiction. As he explained:

> I began to write fiction primarily because of my dissatisfaction with literary history which slid along on generalities and did not clearly represent the people, movements, and development of Russian literature. [...] A need to get to know the [people] better and to understand them more deeply — that's what fiction was for me.[35]

The deep connection between scholarly approaches to historical figures and the genre of the novelized biography was born in Vengerov's seminar. However, Tynianov's works remain a litmus test for readers to this day; those who tolerate fictionalization in biography and who value his other stylistic innovations love Tynianov, while others see his *biographies romancées* as sullying the larger field of biography.

Eikhenbaum: The 'Experimenter'
Already in the 1910s, Boris Eikhenbaum was exploring the idea of biography. He wrote a number of articles using letters and other personal documents on such poets and writers as Gavriil Derzhavin, Fedor Tiutchev, Ivan Goncharov and Anton Chekhov, striving, as his biographer Carol Any has written, to 'discover the particular kind of artistic knowledge possessed by each writer'. These were, she explains, 'mini-investigations of how the writer's personality, or "soul", to use Eikhenbaum's word, is reflected in his art'.[36] In 1913, when Boris Eikhenbaum observed that '*the novel is moving toward biography*', he had already begun to theorize about a paradigm shift.[37] When he saw his friend and colleague Tynianov writing biographical fiction in the mid-1920s, he was not surprised.

Indeed, in 1924 Eikhenbaum wrote to his friend Viktor Shklovskii that he was longing to immerse himself in the genre of biography: 'History

---

[35] Quoted in V. Kaverin and Vl. Novikov, *Novoe zrenie: Kniga o Iurii Tynianove*, Moscow, 1988, p. 143. The newest biographies of Alexander Griboedov include Sergei Fomichev, *Aleksandr Griboedov: Biografiia*, St Petersburg, 2012, and N. A. Tarkhova, *Letopis' zhizni i tvorchestva A. S. Griboedova*, Moscow, 2017.

[36] See Carol Any, *Boris Eikhenbaum: Voices of a Russian Formalist*, Stanford, CA, 1994, pp. 19, 20. We might see this as related to what David Cecil identified as part of the modernist project of biography, the 'study of "human character"'. David Cecil quoted in Laura Marcus, "The Newness of the "New Biography": Biographical Theory and Practice in the Early Twentieth Century', France and St Clair, *Mapping Lives*, p. 194.

[37] Boris Eikhenbaum, 'Roman ili biografiia?', *Russkaia molva*, 18 February 1913. Reprinted in *O literature. Raboty raznykh let*, Moscow, 1987, pp. 288–89 (p. 288).

has exhausted me, but I don't want to rest, and I don't know how. I have a yearning [*toska*] for action, a yearning for biography.'[38] In his diary in the same years Eikhenbaum both judged his friends and colleagues and sought his own path: 'The choice is clear: either be cynical and do hack work to advance my career, like Tomashevskii, or dry up and become a "professor", like Zhirmunskii, or not insist on doing scholarship, not force myself to do it and switch to something else, like Tynianov.'[39] Eikhenbaum's fellow graduates of Vengerov's seminar were working together at the State Institute of the History of the Arts and they continued — each in his own way — to circle around questions of Pushkin and of biography.

The work that Eikhenbaum imagined was, he thought, 'necessary historically as well as for me personally', and would constitute a new connection of the individual's life with the events around him or her. As he wrote, 'Somehow I keep coming back to the idea of biographies. Of writing a book [...] from the standpoint of the historical milieu. Interweaving the question of how to build one's life [...] with the epoch, with history'.[40] These ideas resonate with Vinokur's programme of rendering individual lives in the context of historical events relevant to those lives. However, Eikhenbaum's vague plans throughout the mid-1920s for what he called a 'book about people' remained unrealized. Instead, he wrote *The Young Tolstoi* (1922), which he expanded further into *Lev Tolstoi* (vol. 1, published 1928; vol. 2, published 1931). Both books focus on Tolstoi's poetics, literary devices and traditions rather than his life.

But in his casting about, Eikhenbaum came to an entirely unexpected resolution for his 'book about people'. The slim volume that emerged was not in the end a biography, but was rather an experiment in a new genre: the genre of the one-man journal. In its pages, Eikhenbaum was striving to understand the relationships between history and plot, between detail and narrative, which he knew had significance for the biographical endeavour as well. *Moi vremennik* (1929), or *My Periodical*, came at the question of the person-in-history from various angles and offered a completely new representation of biography, a personalized version. Consisting of four sections (literature, scholarship, criticism and miscellaneous), the book is a bit of a hodge-podge, dipping into the personal as well as the critical and even including some poetic juvenilia. In the opening essay, a kind of autobiography-cum-historical-family-memoir, Eikhenbaum recovers a lost

---

[38] 'Eikhenbaum, Boris Mikhailovich. Biograficheskaia spravka' <http://philologos.narod.ru/eichenbaum/eichenbio.htm>, paragraph 9 of 11 [accessed 8 August 2017].

[39] *Diary*, 2 December 1925, quoted in Any, *Eikhenbaum*, p. 93.

[40] Eikhenbaum, *Diary*, 15 December 1925, quoted in ibid., pp. 102–03.

literary artefact: a poem about chess penned in Hebrew by his grandfather Iakov Eikhenbaum.[41] In addition to the literary and personal revelations in this piece, in it an overarching theme for the entire volume is proposed: 'As far as the author of the poem itself, he has been transformed into a scholarly matter. Isn't that how many scholarly matters emerge? Doesn't scholarship [itself] develop on a foundation of oblivion?'[42] Throughout the first, most autobiographical, section of *My Periodical*, Eikhenbaum explores the relationship between facts and lives, and between history and literature. 'Every kind of past,' he writes, 'is in and of itself emplotted [*siuzhetno*]. The dust of time makes the most ordinary things into museum pieces.'[43]

In *My Periodical*, Eikhenbaum defined history as 'prophesying backward', but also recognized that the role of historical detail itself had changed after the revolution: 'the revolution brought with it,' he wrote, 'the need for the creation of different forms of the literary everyday [*literaturnyi byt*] [and] a heightened interest in literary memoirs and biographical materials.'[44] This heightened interest, he insisted, was a natural result of literary processes and facilitated the development of a 'biographical chronicle at the heart of which lay the question of human fate'.[45] For Eikhenbaum at the end of the 1920s, biography and the literary everyday were tightly entwined. He could not imagine the lives of Gogol', Turgenev, Nekrasov, Leskov, Tolstoi, or even Gor'kii without the conditions of *byt* under which they lived, perhaps because the facts of his own literary everyday were pressing on him even as he imagined new kinds of writing about lives.

At the same time, in his literary, historical and personal autobiographical investigations, Eikhenbaum continually strove to understand the relationship between 'accidental occurrences' (*sluchainosti*) and history. He ascribed the events of his own life and the life around him to the category of *sluchainosti*: events of the 1910s including war, revolution, the deaths of his parents, the October revolt, the cold and hunger of those difficult years, his son's death, and life huddled around a stove; and events of the 1920s, including the institutions where he ate, lived and worked (the House of Scholars, the House of Writers, the Institute of the History of the

---

[41] Brian Horowitz calls the volume 'part autobiography, part notebook, and part chronicle of his life and times' in his article about the essay on Eikhenbaum's grandfather, 'Battling for Self-Definition in Soviet Literature: Boris Eikhenbaum's Jewish Question', *Znanie. Ponimanie. Umenie*, 2, 2015, pp. 379–92 (p. 379).

[42] Boris Eikhenbaum, *Moi vremennik*, Leningrad, 1929, p. 16.

[43] Ibid., p. 18.

[44] Eikhenbaum, 'Literaturnaia domashnost'', in ibid., pp. 82–86, p. 85.

[45] Eikhenbaum, 'Dekoratsii epokhi', in ibid., pp. 126–27 (p. 126).

Arts), plus the deaths of poets Alexander Blok and Nikolai Gumilev (both in 1921); his chance meeting with Viktor Shklovskii and reacquaintance with Pushkin seminar classmate Iurii Tynianov that led to the founding of OPOIAZ. Accidental occurrences were simply events that existed outside a system, and as he went on to argue, 'Outside of theory there isn't even a historical system, because there is no principle of choosing and interpreting facts. [...] History is a specific method of understanding the present with the help of facts from the past'.[46]

With *My Periodical*, Eikhenbaum launched an experiment, aiming to combine literature and theory, autobiography and family memoir, criticism and biography. In several places he emphasizes the connections: 'history is a specific method of studying or interpreting contemporary life. It is difficult to make generalizations using contemporary material — it is essential to enlist the help of the past and find in it analogies.'[47] The project itself, as Vladimir Orlov argues, is a seeking in the past, a throwback to the eighteenth century, but at the same time we might see it as an attempt to cast light on questions of lives and facts from various — both personal and generic — points of view.[48]

Feider: The 'Compiler'

Having begun this article by looking at Semen Vengerov and his 'two million filing cards', it is appropriate to end with another bibliographer, Valeriia Feider. Whether or not she studied with Vengerov — and she certainly might have attended one of the affiliate 'Pushkin Seminars' at the Women's Higher (Bestuzhev) Courses or the Psycho-Neurological Institute, for example, although there is no record of her educational background — Feider developed a method of which the 'old guard' himself might have approved.

Feider's biographical approach, the compilation method, differed from Vengerov's encyclopaedism primarily in its scope. Vengerov had got bogged down in wanting to catalogue the process of literary production and

---

[46] Ibid. pp. 45–46, 49. The list I translated above is laid out in poetic form and concludes the *Slovesnost'* section with a set of poems entitled *Stikhi i stikhiia*. In the final lines Eikhenbaum writes: 'These were historical accidents and unexpected events. These were the muscular movements of history. This was element[al] [*eto byla stikhiia*].'

[47] Ibid., p. 86.

[48] Vladimir Orlov, preface to B. M. Eikhenbaum, *O poezii*, Leningrad: Sovetskii pisatel', 1969, p. 7. Not that Eikhenbaum gave up on conventional biography altogether. In 1933, he published a novel in the same vein as Tynianov, *Marshrut v bessmertie. Zhizn' i podvigi chukhlomskogo dvorianina i mezhdunarodnogo leksikografa Nikolaia Petrovicha Makarova*. Republished in Eikhenbaum, *Moi vremennik. Marshrut v bessmertie*, Moscow, 2001.

everyone associated with it: we might recall that one of his encyclopaedic projects was entitled *Russian Books: With Biographical Data about their Authors and Translators*. In contrast, Feider and another compiler of her era, Vikentii Veresaev (1867–1945), were more disciplined in their work. With a focus on a single classical Russian author per volume, these compilers looked backward with a specific purpose: to understand the life trajectories of these literary greats using as much as possible only the voices of the past. Unlike Eikhenbaum, Feider and Veresaev did not explicitly claim to link the past to the present. Laying out the materials they found seemed to them enough of a service to their contemporary moment.

Interestingly, Feider published her *A. P. Chekhov: Literaturnyi byt i tvorchestvo po memuarnym materialam* (A. P. Chekhov: Literary Life and Work according to Memorial Materials) with Academia, the same publisher who brought out theoretical works by many other Vengerov pupils, and it was the first in Academia Press's series 'Literary Life and Work of Russian Writers'.[49] This publisher began life as an independent entity in 1921, was subsumed under the State Institute for the History of the Arts in 1923, moved to Moscow in 1928 shortly before that Institute was forcibly closed, and ended its existence in 1937, having published just over 900 volumes. It overlapped in authors, directors and publishing programmes with the ascendant publisher of biographical works: the 'Lives of Remarkable People' series at Molodaia gvardiia press, founded in 1933 by Maxim Gor'kii.[50] We will return to the 'Lives of Remarkable People' in the conclusion.

[49] These volumes include, among others, Eikhenbaum's *Skvoz´ literaturu* (a collection of essays), Tynianov's *Problemy stikhotvornogo iazyka*, Tomashevskii's *Russkoe stikhoslozhenie. Metrika* and even Zhirmunskii's *Pushkin i Bairon*. Feider wrote or participated in other bio-bibliographic works as well, including several about A. P. Karpinskii (1936, 1938), the 'father of Russian geology' and first elected head of the Russian Academy of Sciences, another dedicated to geologist F. N. Chernyshov (1961), and an edition dedicated to the 75th anniversary of the death of V. G. Belinskii (1923). In 1923 she also published *Revoliutsiia 1848–49: obzor literatury* and *Khrestomatiia po istorii klassovoi bor´by* — the work, along with *A. P. Chekhov*, for which she is best known — with the revolutionary publisher Priboi.
[50] Gor'kii served on the Editorial Council of Academia press from 1927 until its demise. Academia's director from 1932 to 1934, Bolshevik party leader and politician L. B. Kamenev, maintained the aesthetic and ethical goals of the publishing house, including launching the series 'K stoletiiu smerti A. S. Pushkina', thinking up a new series entitled 'Biografiia idei' (which did not come to fruition), and even himself writing a biography of Nikolai Chernyshevskii, which was published in the ZhZL series in its first year, 1933 (this while continuing his work on Pushkin and briefly being exiled between October 1932 and April 1933). Arrested again on 16 December 1934, Kamenev was shot on 24 August 1936. See V. V. Krylov and E. V. Kichatova, *Izdatel´stvo 'Academia': Liudi i knigi 1921–1938–1991*, Moscow, 2004, and L. F. Kadik and V. V. Krylov, 'Kamenevskaia Pushkiniana', *Istoricheskii arkhiv*, 3, 1999, pp. 25–36.

As mentioned, Feider was not the first to work in the 'compilation' method. Veresaev, who was an author and medical doctor, also strove to create strictly 'objective' representations without adding his own voice, attempting to render portraits of the authors using primary materials chosen from among writings by their contemporaries.[51] His first such attempt, *Pushkin in Life: Character, Moods, Habits, Physical Appearance, Clothing, Situation (A Systematic Collation of Authentic Testimony of his Contemporaries)*, came out in 1926 with the Moscow publisher Nedra. By its fifth, expanded edition in 1932, this book had been taken over by Academia in Leningrad and Moscow, where in 1933 the companion, *Gogol´ in Life*, was also published. These two books were collections of anecdotes, rumours, opinions and reminiscences about the two Russian writers.

But if Veresaev used the word *svod*, 'collation', to describe his gathering of testimony, Feider preferred the sobriquet *sostavitel´*, 'compiler'. Her volume *A. P. Chekhov*, published in 1928, was even more characteristic of this style of biography. Feider seems to have been a different kind of author than Eikhenbaum, Tynianov, et al. who lectured and worked at the State Institute of the History of the Arts: she was a bibliographer, a collector of data like Vengerov. As Feider explains in her short introduction to the volume, she deliberately excluded the private, public, political and ethical sides of Chekhov in an effort to focus on Chekhov's *work* rather than his *biography*. At the same time she recognized that the 'living cloth' of the writer might be 'deprived of its blood' if she left out all the biographical details, so she does indeed present a certain 'mosaic' of chronological life events.[52]

The approach was designed to be scientific and materialist. In this book on nineteenth-century author and playwright Anton Chekhov, Feider excerpted and arranged letters to and from the author, biographical pieces by friends and relatives, his autobiographical writings and his

---

[51] Veresaev had a mixed reception even in his own time. Eikhenbaum found Veresaev's attempts at literary criticism to be offensive and worthy of being dismissed (see *Moi vremennik*, 1929, p. 134). Vladislav Khodasevich ridiculed his approach to biography (see Brintlinger, *Usable Past*, ch. 1 as well as Irina Paperno, 'Pushkin v soznanii cheloveka serebrianogo veka', in Boris Gasparov, Robert P. Hughes, and Irina Paperno [eds], *Cultural Mythologies of Russian Modernism: From the Golden Age to the Silver Age*, Berkeley, CA, 1992, pp. 26–32), and Mikhail Bulgakov struggled with his literalism during their collaboration on a 1936 biographical play about Pushkin (see Brintlinger, *Usable Past*, ch. 7), but Veresaev's work was widely distributed and influential in the Soviet Union and in Russian communities abroad.

[52] Feider, *A. P. Chekhov: Literaturnyi byt i tvorchestvo po memuarnym materialam*, Leningrad, 1928, pp. viii–ix.

fiction, to present a life of Chekhov that supplemented biographical 'facts' with descriptions from Chekhov's fiction which she thought had autobiographical resonance.[53] Feider opens her introductory essay with a lengthy quote about the scientific method from Chekhov's November 1888 letter to his friend and publisher A. S. Suvorin, which reads in part: 'today's hotheads want [...] to find the physical laws of creativity, to capture the general law and formulas according to which an artist — who feels them instinctively — creates pieces of music, landscapes, novels, and so on.' This insertion exemplifies the compilation method Feider used throughout the volume: even her own introduction features first and foremost the voice of her subject, rather than her own voice, although the excerpt implies that in the 1920s, as in Chekhov's time, the desire to approach creativity in a scientific manner is irresistible.

In an effort to be maximally objective, as scientific as possible, Feider removes herself to the background. In her book each biographical and creative moment of the subject's life, from his birth in Taganrog (chapter 1) and impressions of childhood there through to his death at the Badenweiler spa (chapter 34), is told using the voices of Chekhov, his family members, friends, contemporaries and characters, with the compiler's voice virtually absent. Only in the introduction and in the dry explanatory and identificatory footnotes does the reader hear from her, and we discern her hand only in the arranging of material into chapters.[54]

For Feider, this was a deliberate move. She explains that although the internal world of an author remains inaccessible to readers and historians, the material conditions of his life and creative path, 'the external situation and external process of writing are in significant measure "visible to the eye"'.[55] This 'materialist' approach to writing lives brought Feider into what she termed the 'literary workshop' of an individual, peering into the methods to discern how things were done. This focus on the so-called

[53] In his *Chekhov v zhizni: Siuzhety dlia nebol'shogo romana*, Moscow, 2010, Igor Sukhikh points to Feider's book as 'not widely noticed' in its time or afterward (p. 5), although it was published in 5000 copies. At this point in its history 'Academia' was affiliated with the State Institute of the History of the Arts where Eikhenbaum and Tynianov worked.

[54] In this Feider differs from Veresaev, who eschewed any and all footnotes or explanations. The only evidence of his 'voice' are the prefaces to each edition and the headings (i.e. the first three sections of volume 1 of *Pushkin v zhizni*: 'Predki Pushkina', 'Detstvo', 'V litsee', etc.) as he marched his reader through the subject's life. Beginning with the second edition (October 1926) and at the request of readers, he also began to mark 'questionable' information with an asterisk, which he did with more and more frequency with every edition.

[55] Feider, *A. P. Chekhov*, p. vi.

'literary everyday' (*literaturnyi byt*) — which was, after all, the name of the Academia book series — rather than just the 'life' of the author, was meant to animate the subject's creative process. Or, as Feider explained in her introduction, to 'give a living picture of the creative activity of the writers we have chosen'.[56]

Describing her method, Feider wrote of the struggle later generations must engage in to understand and assess opinions and unreliable sources in both actual and metaphorical 'biographical archives'. She pointed to her technique of confrontation and comparison — of the 'ochnaia stavka' she staged between testimony from various 'witnesses' as well as witnesses' versions of events with Chekhov's own writings — as a way to dispense with 'everything dubious, apocryphal, and anecdotal'. Interestingly, it is in asserting that she had removed the social, political, ethical and personal aspects of Chekhov's life that Feider explicitly defined the series' goals and her own work *in contrast to traditional understandings of biography*: if we had not thrown these (admittedly extremely interesting) elements out, she claimed, our work 'would have turned into a *biography*, and the topic we chose — creative works — would have lost its contours'.[57]

Feider's emphasis on her representation of concrete material and the resulting benefit for the reader highlights the conversation to which her book contributed. Her rejection of 'biography' in favour of the topic of 'creative works' is also telling. A few years earlier, Anatolii Lunacharskii had asked, 'How might Chekhov be useful for us?', and with her book Feider aimed to help readers understand how Chekhov's struggles in late tsarist times could aid in the building of a new culture among 'the literary young people, workers' intelligentsia, and teachers' of the young Soviet Union.[58] Similar questions were being asked and answered about other nineteenth-century literary figureheads. What would past Russian literature contribute

---

[56] Ibid., p. vi. This instinct, to peer into a writer's workshop, to look over his shoulder, if only retrospectively, was exemplified by the 1930 book, *Kak my pishem*. In the volume writers ranging from Andrei Belyi and Maksim Gor′kii to Iurii Tynianov and Viktor Shklovskii wrote about the 'technology [or techniques] of the literary trade'. See *Kak my pishem*, 1930, p. 5.

[57] Feider, *A. P. Chekhov*, pp. viii–ix. Not that the personal was completely absent from the book. For example, when in the chronology of Chekhov's life his brother Nikolai dies, the reader learns about it in a letter from Chekhov to Suvorin: 'Poor Nikolai died. I feel stupid and dull. Hellish boredom, not a penny of poetry in life, no desire whatsoever, etc. etc. In a word, the hell with him…' Feider's footnote reads: 'A. P.'s brother, the artist Nikolai Pavl., died from consumption on 17 June 1889 at Luka, where he is buried. A. P., who cared for him during his illness and predicted the inevitable end, was deeply shaken by his death' (p. 159).

[58] Feider, *A. P. Chekhov*, p. ix. She cites Lunacharskii's article from *Pechat′ i revoliutsiia*, 4, 1924.

to the education and formation of the newly burgeoning writing classes? Striving to facilitate continuity in literary life, Feider and others like her used their research into facts to reconstitute the literary *byt* of the past and with it lay the foundations for building a literature of the future.

Conclusions

If Dostoevskii is often quoted as having said that all of Russian literature came out from under Gogol''s 'Overcoat', we can say that many of the developments in biography, literary scholarship and literary criticism in the 1920s came out of Semen Vengerov's Pushkin Seminar. The students who emerged from that seminar participated in and created the important approaches to biography in this period which we have detailed above. In general, biography and theory of biography was written by people who had learned their skills of research, compilation and analysis as university students and who travelled in similar circles during the 1920s. These students were trained to undertake versions of what Nathaniel Knight has in this issue called the 'scholarly biography'.

For academically-trained scholars and biographers, documents had a kind of power all their own, and learning how to treat those documents was part of what remained of the university curriculum's nineteenth-century heritage: a need to organize and display facts so as to give each its proper due.[59] These skills — finding the primary material, compiling and reorganizing it, and analysing it carefully and conservatively if at all — were taught, and they could be applied to all manner of subjects: writers, poets, journalists and historical figures of all kinds included. Just as importantly, given that their years at university in many cases overlapped with the revolutionary era, these scholars learned to balance their own research interests with the desires of their audience and the increasingly specific publishing possibilities in the new Soviet state.

Contemporaries remembered Vengerov fondly. In a 1922 recollection, his student and personal secretary Aleksandr Fomin emphasized that although Vengerov's own approach to studying the past involved primarily the social and historical contexts of the data he was collecting, as an educator the professor was more flexible. In the seminar he permitted students to choose their own topics and himself came to be influenced by certain students who focused on form rather than content.[60] In Fomin's

---

[59] Steven Conn has written about this nineteenth-century 'object-based epistemology' in the context of American museums and their underpinning philosophy. See his *Museums and American Intellectual Life, 1876–1926*, Chicago, IL, 1998.

[60] Several of these students put off their interest in biography to found the 'Formalist'

view, these seminars were a wonderful mix of professorial guidance toward historical detail and student inclinations to move literary studies in new directions. Without the 'data' preferred by their professor, the biographies produced by the students would have lacked precision and verisimilitude; however, at the same time, the students moved past Vengerov's fact-bound research to try to draw connections and make judgments about the psychological reasoning behind the actions of historical individuals.[61] As Fomin described it in great detail in his memorial essay, the venerable Vengerov went out of his way to encourage and develop literary and scholarly talents in his students, but he did not 'found his own historico-literary school'. Rather, he 'aroused in several generations of students a serious interest in literature, a love for it, motivated them to engage in academic work, and inculcated scholarly habits'. Then the students took their own paths.[62]

Thus over the course of the 1920s, Vengerov's students and other scholars and biographers continued to explore new avenues, including sociolinguistic approaches and fresh kinds of taxonomy. Lives and facts were the raw data, but in conceiving of and retelling those lives, methods varied, from fictional representation to compilation to the *sui generis* mix that was the one-man journal. This focus on biography in most cases represented the future as emerging from the past.[63] Beyond metaphysical issues about the nature of a life and how to discover and reveal its plot — the quintessential questions of biography and life-writing — writers and publishers also considered more quotidian matters, such as reader interest and potential audience. Interest in biography and the methodology of constructing a biography ran up in the 1920s against not only theoretical but also practical moments related to the meaning of the past.

---

school of literary theory. It perhaps redounds to Vengerov's credit that they all returned to biography in some way. For more on the seminar, see Catherine Depretto, 'Le séminaire de Vengerov sur Puškin (1908–1918)', in *Le formalisme en Russie*, Paris, 2009, pp. 68–76.

[61] Compare with the 'archeographic' movement of the nineteenth century described by Nathaniel Knight elsewhere in this issue.

[62] A. Fomin, 'S. A. Vengerov, kak professor i rukovoditel' pushkinskogo seminariia', in *Pushkinskii sbornik pamiati professora Semena Afanas'evicha Vengerova*, St Petersburg, 1922, pp. x–xxxiii (p. xxxii).

[63] After Feider's 1928 *A. P. Chekhov*, Academia published *Liubov' liudei shestidesiatykh godov*, in 1929, with an introduction by Nikolai K. Piksanov, edited by T. A. Bogdanovich, in a print run of 7,200. This book included two parts: general comments about the era followed by three chapters about four specific 'Men of the Sixties': N. G. Chernyshevskii, N. V. Shelgunov, I. M. Sechenov, and P. I. Bokov. Part two consisted of excerpts from letters and memoirs, but part one is narrative in nature. Thus the second book in the series differed from *A. P. Chekhov*, with more analysis of the subjects, and bore more of a resemblance to the 'short biographies' Polly Jones writes about in this issue.

Eikhenbaum, who remained both practitioner and theorist of the relationship between biography and social context, made numerous attempts over the course of the decade to understand and explain the connection between history and individual lives. We might turn to his *My Periodical* for a final exploration of facts and lives. In the miscellany section of his one-man journal, Eikhenbaum juxtaposed two book reviews. Insisting on the importance of the 'historical novel of the "memoir" type', he noticed a couple of things.[64] By the end of the 1920s literature in Soviet Russia had undergone some significant changes, and Eikhenbaum believed that the answer was in *byt* and in a change of genre:

> Literature is now living an itinerant life. It is snuggling up to *byt*, living like a tramp, here and there. [You can find it] in the feuilleton, the essay, the humoresque, the memoir, the biography, the anecdote, even in the personal letter.[65]

Thus after the complexities — and the hunger and cold — of the revolutionary era, one place literature had come to shore was in the biographical novel. Reviewing Olga Forsh's 1926 *The Contemporaries* (*Sovremenniki*), Eikhenbaum compared it to similar works coming out in France and Germany: 'The prevailing material is not historical events, but the outstanding people who are constructing their own fates: writers, musicians, artists.'[66] Eikhenbaum's other review looked at Stefan Zweig's book on Tolstoi, translated into Russian as *Singer of His Own Life: Lev Tolstoi*, and perhaps as a biographer of Tolstoi himself, Eikhenbaum chose to engage less with that book's content than with Zweig's style.[67] Zweig, Eikhenbaum asserted, did not seem German in his writing, but rather French: 'Reading Zweig's book (especially since it is about Tolstoi), you keep wanting to translate it into Russian, not in the way that the publishing house *Vremia* did, but in another, more metaphorical sense: to replace the exquisite lace of its words with a simpler and coarser fabric.'[68]

---

[64] Eikhenbaum, *Moi vremennik*, 1929, p. 127.
[65] Eikhenbaum, 'Vmeste "rezkoi kritiki"', p. 125, in ibid., 1929, pp. 123–25.
[66] Eikhenbaum, 'Dekoratsii epokhi', p. 126. Forsh was also the author of *Odetye kamnem*, 1925, about the revolutionary M. Beideman, and in 1930, *Sumasshedshii korabl'*, about her own contemporaries who lived in the Petrograd/Leningrad House of Arts. On Forsh, Eikhenbaum, etc., see Martha Weitzel Hickey, *The Writer in Petrograd and the House of Arts*, Evanston, IL, 2009.
[67] Stefan Tsveig, P. S. Bernshtein, and B. Eikhenbaum, *Pevets svoei zhizni: Lev Tolstoi*, Leningrad, 1928.
[68] Eikhenbaum, 'S. Tsveig o Tolstom', in *Moi vremennik*, 1929, pp. 128–30 (p. 128).

For Eikhenbaum and others this simpler fabric translated to a desire for less analysis, less imagination, and more straight material. The compilation approach to biography had broad appeal, as we have seen, in part because it removed the voice of the expert, and readers could form their own opinions about what they were reading. But too much raw material meant that biographers were abdicating their responsibilities, or so Vinokur believed. Certainly they were abdicating analysis and interpretation. This was the balancing act they had to do in the era of lives and facts: each biographer and theorist tried to understand how *byt* and other literary-historical facts affected the lives of their subjects and, if only implicitly, what that meant for their own time.

In the 1920s, biography as a genre prospered even while the socialist experiment gained steam and the very concept of an individual human being, and his biography, was losing value. Ironically, both these tendencies fed into and shaped the doctrinal strictures of Soviet literature, culminating in the hero-driven, historically-grounded (if ideologically contingent) fictional works that by 1934 would come to be known as the Socialist Realist novel. A further irony was that if the 1920s demanded a 'simpler and coarser fabric' and an approach to writing biography that enabled readers to look into the 'writer's workshop' as they did with Tynianov and *How We Write*, biography's fate in that decade also set the stage for a resurgence of officially sanctioned biographies, with their real life 'positive heroes', in the series known as 'Lives of Remarkable People' which was relaunched by Maksim Gor´kii in 1933.[69] The ZhZL approach to biography emerged in some ways from the debates and practices of the 1920s and was to reign on the Russian scene until the demise of the Soviet Union and beyond.

---

[69] See the forum on the 'Lives of Remarkable People' series in *Slavic & East European Journal*, 60, 2016, 2, especially the introduction by Ludmilla Trigos and Carol Ueland, as well as their contribution to this issue of *SEER*.

5

The Antifascist Pact:
Forging a First Experience of Nazi Occupation in the Wartime Soviet Union

JOCHEN HELLBECK

I was born in Dikanka in 1927. I went to school through the fifth grade, and then I worked at the communal farm. I worked with my mother, who was in charge of the orchard there. We had a good life. There was plenty of milk and bacon [*salo*]. When they took me to Germany my mother was so heartbroken, she completely lost it. I didn't think she could handle it. It was March 1943 when they took me. I didn't go until the third time they called, when they said they were going to take my mother too. They loaded us into freight cars. They took us to Kiev, and from there to Poland and Germany.[1]

THUS begins the testimony of Ol´ga Sukhostat, a 17-year-old Ukrainian girl who was interviewed by Berta Likhter, a historian from Moscow, in Sukhostat's home village in the Poltava region on 17 February 1945 — just weeks after her rescue from Nazi Germany to where she had been deported as a slave labourer. Ol´ga Sukhostat was one of many Soviet citizens who shared accounts of their lives under Nazi occupation with Likhter and several other Moscow historians. Within months after the German attack on the Soviet Union in June 1941, these historians had constituted themselves as a 'Commission on the History of the Great Patriotic War', to assemble documentary material for a future chronicle of the Soviet Union's historic

---

Research for this article was conducted within the framework of a collaborative project devoted to the 'Commission on the History of the Great Patriotic War', directed by the German Historical Institute in Moscow and the Institute of Russian History of the Russian Academy of Sciences, with funding from the Fritz Thyssen Foundation. I want to thank these institutions for their partnership and critical support.

[1] Nauchnyi arkhiv Instituta Rossiiskoi istorii Rossiiskoi Akademii nauk (hereafter, NA IRI RAN), f. 2, razd. VI, op. 9, d. 10.

struggle against the Nazi invaders. As early as December 1941 — German troops had suffered their first setback near Moscow and were forced to retreat — the historians resolved to include the history of 'German-fascist' occupation into their documentary initiative. From January 1942 through the remainder of the war, tandem teams composed of a historian and a stenographer each trailed the Red Army on its path of liberation or reconquest. In smouldering towns and villages throughout western Russia, in Ukraine, Belorussia and elsewhere, they gathered testimonies from more than 1,000 witnesses and survivors of Nazi rule, often within weeks or months of the Germans' departure. The interviews were never published; within a few years of creating them, the commission had to close shop, and its documentary holdings were consigned to the archive — off limits to researchers. The team of Russian, Ukrainian and German historians working under my direction is the first group of researchers to be given full access to the interview transcripts, which are presently located in archives in Russia, Ukraine, Belarus and Crimea.

As I engage with the remarkable fieldwork generated by the historical commission, my goal is to map the largely unknown first Soviet experience of Nazi rule. This experience presents itself as a chorus of voices — those of workers, engineers, scientists, teachers, peasants, partisans, Communists who had stayed behind enemy lines and returning evacuees who were setting out to rebuild the Soviet order in the liberated regions. Many of the interviewees were women and elderly people, groups in society that as a rule were not evacuated and suffered the brunt of the occupation regime. Until now, their voices were markedly absent from the historical record.

The oral records of the experience of German occupation were only part of a much larger initiative pursued by the commission. Its founder, the Moscow historian Isaak Izrailevich Mints, aspired toward creating a *histoire totale* of the war. Mindful of how little of the war experience would be reflected in official state records once the war would be over, he called on his associates to collect or produce human documents that would ordinarily not be deposited in historical archives. The trademark of the commission was the stenographed interview. Over the course of the war members of the commission produced close to 5,000 such interview protocols, recording their conversations with a wide array of people — men and women serving in the Red Army, partisans, workers, directors, engineers, survivors of enemy occupation as well as returning evacuees who were setting out to rebuild the Soviet order in the liberated areas. Every interviewed person talked about their life and activities during the war, often embedding their accounts in a larger presentation of their biography. The interest in the autobiography of the historical subject was another characteristic of the Mints Commission.[2]

In fact, Mints's documentary quest amounted to a large-scale biographical enterprise. When it came to the theme of Nazi occupation, one of his core objectives was to generate life stories of exemplary Soviet citizens who had heroically battled the enemy by forming underground cells, joining the partisans, or enduring acts of torture. The circulation of such exemplary accounts, Mints and his fellow historians reckoned, would give Soviet readers a model to emulate and mobilize them to fight the hated invader with redoubled force. And yet, the actual transcripts that they obtained — long, complex and richly shaded — cannot be reduced to this propagandistic injunction. Or rather, this injunction meshed with pressing political and existential concerns on the part of the interviewees. Many of them keenly sensed the exceedingly high standards against which their performance under enemy occupation would be measured, and they positioned themselves accordingly, dwelling on acts of active resistance or explaining their incapacitation by forces beyond their control. But many also eagerly grasped the opportunity to speak out and share traumatic memories of a distressing time. Some interviews were conducted in close proximity to murder sites — trenches with exhumed bodies, gallows on which Nazis had hung suspected partisans, cellars in which the Gestapo had tortured and killed people. As the interviewees recalled these horrors and traced the story of their own survival, they effectively bespoke their rehumanization in the aftermath of Nazi occupation. In this instance, the personal and the political fused, as 'humanity' and 'humanism' were themselves important tropes in the ongoing Soviet ideological battle against fascism. In sum, autobiographical storytelling about life and death under Nazi rule amounted to an antifascist pact between survivors of enemy occupation and their audiences — a pact that proved crucial for the reconstitution of life and the rebuilding of Soviet authority in the very

---

[2] The Moscow, or 'Central', commission took the lead in this effort. It initiated the founding of similar commissions on the levels of union republics and autonomous republics. On the creation, work, and output of the Moscow commission, see Jochen Hellbeck, *Stalingrad: The City that Defeated the Third Reich*, New York, 2015, pp. 68–84; D. D. Lotareva, 'Komissiia po istorii Velikoi Otechestvennoi voiny i ee arkhiv: rekonstruktsiia deiatel´nosti i metodov raboty', *Arkheograficheskii ezhegodnik za 2011 g.*, Moscow, 2014, pp. 123–66; 'Komissiia po istorii Velikoi Otechestvennoi voiny AN SSSR 1941–1945 gg.' <http://komiswow.ru/> [accessed 17 January 2017].

moment of liberation.³ The meaning of 'liberation' itself was underwritten by such life stories.

Autobiographical storytelling of the kind practised by the Mints Commission was rooted in Soviet political and cultural life. From the start of the Communist project, Bolshevik leaders embraced the autobiographical form as a means of moulding their political following. Whether they joined the Communist party or its youth movement, enrolled in a university or took up a government job, Soviet citizens had to present their 'autobiography', a short account in prose that listed educational and professional achievements but at its core focused on the formation of its author's personality as an unfolding subject of revolutionary consciousness. Party purges were dramatic moments when a candidate's autobiography was either affirmed or challenged by the testimonies of other Communists who knew the candidate and were asked to comment on his or her life narrative. Communists were expected to be model Soviet citizens, and a Communist autobiography was to extol exemplary Soviet features: an active and strong will that aligned with the objectives of the Soviet state and, ultimately, the course of history itself. Communists were allowed to wander and err, but only intermittently, as the road on which they travelled was preordained as a trajectory that led from historical darkness to the Communist light.⁴

As the first interviews after liberation carried out by the Mints Commission make clear, the practice and significance of Soviet autobiographical storytelling continued into wartime. The testimonies did more than describe the deprivations and sufferings endured by a given survivor; they performed self-constituting work, moulding the speaker into a distinctly Soviet person. Many of the interviews contain elements of progression of consciousness and even conversion that characterized

---

³ 'Antifascist pact' paraphrases Philippe Lejeune's notion of the 'autobiographical pact', by which Lejeune means the reader's acceptance of the truth claims made by the author of an autobiography. Lejeune uses the term to destabilize the relationship between the subject of the autobiographical narrative and the autobiographical speaker, which readers are to accept as identical. Many of the witnesses of Nazi occupation expected their Soviet listeners to perform a similar leap of faith when listening to their testimonies of suffering. As for the 'pact', the question this article seeks to explore is whether the semantics of Soviet liberation were imposed by the interviewing (some might instead want to say, 'interrogating') historians or whether both sides adopted the term willingly, and jointly negotiated its meaning, even if on unequal grounds. Philippe Lejeune, 'The Autobiographical Pact', in Lejeune, *On Autobiography*, Minneapolis, MN, 1989, pp. 3–30.

⁴ Igal Halfin, *From Darkness to Light: Class, Consciousness, and Salvation in Revolutionary Russia*, Pittsburgh, PA, 2000, pp. 283–336; idem, *Terror in My Soul: Communist Autobiographies on Trial*, Cambridge, MA, 2003, pp. 43–95.

the Soviet autobiographical form. The survivors not only inscribed their wartime experiences into the loose interview matrix provided by the historians from Moscow (which in turn was shaped by Soviet autobiographical practices), but avowed their Sovietness through choice of words, images, or narrative style. While some of the interviewees averred a steady, unshaken Soviet orientation throughout the travails of the war, others indicated that the hasty and unequal terms of the Soviet evacuation effort in 1941 sparked confusion and resentment among those left behind, making at least some of them receptive to the prospect of German rule. Yet the practice of German occupation, in particular the Germans' exceeding cruelty toward the local population, reconverted these speakers to the Soviet cause. To be Soviet in the moment of liberation meant to be an active and politically conscious fighter in the struggle against fascism; this was a position that the Soviet witnesses and survivors of German rule eagerly embraced in 1942, 1943 or 1944, depending on the time of the interview and the reconquest of their given locality from German rule.

Isaak Mints and his co-workers were not the only people interested in the biographies of Soviet citizens who had lived under German occupation, nor were they the first ones to talk with them. NKVD operatives were the first to swarm through liberated towns and villages, with orders to arrest collaborators and uncover spies working for the enemy. Collaborators, referred to as 'traitors to the homeland', were defined as individuals who had formally worked for the German administration, joined their police units or the army, or had denounced Soviet citizens to the Germans. According to varying calculations, between 320,000 and 500,000 Soviet citizens were arrested on charges of collaboration.[5] Captured collaborators

---

[5] These figures apply to a ten-year period, 1943–53. The sentences meted out to arrested collaborators appeared to have been harshest during wartime; they were fed by orders from the Soviet military prosecutor to discover and prosecute crimes swiftly and not allow for any leniency. If a suspected collaborator survived this early phase, his or her chances to appeal the initial verdict rose significantly over time. Sergey Kudryashov and Vanessa Voisin, 'The Early Stages of "Legal Purges" in Soviet Russia (1941–1945)', *Cahiers du Monde russe*, 49, 2008, 2/3, pp. 263–95; Tanja Penter, 'Local Collaborators on Trial: Soviet War Crimes Trials under Stalin (1943–1953)', *Cahiers du Monde russe*, 49, 2008, 2/3, pp. 341–64. As in other European countries, convictions of collaborators did not always proceed on a legal basis during wartime and the immediate post-war years. It was not uncommon for NKVD special units to shoot collaborators without any trial. Soviet partisans trained their ire in particular on Soviet collaborators (often these were people they knew personally as former neighbours or fellow villagers), more so than on German soldiers. They would sentence captured collaborators in improvised 'Soviet' field courts and shoot or hang them in great frequency. Masha Cerovic, 'The Joys of Killing: Partisans at War 1941–1944', paper presented at the Annual Convention of the Association of Slavic, East European and Eurasian Studies (ASEEES), Philadelphia, 21 November 2015.

were on occasion able to mitigate the charges brought against them, if they could prove that during their formal services to the enemy they had actively and consciously helped the Soviet war effort. As with pre-war interrogations of suspected 'enemies of the people', NKVD interrogations of collaborators during wartime could thus evolve as a form of contested biographical/autobiographical storytelling in which the defendant's entire moral personality was at stake.

Communist party commissions proceeded to examine the credentials of party members who had remained on occupied territories. As early as 1 November 1943 (this was before the liberation of Kiev, which took place from 6–13 November), Ukrainian Communist leaders decreed that every single Communist who had been on occupied soil be subjected to a thorough verification process.[6] Such verifications took place in the presence of fellow party members who knew the individual, and they were often presided by partisan commanders who had distinguished themselves in battle. 'Why did you choose to remain on the occupied territory?', the investigators would ask, thus suggesting that the suspect had made a voluntary choice and not been forced by circumstances beyond his control. Only irrefutable evidence of active struggle against the Germans could absolve the Communist in question from general suspicion that he was a coward or, worse, had sold out to the Germans, becoming their accomplice (*posobnik*). These internal verifications in fact yielded few charges of active collaboration with the occupiers. The most frequent verdict was the Communist's failure to act. Passivity disqualified a person from membership in the party.[7] In other European societies, the process of liberation also entailed a reckoning with indigenous people believed to be Nazi collaborators.[8] But the situation in the Soviet Union was unique in that Soviet authorities did not acquiesce to the definition of collaboration as a by-product of the war, and did not treat it as a topic too pervasive and unwieldy to be effectively confronted. On the contrary, they took up their search for hidden enemies with renewed inquisitorial zeal.[9]

A third agency gathering records in liberated Soviet towns and villages was the 'Extraordinary State Commission for Ascertaining and Investigating Crimes Perpetrated by the German-Fascist Invaders and

---

[6] Amir Weiner, *Making Sense of War: The Second World War and the Fate of the Bolshevik Revolution*, Princeton, NJ, 2002, p. 86.

[7] Ibid., pp. 83, 86, 109.

[8] Tony Judt, *Postwar: A History of Europe since 1945*, New York, 2005, pp. 41–62; Weiner, *Making Sense of War*, p. 137.

[9] Ibid. An amnesty act on wartime collaboration was not passed until 1955.

FORGING BIOGRAPHY UNDER NAZI OCCUPATION

their Accomplices' (ChGK), a government body constituted in November 1942 with the task to investigate fascist atrocities and collect for the purpose of future trials and reparation claims documents and reports on crimes and losses caused by the invaders.[10] The organization had its headquarters in Moscow, but its principal work was shouldered by thousands of Soviet activists on site. Commission members listed or briefly recorded acts of murder, theft and pillage in the form of protocols (*akty*). The protocols also contain testimonies from eyewitnesses and on occasion also drawings and photographs of destroyed buildings or murder sites. Nathalie Moine, who has done pioneering work exploring local ChGK records, notes that many local commission members, most of them women, were relatives of Red Army soldiers, deported slave workers, or partisans who had been executed by the Germans, and that their documentary records brim with accusations and a thirst for justice and revenge.[11]

[10] When, in the course of 1942, Isaak Mints sought to persuade Soviet state leaders to create the ChGK, he pointed to the First World War as a precedent. In 1915 Russia had created an Extraordinary Commission on the Investigation of Violations of Laws and Customs of War. As Mints wrote, this commission did poor work, recording only isolated atrocities performed by the German army. During the Civil War, the Soviet state did not have an organization that recorded the atrocities and the plunder committed by foreign intervention troops. Only after the end of the Civil War was a Commission on the Calculation of the Effects of the Intervention created. Given the shoddy documentation on which they rested, the reparation claims that Soviet diplomats presented at the Genoa conference in 1922 were rejected by their Western counterparts. History, Mints concluded, taught a lesson: the ChGK had to be created early on and do comprehensive and thorough work. Mints himself had researched the World War One and Civil War commissions as well as the Genoa conference as part of his historical work on the Civil War. Drozdov, 'Chrezvychainaia Gosudarstvennaia Komissiia'. See also, Nathalie Moine, 'La commission d'enquête soviétique sur les crimes de guerre nazis. Entre reconquête territoire, fixation officielle de la mémoire et souci de justice', *Le mouvement social*, 1, 2008, pp. 81–109 (pp. 83–84).

[11] Ibid. The ChGK has a poor reputation, chiefly because of the International Military Tribunal at Nuremberg where the commission presented the 1940 Soviet mass murder of Polish officers at Katyn as part of a long list of alleged 'German-fascist' crimes. Yet the position of some scholars who discount the organization and its entire work as a single exercise in playing to, and deluding, foreign opinion is excessive. Marina Iu. Sorokina, 'People and Procedures: Toward a History of the Investigation of Nazi Crimes in the USSR', *Kritika: Explorations in Russian and Eurasian History*, 6, 2005, 4, pp. 797–831; Marian R. Sanders, 'Extraordinary Crimes in Ukraine: An Examination of Evidence Collection by the Extraordinary State Commission of the U.S.S.R., 1942–1946', unpublished PhD dissertation, Ohio University, 1995. Western distrust toward Soviet records is deep-seated and it preceded Nuremberg. It was not unfounded: recall the staged confessions of the Moscow show trials from the late 1930s. When Alexander Werth, a noted British writer and war correspondent stationed in Moscow, sent the BBC a detailed report on the discovery of the death camp of Majdanek in August 1944, his editors in London turned it down, thinking it was another Soviet propaganda stunt. It was not, Werth remarks in his memoirs, until the 'discovery in the West of Buchenwald, Dachau

Sharing the stage with these other agencies were the historians working for the Mints Commission. When they arrived in a liberated town or village, the NKVD had already completed its first wave of interrogations and arrests.[12] The ChGK and the historians worked side by side, but the historians did not collaborate with, or aid, the ChGK, nor is there any indication that their materials were ever sought or used by the NKVD or party officials. Like their counterparts in the ChGK, the historians of the Mints Commission sought to build a network of local and regional co-workers to render their documentary work more efficient and comprehensive. Throughout the war years, Mints campaigned for the formation of republican and regional historical commissions and shared ideas about the type of work they should do.[13] As de facto head of the 'Central Commission' in Moscow, Mints had ample experience in the generation of historical testimony. Since 1931 he had worked as chief editor of a massive documentary project launched by writer Maksim Gor′kii in the same year. Entitled, 'The History of the Russian Civil War', it was not intended to be a military history in the traditional sense. Rather, it aimed to depict the heroic individuals who fought in the Civil War, be they workers, peasants, or soldiers. A Nietzschean and a socialist, Gor′kii believed that every person came into the world a hero, but that this heroic essence would unfold only if it received proper support.[14] Ordinary workers could be

and Belsen that Western media became convinced that Majdanek and Auschwitz were also genuine'. Alexander Werth, *Russia at War, 1941–1945*, New York, 1964, p. 890. Today, the entire archive of the ChGK is fully accessible to researchers, but beyond scholars exploring the Soviet Holocaust, it draws remarkably little attention. Yad Vashem's impressive online platform, 'The Untold Stories: The Murder Sites of the Jews in the Occupied Territories of the Former USSR', builds in great measure on holdings from the Moscow archive <http://www.yadvashem.org/untoldstories/homepage.html> [accessed 17 January 2017].

[12] The intervals between the Red Army's liberation of a given locality and the arrival of the historians on the scene varied: in Khar′kov, the historians arrived in September 1943, six weeks after the Red Army had reconquered the city; in Kiev, they began their work in February 1944, three months after the city's liberation; yet the historians covered the Poltava region only in February 1945, almost a year and a half after the Germans had been driven away.

[13] How many of these republican and regional commissions were in fact created and what they accomplished remains to be explored. Two organizations, the Ukrainian and the Crimean commission on the History of the Great Patriotic War, with headquarters in Kiev and Simferopol, respectively, carried out impressive documentary work.

[14] Bernice Glatzer Rosenthal, *Nietzsche and Soviet Culture: Ally and Adversary*, Cambridge, 1994; Hans Günther, *Der sozialistische Übermensch: M. Gor'kij und der sowjetische Heldenmythos*, Stuttgart, 1993. On Gor′kii's documentary projects of the 1930s, see Katerina Clark, 'The History of the Factories as a Factory of History', in Jochen Hellbeck and Klaus Heller (eds), *Autobiographical Practices in Russia*, Göttingen, 2004, pp. 251–54; Sergei Zhuravlev, *Fenomen 'Istorii fabrik i zavodov': Gor′kovskoe nachinanie v kontekste epokhi 1930-kh godov*, Moscow, 1997.

made into 'HUMAN BEINGS in capital letters' if they were made aware of the world historical significance of their actions. The catalyst of this awareness was the biography of the subject, or even better, the subject's autobiographical self-presentation. Working under Gor'kii's aegis, Mints directed a team of historians who interviewed scores of participants in the civil war, relying on the stenographed interview template. Mints himself had served as a political officer in the Civil War, before training as a historian and becoming the Civil War's chief historian.[15]

When Germany invaded the Soviet Union in 1941, Mints on his own initiative redirected his staff to work on a new project, documenting the Great Patriotic War. He conceived of the new project in the same Gor'kiian terms, and he continued to be guided by the spirit of revolutionary documentarism that had swept the Soviet 1920s and 1930s.[16] It was a belief that the most important aesthetic of the day was the documentary, as a chronicle of the evolving new world. Revolutionary documentary work helped to move history forward: beyond representing reality, it ordered raw facts into a meaningful framework. Documentarians were 'operatives', to use the words of critic Sergei Tret'iakov, participating in the 'life of the material' and engineering a new world.[17] In a palpable way, Mints and his co-workers worked as 'engineer of souls', as Stalin put it in an address to Soviet writers in 1932. One project particularly dear to Mints's heart during the war was the presentation of a 'Gallery of Heroes' — self-narratives of exceptional, highly decorated Soviet soldiers whose autobiographical accounts were to inspire a mass wartime readership and thus produce a growing spiral of more heroes and heroic narratives. The members of the historical commission thus brought a biographical interview form to the front lines of the Great Patriotic War to transform ordinary soldiers (as well as the readers of their testimonies) into heroes. They were heavily steeped in the transformative, subjectivizing work that characterized the Soviet Communist project as a whole.[18]

[15] Elaine MacKinnon, 'Writing History for Stalin: Isaak Izrailevich Mints and the *Istoriia grazhdanskoi voiny*', *Kritika: Explorations in Russian and Eurasian History*, 6, 2005, 1, pp. 20–21.
[16] Elizabeth Astrid Papazian, *Manufacturing Truth: The Documentary Moment in Early Soviet Culture*, DeKalb, IL, 2009.
[17] The words of Sergei Tret'iakov are cited in Maria Gough, 'Paris: Capital of the Soviet Avant-Garde', *October*, 101, Summer 2002, p. 73. See also, N. F. Chuzhak (ed.), *Literatura Fakta*, Munich, 1972 (1929), pp. 31–33. Tret'iakov's notion of the 'operative' strongly influenced Walter Benjamin. See, especially, his essay, 'The Author as Producer' (1934), in *Reflections: Essays, Aphorisms, Autobiographical Writings*, ed. Peter Demetz, New York, 1986, pp. 220–38.
[18] See Hellbeck, *Stalingrad*, for interviews conducted with Soviet soldiers and civilian

The historians obtained their first testimonies about Nazi occupation in the aftermath of the Red Army's counteroffensive near Moscow. They produced a particularly rich set of interviews over a two-day-long conversation with five *kolkhoz* workers and peasants from the Tula region in late March 1942.[19] All of the five witnesses, three men and two women, addressed at length the occupiers' record of violence. Stepan Baranov, a *kolkhoz* chairman and party member, the first to appear in the stenographic transcript, called the attitude of the enemy soldiers 'beastly' and used episodes that he personally witnessed to underscore his judgment: a few village boys searching for firewood were shot at by a German or Finnish soldier. One of the boys died. Baranov's own son, suspected of having participated in an attack on German soldiers, was executed. Baranov then widened the lens to address the aggregate trail of violence in the district:

> In the village of L'govo 35 Red Army prisoners of war were burnt to death in a barn. At the Khrushchevo collective farm Kolia Efremov was shot because he left his home after 4 PM. They shot a 13-year-old boy! In the villages of Shakhovo, Isakovo, Rodionovo and Lavrushkino 25 people were hanged or shot. In the village of Glinishcha the two sisters were shot, Vera Sergeevna and Evdokiia Sergeevna. The reason is unclear. Possibly they had been harassed.

The next to speak was Maria Kozyreva, a non-party member and *kolkhoz* worker (from a different collective farm), 40 years of age. She described how the Germans came into her village on 21 November 1941 and arrested her son, believing him to be a partisan. They deported him when they retreated from the advancing Red Army in early December. Only after the rout of the Germans did she discover her son's dead body, near a village that the enemy had burned to the ground. The Germans also took her cow.

The beginning and the end of the interview are significant. 'I'm an ordinary collective farm worker,' Kozyreva began. 'Our collective farm was a very good one. We lived well, had farms with horses, cows, calves, pigs, and sheep. Every *kolkhoz* worker had a cow, a calf and a piglet, sometimes even two, and we had up to four, seven, eight sheep. We lived very well on the collective farm until the arrival of the Germans.' The point Kozyreva

---

defenders of Stalingrad in the course of 1943.

[19] This interview is unusual in that it took place in the Moscow offices of the commission and in the presence of a larger group of Mints's associates. Evidently, the commission was still practising the interview form and thus involved more staff. Later interviews as a rule would be gained through field work expeditions of small teams (1–2 historians, accompanied by 1–2 stenographers).

seemed to make was that before the war she and her fellow villagers had something — the Germans took it all away. This 'something' figures as a nostalgic memory of material plenty, rendered even more potent by the fact that her home village was now in ruins. The history of German occupation, told through a personal lens, established pre-war Soviet life as a good life, even though it may have been a very difficult one.

Kozyreva ended the interview with a view to the present need to rebuild the village and the *kolkhoz*, a task that was not made easier by the fact — expressly mentioned by her — that the Red Army had helped itself to the few good horses that had remained in the village. But the fight against the hated invaders was the overriding imperative; it deflected her from personal despair and spurred her on:

> Everyone is getting ready for the spring sowing campaign because we need to work in order for the German not to step back onto our soil once more. We women like to say that if the German comes we will take our pitch forks and confront him. I will tear any German to pieces because of how he inflicted 18 wounds on my son and left him there to die.

As with countless other Soviet citizens during the war, Kozyreva described herself as activated by powerful visceral feelings of hatred and revenge.[20] These feelings were not entirely self-generated, as state authorities and experts worked to sow hatred toward the enemy through atrocity propaganda, 'hatred seminars' held at the front, and 'Kill!' columns in *Krasnaia Zvezda*, penned by Il′ia Ehrenburg, Konstantin Simonov and others.[21] The interviewing historians of the Mints Commission, too, contributed to this spiral of hatred production, as they asked their interlocutors pointed questions about the attitudes of the occupiers and their record of violence and destruction.[22]

---

[20] The Communist party vastly extended its ranks between 1941 and 1945, and avowals of hatred toward the enemy and the ability to kill enemy soldiers were prime conditions for a Red Army soldier's acceptance into the Communist party during the war (see Hellbeck, *Stalingrad*, pp. 35–36). Masha Cerovic's work underscores how importantly demonstrations of hatred and cruelty toward the enemy figured as a sign of distinction also among Soviet partisans (Cerovic, 'The Joys of Killing'). On (Soviet) hatred as a moral quality in the context of the Soviet-German war, see Boris Frezinskii's introduction in I. Erenburg, *Lik voiny. Vospominaniia s fronta, 1919, 1922–1924. Gazetnye korrespondentsii i stat′i, 1915–1917*, ed. B. Ia. Frezinskii, St Petersburg, 2013, p. 21.

[21] See Karel Berkhoff, *Motherland in Danger*, Cambridge, MA, 2012, pp. 167–201.

[22] The historians' questions as a rule were erased from the typed interview transcripts. They can often be inferred, however, from the rough transitions in the course of a conversation, and from how interviewees at times began sections of their testimonies with a question — the very question, it appears, that had just been posed to them.

After a more than year-long hiatus, the historians resumed their interviews with civilians in liberated regions in the fall of 1943, as they followed Soviet troops into Ukraine, then onto the Crimea, and further West. These later interviews — the bulk of the historians' record on occupation — differed from the earliest ones in two important ways. The people in these regions were liberated much later, and they had fallen under German occupation earlier, meaning that they had lived under enemy rule for a much longer time, heightening suspicions of their collaboration with the enemy. Many interviews correspondingly ring with an apologetic tone that is virtually absent in the conversations with the *kolkhoz* workers from Tula. But, over the longer period of occupation, the Germans had also performed more and greater atrocities, making for far more distressing memories to be aired and shared.

Only in late 1943 did the Moscow historians resolve to create a distinct 'Department on the Occupation Regime and on Reconstruction'; it was formed in January 1944. During one of the initial meetings of the newly constituted working group, Esfir′ Genkina, the head of the department and one of Mints's closest associates, talked about the challenges awaiting them in these interviews:

> We are talking with people who feel different about themselves than, say, a general or a sniper who talks to us about military affairs.[23] That is why you need to be especially tactful in your interviews. Everyone who has worked with the Germans will say that they committed acts of sabotage and dragged their feet. This requires an active involvement on the part of the interviewers; they will need to obtain factual proof of sabotage or foot-dragging. Remember, we are dealing with a particular human material here, and that necessitates a particularly careful form of factual accounting.

Genkina instructed her group to read up in the Soviet press on a given region before conducting interviews on site, and to talk with a range of people in a given locality so as to be able to triangulate their accounts.[24] Another senior historian on the team reminded the participating stenographers to commit themselves to the same factual standards and record testimonies in unvarnished form. She criticized a stenographer for editing out from

---

[23] Genkina had been part of the small delegation of historians who had travelled to Stalingrad in January 1943 and then again in February 1943, to collect a total of 215 interviews with Soviet defenders of the city. See Hellbeck, *Stalingrad*.

[24] The archive of the commission contains binders of newspaper clippings on the occupation regime and on reconstruction, organized by regions.

her accounts statements that expressed an interviewee's critical attitudes toward Soviet power.[25]

The historians' premonition of what awaited them in the liberated regions was well founded. Many of the interviewed witnesses evidently felt a pressure to justify their life and their actions as they detailed acts of personal resistance or alternatively emphasized their absolute helplessness in face of an overpowering enemy. The inquisitional context of Soviet liberation — the political departments of the Red Army and NKVD operatives had already swept through the respective area, targeting suspected enemies; the Communist Party was preparing to do the same — also shaped the interviews protocols of the Mints Commission. But the records created by the Moscow historians differed significantly from the interrogations conducted by the Party, the NKVD and the ChGK. The historians did not come as judges, and there is no indication that they shared their records with other agencies, or were even asked to do so. None of the typed interviews transcripts bears the blue or red underlinings and signs on the margins that give away documents that had been read by NKVD officers or Soviet state prosecutors — 'operatives' of a different kind. The express aim of the historians was to document plural individual voices, to preserve the individual as such, not to standardize according to a simple template; working toward this purpose, they posed individualized and open questions. Schooled in interview techniques that amounted to Oral History *before the letter*, they were able to create an informal atmosphere, which induced witnesses to express themselves in their own terms and for hours on end.

Most of the interviews followed a timeline, tracing the interviewee's life before the war, the outbreak of the war, defence preparations in their locale, and evacuation policies, before reporting on life under enemy occupation. Virtually all pointed out that the evacuation effort was chaotic and was often tantamount to high officials and their families escaping into safety, while abandoning large segments of the population to their fate. Almost every single interviewee provided an explanation of why she or he was unable to leave (they tried but failed, or they were unable to leave because they were ill or had to care for sick family members) — thus responding to an implicit charge that they chose to stay behind. At the same time, many also talked about other people (very rarely themselves) initially adopting

---

[25] Berta L. Likhter, 'Soobrazheniia o kharaktere materialov, sobrannykh v otdele "Okkup. rezhim i vosstanovlenie" (rasshifrovannykh)', 29 July 1944, NA IRI RAN, f. 2, razd. XIV, op. 1, d. 3, ll. 18-22.

a wait-and-see attitude toward the Germans. A group of engineers, one interviewee from Stalino remarked, expected to do well under the Germans:

> They thought that the Germans would foster private initiatives. Businesses started opening: a bakery, a furniture factory, soap and butter factories, a mill. But as soon as they opened up, the Germans clamped down on them. [...] Within two months, by the time the Germans had shown their face, everyone began to despair.[26]

Virtually all interviewees, regardless of geographical location, age, or occupation, agreed that the practice of the occupation regime revealed to them the inhumanity of fascist rule. Many described the treatment of Soviet POWs as a powerful initial shock. Interviewee after interviewee talked about the rows of POWs that they saw passing by: emaciated men, in rags, barely alive, and mercilessly beaten by the Germans who also struck at civilians who wanted to give them food. Mariia Gaivoronskaia, a researcher in the Stalino Chemistry department who took up work as a schoolteacher to survive, described how contingents of POWs were repeatedly led past her school. Each time her pupils got up to look outside, 'because every one of these school children has a father or a brother who is serving in the army. One time the director forbade us to go outside to look at the prisoners. The children began to cry, it was impossible to go on with the lesson. They were crying, and I was, too'.[27] Many mentioned the mass killings of Jews in their localities as equally unsettling: 'Personally for me, the most harrowing impression came from how the Germans related to the POWs and from the murder of the Jewish population.'[28] For residents of Ukraine, the deportations of slave labourers were another memory filled with violence and pain. But regardless of which particular theme they stressed and in what order, most interviewees described German occupation as a near permanent state of oppression and display of unimaginable cruelty.

[26] NA IRI RAN, f. 2, razd. VI, op. 2, d. 13. Interview with Professor Andrei I. Charugin.
[27] NA IRI RAN, f. 2, razd. VI, op. 2, d. 11. Interview with Mariia Gaivoronskaia. Over the course of the war 5.7 million Soviet soldiers fell into German captivity, the larger part during summer and autumn 1941. 3.3 million Soviet POWs (57.5% of all prisoners taken) died in German custody. Christian Streit, 'Soviet Prisoners of War in the Hands of the Wehrmacht', in Hannes Heer and Klaus Naumann (eds), *War of Extermination: The German Military in World War II, 1941–1944*, New York and Oxford, 2000, pp. 80–91 (pp. 80–81).
[28] NA IRI RAN, f. 2, razd. VI, op. 2, d. 10. Interview with Comrade Mikhail P. Babkin.

Ol′ga Sukhostat, the 17-year-old girl from Poltava with whose testimony this paper began, was brought to Germany and sold to a German farmer whose wife used her as a slave on their farm — she had to sleep in the barn and was not allowed into the house. 'Russian devil', was what the German wife habitually called her. Ol′ga and other Ukrainian girls in the village suffered constant beatings. The Germans in the village 'wouldn't look you in the eye, as if you weren't human. There were times they'd beat us until we were down on the ground'. Etta Maizles, a Jewish survivor of the Minsk ghetto, used drastic words when she talked about the series of mass killings in the ghetto that also claimed the lives of two of her own children: 'He [the German] is a beast, worse than a tiger, worse than anything in the world. You cannot imagine what kind of beasts they are, bloodthirsty to no end, unless you submit to them.' Professor Aleksei Stasov,[29] chair in biochemistry at the Stalino Medical Institute, declared that when the war began he had felt only 'abstract hatred' toward the Germans, but this hatred had now become a 'savage' one: 'Just hearing the word "German" alone is sufficient to make me nauseous.' Praskov′ia Samokoneva, a cleaning lady from Stalino, remembered the German shout, *Geh weg!* ('Go away!'), with disgust. The Germans' 'refined cruelty',[30] experienced first-hand, clarified the moral horizons for many observers and victims of Nazi occupation. The changing military front-line in winter 1942 and the following months only underscored this process. In the wake of the Soviet victory at Stalingrad many witnesses described how they were looking forward to the liberation by 'our' Red Army soldiers, drawing a sharp line between themselves and the German occupiers. Samokoneva ended her interview with the words: 'I kept thinking: "You parasites, your time will come." And now it has.'

Many of the interviewees adopted strikingly Soviet criteria to characterize the 'fascist' regime. They noted critically that the occupiers did not preach high ideals, or in any event no ideals that would appeal to the Slavic or

---

[29] Stasov, and subsequently, Ignat′ev and Pavlov, are pseudonyms. Real names have not been used here in order to protect the actual historical subjects against charges of collaboration with the German enemy.

[30] The quote is from the diary of the Khar′kov professor of medicine, Lev Nikolaev. Nikolaev spoke with members of the Mints Commission, and in addition he gave them a copy of his diary from the period of occupation (NA IRI RAN, f. 2, razd. VI, op. 6, d. 7a u. 7v). See also Lev Nikolaev, 'Pod nemetskim sapogom. Vypiski iz dnevnika: 1941 g.– avgust 1943 g.' <http://magazines.russ.ru/sp/2010/12/ni8.html> [accessed 17 January 2017]. The diary is particularly valuable because it documents the evolving views and moods of Nikolaev and other Khar′kov residents in real time, thus adding a different angle to the retrospective claims found in the interviews, which were conducted after liberation.

Jewish populations; that the Germans neglected schooling and cultural life; and that their way of meting out exceedingly cruel punishments in public overshadowed even the worst excesses of the hated tsarist regime.[31] Maria Nekrasova, a Kiev resident 64 years of age, gave an interview rich in nuance and differentiation, and yet her verdict about the Nazi Germans was unequivocal: 'Before 1914 I travelled abroad at least once a year. The Germans back then and the Germans here — you can't compare them. Back then the Germans were on wonderful terms with the Russians. [...] I never saw that someone [in Germany] would slap another person. But now they are beating [Soviet] workers left and right.' This assessment was confirmed by the Kievan worker Nadezhda Konashko: 'We were speechless when we saw how much and how often the Germans would resort to beatings.'[32]

While not full-fledged autobiographies, these survival accounts contain elements of progression of consciousness and, in many cases, conversion, that characterize the Soviet autobiographical form. Some of the interviews indicate an unchanged moral orientation over time — recall Maria Kozyreva's recollection of the good *kolkhoz* life on the eve of the Germans' arrival. Or Ol'ga Sukhostat and her memories of milk and bacon. These images might not withstand critical scrutiny by a historian who would inquire into how Sukhostat's village of Dikanka fared during the Great Famine of 1932/33, or collect data on socio-economic conditions in Soviet villages in the late 1930s. But the more important point here is that the witnesses establish the good earlier life as a salient reality in the aftermath of Nazi occupation and against its immediate backdrop of violence and destruction. Many other interviewees described the moods in their home towns and villages in summer and autumn 1941 as far from fully Soviet in spirit. But virtually all pointed out how the practice of German occupation (re)oriented themselves and many others powerfully. Interview after interview concluded with fond words about 'our troops' (*nashi*), who are unambiguously cast as liberators. Here is *kolkhoz* chairman Baranov: 'When our troops arrived, everyone came out to meet them, praying, making the sign of the cross, crying — it was a real festival. Our army men all wore white winter capes. Compared to them, the Germans with their side caps looked pitiful. Our men looked amazing — like real Siberians.' The use of *nashi*, in his case and that of many others, referenced the speaker's restoration and self-universalization as a Soviet citizen.

[31] Karel Berkhoff, *Harvest of Despair: Life and Death in Ukraine under Nazi Rule*, Cambridge, MA and London, 2004, pp. 132–40; Bernhard Chiari, *Alltag hinter der Front. Besatzung, Kollaboration und Widerstand in Weißrussland 1941–1944*, Düsseldorf, 1998, p. 191.
[32] NA IRI RAN, f. 2, razd. VI, op. 10, d. 20.

Liberation from German occupation also had a powerful self-activating effect. Maria Kozyreva declared her unquestioned willingness to contribute to the spring sowing campaign and to recultivate a wasteland. Even more graphically, Professor Stasov described how he awoke from the deep depression into which he had sunk during the years of occupation, a descent from his favourite research into a struggle for survival, producing toothpaste and selling it on the black market:

> All my research counted for nothing, all that mattered was to make tooth powder. I developed a terrible migraine and my head hurt every single day because of this terrible depression. I felt as if I was dying spiritually. One more year of the occupation regime and I would turn into a bazaar trader. [...] Now I can't sleep at all. During the occupation, I would go to bed at 8 PM, which doesn't mean that I slept all the time. I would get up at 11 PM and not be able to sleep again until morning. Now my muscle tone is fully restored.

These, I should repeat, were the words of people who stayed behind, experienced occupation first-hand. Their perspectives and, more fundamentally, their self-presentation as reconstituted and activated Soviet citizens were at times challenged by Soviet Communist and state officials who had just returned from evacuation and were also interviewed by the Moscow historians. A case in point is the interview with Fedor Starovoitov, Chairman of the Executive Committee of the City of Stalino. Starovoitov said that he returned to Stalino on 13 September 1943, five days after the Red Army had driven the Germans out of the city:

> I arrived on the 13th. What did I find? To begin with, life in the city was dead. Buildings that the Germans had put on fire were still burning. There were clouds of smoke throughout the city. The crashed wood ceilings were burning — a horrible picture. No water, no electricity. All the stores were closed, and only children were hanging around trading cigarettes. [...] Life in the city had literally died out. You could only see the happiness on the faces of the residents. Some of them were of course happy, and others were worried because they hadn't been able to escape with the Germans. They remained here and the appearance of our soldiers struck them like a bolt from the blue.

Like the survivors of German occupation Starovoitov listed the damage done by the Germans, but he also commented at length on the dissolute state and questionable behaviour of many of the survivors. Life under enemy rule had corrupted them — they had essentially unlearned what it meant to be a Soviet citizen. Proof for this he saw in the fact that children were shouting and hissing during theatre performances — something unheard of in Soviet times. 'They have forgotten the names of Soviet institutions, and created a new lexicon: "Comrade boss, they would write".' What irked Starovoitov in particular was that he had great difficulty mobilizing people to work on the city's reconstruction. People would come up with excuses, claim to be sick or otherwise unavailable. Many of them had 'simply unlearned how to work'.

Starovoitov devoted a good part of the interview talking about the reconstruction of Stalino — under his leadership, of course, and therefore relevant to his own self-presentation. In this connection, he made interesting remarks on Aleksei Stasov — who, we may recall, also talked with the historians and spoke about how his abstract hatred toward the Germans had become beastly over time. Starovoitov lauded Stasov for his activism in rebuilding the city's Medical Institute, but he also referred to the professor's dubious past: Stasov had left Stalino before the Germans came, only to return to the occupied city. The local press controlled by the Germans had published headlines about the 'Return of the famous professor Stasov'. In the weeks since Stalino's liberation, Starovoitov went on, Stasov had demonstrated great activism:

> Is he deceiving us? With many people, the mood has now of course changed, and I think that he will now be one of us [*nash chelovek*].[33] A great many people were just unsteady. Many began to think that Soviet

[33] Starovoitov's generous assessment of Stasov seemed to form an exception. Here is how Stasov addressed the distrust that he felt directed toward him as a survivor of occupation. His description was at the same time an attempt to turn the table on Soviet evacuees as less-than-fully-dedicated, self-sacrificing citizens: 'The only thing that's making work difficult now is the boorish, mean, and disgusting attitude of the people who have returned from evacuation, and that includes even some professors. They are rascals and careerists who only seek to advance themselves. They walk around with confidence and pride, as if they had defended the homeland from behind the Urals. Of course, not everyone is like this. In fact, they're the minority, those who have returned from evacuation and think that they are the only good citizens deserving of attention and respect, and that everyone else is a rascal and counter-revolutionary. They fully ignore that comrade Stalin everywhere in his speeches talks about the attention and the care that needs to be given to the unfortunate citizens who fell under the yoke of the German occupation. [...] For me, the year under the occupation regime was more terrible than the year of evacuation.' (See also below, on how returning Red Army veterans would judge local Soviet officials who had spent the years of the war in evacuation.) Stasov was interviewed on 19 February 1944, Starovoitov on 27 February.

power wouldn't return. Now they have realized that this is not the case, and some of them work hard and well in order to burnish their past.

Among the teachers who were back at work in Soviet schools, Starovoitov commented, there were two, one Ignat'ev and one Pavlov, who had just recently given lectures to mark the second year of 'Ukraine's liberation from Bolshevism'.[34] Starovoitov vowed to intensify the re-Sovietization of Stalino, and he concluded the interview by critically commenting on the party members in the Municipal Committee who had not followed the evacuation orders in 1941 and had only weak excuses to offer when asked why they had stayed behind: 'All of them say — I was sick, or my family was sick. A Communist is a soldier of the revolution. When they draft you into the army they don't ask your family whether they will let you go or not. And when we had to retreat, why did you, a Communist, render yourself into German captivity?'

Thus, survivors of the occupation regime avowed their sovietness, only to see it often questioned by returnees who felt authorized to judge those who stayed behind. At times, this produced a direct clash of perspectives such as in the case of Stalino's attorney general, an evacuee, who told the historians that all talk about Germans having raped Soviet women during occupation was nonsensical: 'In reality, I am convinced of this, it was the women themselves who raped the Germans.' To corroborate his view, the attorney general referred to the many women in liberated Stalino who suffered from venereal diseases, and to the fact that many of the city's women were seeking to shelter Red Army men in their homes. Compare these statements to the testimony of physician Sofiia Neriiavskaia, who had remained in Stalino and watched from close-up how the occupiers forced women into having sex with them. Especially young women had come to her, she said, to obtain certificates that they were suffering from a venereal disease so that they would not be deported to a military brothel.[35]

But there were also points of convergence between the perceptions of returning Soviet officials and the experience of people who had come under enemy occupation. The head of Melitopol''s Municipal Executive

---

[34] Starovoitov practised what Soviet legislation also mandated: you could absolve yourself from past crimes through willing and eager participation in the building of the new life.

[35] NA IRI RAN, razd. VI, op. 12, d. 8. Interview with N.A. Firiabov; d. 16. Interview with S. P. Neriiavskaia. Both testimonies read as self-justifications: Neriiavskaia justified her continued work as a doctor under the Germans, and Firiabov emphasized the challenges of his work as attorney general.

Committee, Vassili Filippovskii, took an active part in the liberation of his home city, and he entered the burnt-out city centre on 24 October 1943, filled with distrust toward his own urban constituents. One of his first political actions was the convocation of a meeting of all residents of Melitopol' on 30 October: 'What we saw exceeded all our expectations. We never expected that they would come with red flags and portraits of the leaders, but that is what they did.' Filippovskii opened the meeting with a brief speech, and he was followed by priests and a few Red Army officers. The last to speak were four partisans — 'two comrades and two girls, all of them from Melitopol'. They joined the partisans after the Germans had shot their families and parents. What we witnessed was not a regular meeting — it was a single roaring and howling. The stories were so horrible, we all stood there, unable to move.'[36] The meeting organized by Filippovskii was not just a display of Soviet power — it also contained an offer to the people of Melitopol' to relay their traumatic experiences of Nazi occupation, or to recognize themselves in the words and emotions of the young partisans. Only this second dimension, this offer of a biographical narrative, explains why the meeting succeeded in touching so many of the present people.

Meetings such as that convened by Filippovskii were held in many liberated cities and towns. A well-documented early case is the liberation of Volokolamsk (a town west of Moscow) in January 1942. Footage produced for the official Soviet newsreel show trucks filled with Red Army men entering the town, past rows of cheering local residents. Soldiers distribute newspapers to the population, and posters go up on building walls, celebrating Communist leaders and exhorting the population to join in the partisan struggle. The silent film then cuts to the town square. A Red Army commander standing on a tank addresses a crowd of local people. Behind the soldier is a gallows. Dangling from it are eight bodies. People in the crowd look shaken, some cry.[37]

---

[36] NA IRI RAN, f. 2, razd. VI, op. 11, d. 2, l. 3.

[37] This scene entered Leonid Varlamov's film, *Razgrom nemetskikh voisk pod Moskvoi* (1942), which was released in the United States as *Moscow Strikes Back*, and won an Academy Award for best documentary. Some visual editing was performed for the American production, and in the process the scene with the gallows in Volokolamsk was inserted into the chapter describing the liberation of Mozhaisk. Similar images figure in other wartime documentaries, including *Bitva za nashu sovetskuiu Ukrainu* (Aleksandr Dovzhenko, 1943). That film features the Khar'kov professor Nikolaev (see note 29), who makes an appeal, speaking into the camera in Ukrainian: 'I was twice brutally struck by SS men, and once, in April 1943, they forced me to dig graves in the Shevchenko Garden. A terrible famine reigned in Khar'kov during that period. My emaciated face shows how

When the Moscow historians came to Melitopol′ in early February 1944 they, too, brought a biographical narrative offer to the survivors with whom they spoke — one that was remarkable on account of its participatory appeal. To an extent, the historians, too, prescribed the transcripts, by choosing with whom they would speak and by projecting their questions and the concepts inherent in them onto their interlocutors. Thus, most interviewees were asked to describe German atrocities and to comment on the actions of heroes (be they partisans, members of the Communist underground, or citizens engaged in resistance on their own) or traitors (meaning: collaborators). But the length and the variable form of the interview transcripts suggest how willingly surviving Soviet citizens inscribed their experience of the past occupation into the loose interview matrix that had been brought from Moscow. The propagandistic value of generating accounts of enemy atrocities intertwined with interviewees' urge, or ability, to share distressing memories about a difficult time, to powerful effect. The transcript of the interview with the schoolteacher Mariia Gaivoronskaia records that she cried when she relayed the story of how her pupils wanted to see the captured Red Army soldiers who were being led past her school in Stalino in winter 1941. A number of the interviews culminated in descriptions of exhumations of mass graves of Jews, partisans and other Soviet citizens who had been murdered by the Germans, and several interviewees identified their own relatives or fellow villagers among the killed.[38]

Thus, we observe a constellation in which the urge of survivors to relate the horrors that they had lived through and justify their own behaviour under occupation became entangled with the intention of the interviewing historians to collect building blocks for a future historical chronicle. This constellation produced a first history of the Soviet experience of Nazi occupation. The history, told through the first person, was narrated in immediate proximity to the time and location of the relayed events, yielding testimonies that stood out on account of their precision, emotional charge and highly variegated form. The latter owed to the fact that at the time of the Moscow historians' visit to Melitopol′ or Kiev, the Soviet state was only in the process of reconstituting itself in these liberated cities. The restoration of Soviet power was coterminous with the attempt to

---

much hunger and deprivations I underwent. I am now standing in front of the Chemistry building of the Medical Institute, a beautiful edifice that the Germans blew up. This is how the Germans related to science and scholars in our country.'

[38] See, for example, NA IRI RAN, f. 2, razd. VI, op. 13, d. 1. Interview with Vladimir Mikhailov (Simferopol′).

normalize the Soviet language and institute binding ways to talk about the past occupation.[39] In the process of such myth-making, orchestrated by the state, Jewish victims were reconstituted as 'innocent Soviet people' and the painful experiences of Soviet POWs disappeared from the historical record. Before long, the stigma of collaboration with the enemy fell on many Soviet citizens who had lived under enemy occupation. Under the circumstances survivors preferred to remain silent about what they had lived through, and the experience of German occupation, to the extent that it departed from the Soviet state mandate, was tabooed until the demise of Soviet power in early 1991.

To flesh out this process of normalization I have sought out serial self-narratives by survivors of Nazi occupation who spoke with the Mints Commission during the war. One that I have found is by Etta Maizles, the Jewish survivor of the Minsk ghetto. Her conversation with the historians — recorded on 20 August 1944 — centres on the horrors she experienced while living in the ghetto and on the mass murder of Jews. Maizles escaped from the ghetto and joined local partisans, and later she transferred to another partisan unit. As she explained, the second partisan group was a 'Soviet' one, and as its member she 'finally felt like a human being, not as a Jew'. The first partisan unit was commanded by a Captain Ostashenok, and he and others would declare that 'the Jews don't want to work or fight. That's why all this is happening to them, etc. They [meaning, Ostashenok and other partisans] would insult and mock us at every step'. In a Belorussian state archive I located another war memoir by Maizles, written in 1959, probably at the behest of the Belorussian Communist Party. The memoir, twelve handwritten pages long, remains fully silent on the horrors of German occupation and Maizles's identity as a Soviet Jew. Its sole focus is on her underground work under the directives of the Communist party. Compared to the wartime interview, the 1959 memoir is impersonal and bland.

Virtually every Soviet citizen who had lived on soil occupied by the enemy, or returned to it from evacuation, had to submit to a sustained biographical reckoning. Recall Fedor Starovoitov, Chairman of the Executive Committee of the City of Stalino. In his February 1944 interview with the historians, this returnee from evacuation appeared as an all-powerful representative of Soviet power and a judge of the compromised lives of the residents of Stalino who had not evacuated. Soon thereafter,

---

[39] This dynamic is well shown in Lisa A. Kirschenbaum, *The Legacy of the Siege of Leningrad, 1941–1995: Myth, Memories, and Monuments*, New York, 2006.

Starovoitov would have to justify his own biography toward veterans of the Red Army (*frontoviki*) who returned from the war as highly decorated soldiers and with political ambitions of their own. As Amir Weiner has shown for the Vinnytsia region, the immediate post-war years produced a significant turnaround in Communist office holders, with the *frontoviki* taking the stage. As they liked to say, they had risked their lives at the front, while people like Starovoitov had spent the years of war safely in evacuation were thus morally not fit to lead the Soviet reconstruction process.[40]

The restoration of Soviet power in the aftermath of Nazi occupation was a complex affair: presented as an antifascist pact, it induced the production of autobiographical narratives of suffering, heroic labour and active self-transformation. For many of those Soviet citizens who spoke out as witnesses to, or survivors of, the German occupation regime, their standing in Soviet society, encapsulated in their 'biography' (*biografiia*) was at stake. This biography was at once a matter of great personal and political significance, and an artefact that proved highly unstable under public scrutiny.[41]

In the final phase of the war, Ol′ga Sukhostat, the 17-year-old girl who had performed forced labour in Germany, was transferred to a Polish village where she had to dig trenches. It was there that she was liberated by the Red Army on 21 January 1945, less than four weeks before the interview with her in her home village in Poltava region:

> The soldiers fed us and sent us by truck to Warsaw, where we took a train over the border. [...] After Warsaw we were taken to Brest. Everyone who had been liberated from German lands was sent to the camps there. We were questioned and checked out. They issued temporary papers to those who needed them. The soldiers gave us lots of sugar, cereals, canned food. They were very good to us. Then this senior lieutenant had us come with him. Other officers went to other groups of girls. The lieutenant took us to the city [the Soviet city of Brest]. He went up to a store, smashed out the window and told us to go inside: 'Take anything you need, girls! Get yourselves some new clothes!' So we all got new clothes and took what we needed. I got three dresses, new shoes, and some stockings. Girls

---

[40] Weiner, *Making Sense of War*, pp. 51–62, 125–27; Mark Edele, *Soviet Veterans of the Second World War: A Popular Movement in an Authoritarian Society, 1941–1991*, Oxford, 2008, pp. 129–36.

[41] See Jochen Hellbeck, 'Galaxy of Black Stars: The Power of Soviet Biography', *American Historical Review*, 114, June 2009, 3, pp. 615–24.

who needed a coat took one, along with whatever else they needed. Our soldiers got us properly fed and clothed and sent us on. After Brest we stopped in Kovel, where they checked and stamped our papers. Then we went to Kiev. We spent days waiting for our train. Eventually we made it to Poltava. My mother was there visiting my sister. It was 7 a.m. I went into the apartment, but no one knew who I was. I said, 'Is that you, Mama?' She didn't recognize me. When it dawned on her she and my sister ran over to me, crying. They'd long since given up hope of seeing me alive. They bathed me, fed me, and put me to bed. My niece — my sister's girl — came to me. They said that her aunt Olya was there. She said, 'Which one?' My mother was a mess, she just couldn't stop crying. When I left for Germany I looked young: plump, with colour in my cheeks. But now my mother and sister said: 'Olya, how you've aged!' My sister is twenty-six, but I'm the one who looks older. When I'm done recovering I'm going to go stay with my sister in Poltava.

On the road back from Germany I kept dreaming about being there. I was still afraid of the bosses. I don't have those dreams anymore. Our entire village was burned down. Our house burned down along with everything in it. We've got nothing now. But so what? I'm just glad to be home.

In Germany they had us wear these badges [the badge is attached]. Anyone caught without one would be beaten or could even be killed.

The badge that Ol′ga Sukhostat handed to the interviewing historians is affixed to the typed transcript of the interview with her (see fig. 1). It is indicative that the interview concludes on the subject of the badge. Though it contains the letters OST (for 'EAST'), the badge served as a visual marker rather than a textual artefact in the context of German imperial and racial rule. Widely visible, the three letters were all that needed to be known about Ol′ga Sukhostat and millions of other forced labourers from the Soviet Union and Poland. The badge certified them as racially inferior, as slaves who were put on even lower food rations than forced labourers from France, the Netherlands and other European countries who did not wear identifying markers, and as cattle that could be exploited and beaten at will. In this context, the Soviet sense of self was not only a matter of Soviet politics (a vector that has been much studied, and probably too exclusively); it was also nourished by German practices of anti-biography, and as such it carried a palpable moral charge.

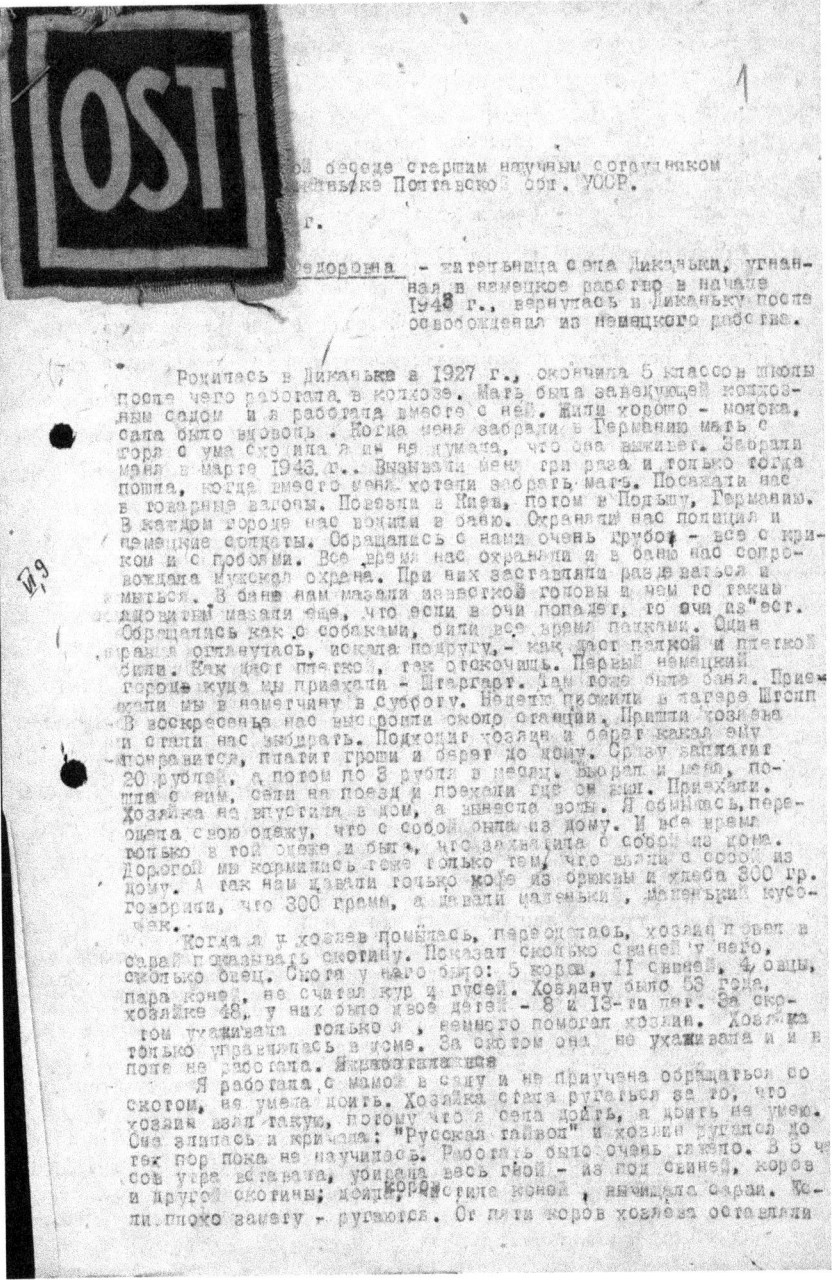

Fig. 1. Typescript of Ol′ga Sukhostat's interview, with her OST badge attached (top left). © Institute of Russian History, Russian Academy of Sciences

What happened to Ol′ga Sukhostat later on? Her first encounter with Soviet authorities post-liberation was easy, perhaps deceptively so. How much more biographical testing did she have to undergo after returning to her home village, and how did she fare? Virtually no Soviet women had served in the German army or the police force during the period of Nazi occupation, and so repatriated women faced much fewer formal penalties compared to their male counterparts.[42] But badmouthing and recriminations on the local level were another matter.[43] Ol′ga likely had to contend with the suspicion, sown by the Communist authorities and spread by fellow villagers, that she had dishonoured herself as a Soviet citizen while under German captivity, for why else was she still alive? And so, she likely came to regard her suffering under German rule, which was so central to her self-narrative in 1945, as a compromising chapter that had to be erased from her life story.

This story has a postscript. In 2000, after years of pressure from international governments and NGOs, Germany agreed to recognize surviving foreign forced labourers as victims of Nazi injustice and offer them financial compensation for their suffering. If she had lived long enough to make the claim and knew about the initiative in the first place, Ol′ga Sukhostat would have been entitled to a 'Category B' lump sum compensation in the amount of €2,556. To be heeded, the claim had to include detailed documentation of the deportation to forced labour. If any such documents existed, they were mostly of German origin. All claims had to be turned in by September 2006. The law that sanctioned the initiative expressly stated that receipt of compensation payment precluded

---

[42] Scholars disagree about the extent of repressive policies meted out against repatriated Soviet citizens. Vladimir Naumov and Leonid Reschin suggest that virtually all male returnees, 4.269 million people, had to perform forced labour after their repatriation. Vladimir Naumow and Leonid Reschin, 'Repressionen gegen sowjetische Kriegsgefangene und zivile Repatrianten in der USSR 1941 bis 1956', in Klaus-Dieter Müller et al. (eds), *Die Tragödie der Gefangenschaft in Deutschland und der Sowjetunion, 1941–1956*, Cologne, 1998, pp. 335–64 (p. 350). Pavel Polian's painstaking study provides lower numbers. It situates the overall number of returnees, men and women, at between 4.2 and 5.2 million people. Of the male repatriates, Polian writes, 'up to 50%' were reintegrated into the Red Army. These were POWs of fighting age who had not turned sides during their captivity and joined the German police or armed forces. Close to another 20% were sentenced to forced labour terms. These probably included the 6.5% of repatriated Soviet citizens who were sentenced to long labour camp terms for having collaborated with the German authorities. Pavel Polian, *Deportiert nach Hause. Sowjetische Kriegsgefangene im 'Dritten Reich' und ihre Repatriierung*, Munich and Vienna, 2001, pp. 174–75, 182.

[43] A Supreme Soviet decree of 1 December 1945 restored the voting rights for repatriated Soviet citizens. Yet in many localities they were treated as second-class citizens or, worse even, suspected to be traitors and spies. Ibid., pp. 180, 187.

any further compensation claims for forced labour.[44] And so the German law at once authorized the presentation of fuller life stories, complete with chapters that had been silenced by political pressures in post-war Soviet society, and sought to harness and close the voicing of claims that lay at the inception of such storytelling. To this day, the government agency created for the purpose of making financial compensation available to former slave workers carries out initiatives to memorialize the lives of former Nazi slave labourers, but the biographical accounts generated in the process have lost their legal purchase.[45]

---

[44] Anika Walke, 'Remembering and Recuperation: Memory Work in the Post-Soviet Context', *Zeitgeschichte*, 36, 2009, 2, pp. 69–87 (pp. 75–76).

[45] The foundation is called 'Remembrance, Responsibility and Future'. See <http://www.stiftung-evz.de/eng/home.html> [accessed 17 January 2017]. Former POWs in German captivity and Soviet citizens who suffered under Nazi occupation on Soviet soil were excluded from the claims process. The reasoning that was offered was that the status of a POW in itself did not offer grounds for compensation, and that the starved, humiliated and beaten civilians had not endured formal captivity or been deported. For a critical view, see the website of the NGO 'Kontakte-kontakty' <http://www.kontakte-kontakty.de/deutsch/ns-opfer/kriegsgefangene/> [accessed 17 January 2017].

6

'Life as big as the ocean':
Bolshevik Biography and the Problem of Personality from Late Stalinism to Late Socialism

POLLY JONES

'THE biographical sketch is the most accessible form of propaganda to educate young people about the heroic traditions of our party. The dry, Talmudic narration of party history has harmed and hampered the cause of studying party history. In biographical sketches, a good author, if also a writer, can put together a description of a period of party history in a much brighter and more interesting way. Good biographical sketches can be many times more forceful than thick, fat monographs.'[1] This statement, by an editorial board member at the State Political Literature publishing house (Politizdat) in 1965, was made at one of the many in-house discussions of biography that the publisher held in the Khrushchev and Brezhnev eras. Biography now promised a personalized, livelier alternative to traditional party history — or at least, an alternative way of narrating it that would be more 'forceful' in its effects on its mass audience.

However, it was also subject to strict criteria, as the speaker Lobarev, a manager at Politizdat, went on to explain: 'Here's how to write an artistic biography of revolutionaries: historically accurate, multi-dimensional, with skilful typification of characters and images. And the language should be such that not even the most pernickety reviewer can find anything to complain about.'[2] This ambitious biographical ideal harboured several unresolved tensions. Was biography primarily the life-story of an

---

I would like to thank the participants of the conference 'Writing and Reading Russian Biography in the 19th and 20th Centuries' (University College, Oxford, 2014), the anonymous reviewers for *SEER*, Anatoly Pinsky, Simon Huxtable and Anna Krylova for their help with this article. The research for this article was funded by the Leverhulme Trust, British Academy and John Fell Fund, Oxford.

[1] Rossiiskii gosudarstvennyi arkhiv sotsial´no-politicheskoi istorii (hereafter, RGASPI), f. 623, op. 1, d. 305, l. 5.
[2] Ibid., l. 6.

individual, or a way of teaching broader historical developments? How could the inherent individualizing impulse of biography be squared with the need for 'typical' heroes? Would assumptions of education and 'forceful' propaganda hamper realistic portraiture? And should biographies contain only verifiable historical fact, and would 'skilful' writers be interested in writing them if so?

These were dilemmas that had faced Soviet biography throughout its existence, but they became especially urgent after Stalin's death and particularly for biographies of Bolshevik heroes. Between Stalin's death and the start of the Brezhnev era, Bolshevik biographies were identified by publishers and critics as the most 'dry' and 'Talmudic' of all Soviet life stories, yet also amongst the most important for disseminating Soviet values and propagandizing party traditions, especially as the Soviet project and Soviet past were being re-defined in light of Stalin's death and de-Stalinization. In what follows, I analyse the substantial changes to the theory and practice of publishing Bolshevik biographies from the end of World War Two to the early Brezhnev era within their two main producers: the main Soviet political literature publisher Politizdat and the Komsomol's publishing house, Molodaia gvardiia (home since 1938 to the 'Lives of Remarkable People' series).

It is late Stalinist and Bolshevik biographies that have both been most harshly criticized in Western scholarship, as formulaic, de-personalized and hagiographic, although many analyses dismiss *all* Soviet and indeed socialist biography in these terms, without regard for periodization.[3] Only occasionally have attempted or actual reforms been acknowledged, such as the shift towards more personalized and popular biography writing after 1978 in China, the launch of new biographical projects in late socialist East Germany in order to reconnect the population, especially youth, with the revolutionary past, or the flourishing of biographical collections and series in post-Stalinist Hungary and other parts of the Eastern bloc.[4] Such

---

[3] William Ayers, 'Current Biography in Communist China', *The Journal of Asian Studies*, 21, August 1962, 4, pp. 477–85; John A. Garraty, 'Chinese and Western Biography: A Comparison', *The Journal of Asian Studies*, 21, 1962, 4, pp. 487–89; Nigel Hamilton, *Biography: A Brief History*, Cambridge, MA and London, 2007; Daniel Madelénat, *La biographie*, Paris, 1984; János Bak, 'Political Biography and Memoir in Totalitarian Eastern Europe', in George Egerton (ed.), *Political Memoir: Essays on the Politics of Memory*, London, 1994, pp. 293–301.

[4] Dai Wenbao, 'Biography of China in the Last Ten Years', in *Biography East and West*, Honolulu, 1989, pp. 50–62; Josie McLellan, 'The Politics of Communist Biography: Alfred Kantorowicz and the Spanish Civil War', *German History*, 22, October 2004, 4, pp. 536–62; Catherine Epstein, 'The Production of "Official Memory" in East Germany:

studies suggest that the post-Stalinist period was a time of particularly intense attempts at biographical innovation, driven by mounting anxieties about the efficacy of propaganda and by the turn to more individualized forms of transmission of socialist values. At the same time, they emphasize the influence of underlying assumptions about the poetics and purposes of socialist biography, which limited substantive change and thus often fuelled the very disillusionment that they had tried to address.

This article analyses similar tensions in Soviet biographical publishing from late Stalinism to the dawn of late socialism. It examines public and private discussions of Bolshevik biography, and of its (in)ability to evoke personality, and publishers' attempts to eliminate their texts' late Stalinist flaws and create true portraits. Criticisms of Bolshevik biography's formulaic, clichéd narrative and tendencies to de-personalization — rather similar to criticism outside the Soviet bloc, except that biography's propaganda functions were derided by these critics but never questioned in the Soviet debate — started to be articulated and debated by Soviet publishers and critics themselves soon after Stalin's death. This growing awareness of the crisis of Bolshevik biography disrupted further standardization and de-personalization along late Stalinist lines, instead spurring rapid growth in numbers of Bolshevik biographies, and experimentation with their genres and forms. Such reforms consistently stayed close to the top of publishers' agendas because biography possessed such potential to be effective propaganda, especially in an era when the blossoming of the individual socialist person(ality) emerged as the central promise of the Soviet project.[5]

What really drove these changes to Bolshevik biography, then, was concern about the recreation of the subject's personality. This has been the most nagging concern in biography and biographical criticism, especially in the twentieth century: theorists (and practitioners) of the form have repeatedly lamented the failure of biography to evoke the real, living self, noting that political biography is particularly prone to such failures.[6]

Old Communists and the Dilemmas of Memoir-Writing', *Central European History*, 32, January 1999, 2, pp. 181–201; Bak, 'Political Biography and Memoir'; Balázs Apor, 'Leader in the Making: The Role of Biographies in Constructing the Cult of Mátyás Rákosi', in Balázs Apor et al. (eds), *The Leader Cult in Communist Dictatorships*, Basingstoke, 2004, pp. 63–80.

[5] For example, Fedor Vasil'evich Konstantinov, *Lichnost' pri sotsializme*, Moscow, 1968.

[6] The literature is enormous, and analysed further below, but some of the best-known meditations on the problem of personality include Leon Edel, *Writing Lives: Principia Biographica*, New York and London, 1987; John A. Garraty, *The Nature of*

These Western critics' concerns were driven by a commitment to the unique human personality — and its portrayal for its own sake — that was considerably more liberal and less pragmatic than that of Soviet publishers. Nonetheless, the Soviet discussion of biography's failings and renewed ambition to bring Bolshevik subjects to life, discussed below, suggest some striking parallels. This article thus aims to inscribe Soviet biography into the broader currents of twentieth-century life writing and biographical criticism: from concerns about the evocation of personality, to the ever tighter embrace of literary technique and even fictionalization to achieve that end.

Bolshevik Biography from Revolution to Late Stalinism
Biography was theoretically problematic for a regime based on an ideology of collective class consciousness and behaviour and supra-personal historical laws. However, by the early 1930s, both the early Bolshevik prioritization of the masses over the individual and the ultra-anonymized masses of Cultural Revolution propaganda had been downplayed and displaced in favour of an emphasis on individual heroes, who were supposed to encourage citizens to work towards such devotion to the cause and coming to consciousness.[7] Scholars have disagreed over whether these individualized visions of Stalinist identity emphasized the flourishing of the complex, individual self (in a neo-Romantic vein, especially in the mid-1930s) or implied a more traumatized or atomized subjecthood.[8] Despite

Biography, London, 1958; André Maurois, *Aspects of Biography*, Cambridge 1929. On political biography's particular problems with personality see, for example, Lucy Riall, 'The Shadow of History? The Substance and Future of Political Biography', *The Journal of Interdisciplinary History*, 40, January 2010, 3, pp. 375–97; Hans Renders and Binne De Haan, *Theoretical Discussions of Biography: Approaches from History, Microhistory and Life Writing*, Leiden, 2014.

[7] Katerina Clark, 'Little Heroes and Big Deeds: Literature Responds to the First Five Year Plan', in Sheila Fitzpatrick (ed.), *Cultural Revolution in Russia, 1928–1931*, Bloomington, IN, 1978; Katerina Clark, *The Soviet Novel: History as Ritual*, 3rd edn, Bloomington, IN, 2000; David Brandenberger, *Propaganda State in Crisis: Soviet Ideology, Indoctrination, and Terror under Stalin, 1927–1941*, New Haven, CT and London, 2011; David Brandenberger, 'Stalin as Symbol: A Case Study of the Cult of Personality and Its Construction', in Sarah Davies and James Harris (eds), *Stalin: A New History*, Cambridge, 2005, pp. 249–70; Jochen Hellbeck, 'Galaxy of Black Stars: The Power of Soviet Biography', *American Historical Review*, 114, June 2009, 3, pp. 615–24; Anna Krylova, 'Imagining Socialism in the Soviet Century', *Social History*, 42, 2017, 3, pp. 315–41.

[8] On neo-Romanticism, see Katerina Clark, '"Wait for Me and I Shall Return": The Early Thaw as a Reprise of Thirties Culture?', in Denis Kozlov and Eleonory Gilburd (eds), *The Thaw: Soviet Society and Culture in the 1950s and 1960s*, Toronto, ON, 2013; Anatoly Pinsky, 'The Origins of Post-Stalin Individuality: Aleksandr Tvardovskii and the Evolution of 1930s Soviet Romanticism', *Russian Review*, 76, July 2017, 3, 458–83. Trenchant

these ongoing disagreements over Stalinist subjectivity, it is clear that the individual hero loomed large in Stalinist culture, and accordingly so did the biographical principle (on the collection of citizens' biographical narratives of World War Two, an undertaking underpinned by similar principles, see Jochen Hellbeck's contribution to this issue).

Biographies were produced in large numbers by Soviet publishers throughout the post-Revolutionary period, and biographies of Bolshevik leaders were always listed as the top priority in publishing plans. However, Bolshevik biography was also beset by a number of inherent difficulties that made delivery of these plans difficult, sometimes in terms of quantity and, as we will see, very often in terms of quality. The personality type of the 'professional revolutionary', established and disseminated in biographies and *Bildung* fiction even before the Revolution, was based on hard work, determination and the suppression of individual needs.[9] This usually dictated the lack (or at least extreme limitation) of personal life and personal concerns, and although work for the party was supposed to generate enough drama, passion and happiness to compensate for (and indeed eclipse) such sacrifices, it often made for flatly 'iconic' figures whose life stories varied only in minor details.[10] Additionally, while Bolsheviks' devotion to the cause could be dramatized for the pre-Revolutionary, Revolutionary and Civil War periods, with their 'adventure story' potential, the more bureaucratic party work after the Civil War was inherently harder to enliven.[11] In this sense, Bolshevik biography represented a peculiarly troublesome iteration of the broader, ongoing dilemmas of Soviet conceptualizations of the individual personality (*lichnost'*): should heroes adhere to a type or set of ideal characteristics or could they express their individuality? To what extent should the masses take priority over the individual? How much agency and importance should be accorded to an individual in the working out of historical dialectics?[12]

---

analyses of the peculiar subjectivity of the Stalin era include Svetlana Boym, 'How Is the Soviet Subjectivity Made?', *Ab Imperio*, 3, 2002 <http://abimperio.net/cgi-bin/aishow.pl?state=showa&idart=68&idlang=1&Code=> [accessed 30 October 2017]; Aleksandr Etkind, 'Soviet Subjectivity: Torture for the Sake of Salvation?', *Kritika: Explorations in Russian and Eurasian History*, 6, 2005, 1, pp. 171–86.

[9] Clark, *Soviet Novel*; Rufus W. Mathewson, *The Positive Hero in Russian Literature*, 2nd edn, Stanford, CA, 1975; Irina Paperno, *Chernyshevsky and the Age of Realism: A Study in the Semiotics of Behavior*, Stanford, CA, 1988.

[10] Clark, *Soviet Novel*.

[11] Matthew E. Lenoe, *Closer to the Masses: Stalinist Culture, Social Revolution, and Soviet Newspapers*, Cambridge, MA, 2004; Brandenberger, *Propaganda State in Crisis*.

[12] Jochen Hellbeck and Klaus Heller (eds), *Autobiographical Practices in Russia = Autobiographische Praktiken in Russland*, Göttingen, 2004; Pinsky, 'Origins of Post-Stalin

At the same time, the problem of how to represent personality was by no means exclusive to the Soviet context; biography as a genre continues to confront the problem wherever it is produced. These dilemmas came into particularly sharp focus during the 1920s, in Russia (as Angela Brintlinger's article in this issue explores) and in the myriad visions of a 'new biography' that sprang up across much of Western Europe in reaction to the failures of Victorian-era biography to capture the unique personality.[13] However, in the 1950s and 1960s, at the same time as the Soviet debate over biographical form and personality really took off again, Western critics of the biographical genre largely concurred that biographies still often failed to bring to life the personality of their subjects.[14] Both these waves of Western criticism blamed above all the inertial force of several typical features of biographical narrative: linear chronology; the 'chronicle' and 'compilation' form; and, above all, an intense wariness of literary devices, let alone any extrapolation or fictionalization.[15] As explored below, the post-Stalinist debates about Bolshevik biography that took place in the press and in internal publishers' discussions identified all of these problems from an early stage, and took determined (if embattled) measures to eliminate them.

Despite, or perhaps because of the particular challenges of creating a compelling Bolshevik life story, a wide range of sub-genres was deployed by biographers from the start, from life summaries for agitprop meetings to journalistic sketches (*ocherki*) and more fictionalized or dramatized biographical tales (*povesti*) usually consumed in more private settings. In the first post-Revolutionary decade, sketches, such as those by Gor'kii and Lunacharskii, were a particularly popular form of biography-writing used to acquaint the party and general population with the leading personalities of the new regime, though large biographical dictionaries of Bolsheviks also started to appear by the mid-1920s.[16] After the Cultural

Individuality'; Krylova, 'Imagining Socialism'.

[13] Ruth Hoberman, *Modernizing Lives: Experiments in English Biography, 1918–1939*, Carbondale, IL, 1987; Laura Marcus, *Dreams of Modernity*, Cambridge, 2014; Maurois, *Aspects of Biography*.

[14] For example, Leon Edel, *Literary Biography: The Alexander Lectures, 1955–56*, London, 1957; Garraty, *The Nature of Biography*. See James L. Clifford, *Biography as an Art: Selected Criticism, 1560–1960*, London, 1962, pp. 185–239, for a selection of mid-century critiques, many of which revolve around the problem of personality.

[15] See previous note's references, and also Paul Murray Kendall, *The Art of Biography*, London, 1965.

[16] Anatoly Lunacharskii, *Revoliutiosionnye siluety*, Moscow, 1923; Brandenberger, 'Stalin as Symbol'.

Revolution of the early 1930s briefly but radically downplayed the role of the individual, one of the key auguries of the new age of biography was the 1933 realization of Maksim Gor'kii's long-standing dream of reviving Florentii Pavlenkov's pre-Revolutionary 'Lives of Remarkable People' (LRP) series (the subject of Ludmilla Trigos and Carol Ueland's contribution to this issue); Gor'kii's broader 'biographical anthology' of the 1930s also included the monumental *History of Factories* and *The History of The Russian Civil War* projects.[17] Another sign of the blossoming of biography was the proliferation of sketches and tales about Bolshevik heroes, which resumed early post-Revolutionary efforts at commemoration, and added new figures, such as the more recently deceased Kirov and Frunze, to their roster.[18]

However, though the basic 'use' of biography for inspiration and emulation never disappeared once thus established, this intense interest in, and optimism about, the genre did not last long.[19] The terror of the late 1930s significantly disrupted the official narrative of party history, and sharply reduced the canon of heroes deemed worthy of public celebration; as a result, hundreds of Bolshevik biographical texts were stopped midway through drafting, heavily revised or removed from public circulation in the last years of the 1930s.[20] At the same time, the installation of Stalin as *primus inter pares* of Bolsheviks, through publication of his *Short Biography* in 1939, eclipsed his colleagues' biographies.[21] Stalin's biography set a template for the narration of Stalin's life in other publications and propaganda, for biographical propaganda across the newly Sovietized Eastern bloc, and for the limited number of biographies of other Bolsheviks produced domestically after it: impersonal, hagiographic, heavy on historical context, and dominated by chronological enumeration of party and state work.[22]

---

[17] Clark, 'Little Heroes and Big Deeds'; Clark, *The Soviet Novel*, pp. 118–24; Inna Bulkina, 'The Lives of Remarkable People: Between Plutarch and Triapichkin', *Russian Studies in Literature*, 49, April 2013, 2, pp. 87–95; S. Semanov et al., *ZhZL. Katalog, 1933–1973*, Moscow, 1974, pp. 5–18; G. E. Pomerantseva, *Biografiia v potoke vremeni: ZhZL, zamysly i voploshcheniia serii*, Moscow, 1987.

[18] Clark, *The Soviet Novel*, pp. 122–24; Claude Pennetier and Bernard Pudal, 'Stalinism: Workers' Cult and Cult of Leaders', *Twentieth Century Communism*, 1, June 2009, 1, pp. 20–29.

[19] It has often been pointed out that biography is 'used' in many, perhaps all, cultures for similar purposes. Edwin Paxton Hood, *The Uses of Biography: Romantic, Philosophic, and Didactic*, London, 1852; Peter France and William St Clair (eds), *Mapping Lives: The Uses of Biography*, Oxford, 2002.

[20] Pennetier and Pudal, 'Stalinism'; Brandenberger, *Propaganda State in Crisis*.

[21] Brandenberger, 'Stalin as Symbol'.

[22] Ibid.; Pennetier, 'Stalinism'; Apor, 'The Role of Biographies'. A good example of

The war further interfered with biographical publishing. LRP stopped publication in 1939, and did not resume until 1946, though short-lived biographical collections of 'great Russians' appeared in the last two years of the war under the umbrella of the series.[23] Nonetheless, as Jochen Hellbeck and others have argued, biography was a key feature of the war effort, including biographical sketches of Soviet citizens by war journalists and book-length accounts of pre-Revolutionary heroes that proliferated with the rise of 'national Bolshevism', such as the biographies of Aleksandr Nevskii and Ivan III and IV published by Politizdat.[24]

The cumulative effects of the Stalin cult, terror and war on Bolshevik biography left it in a troubled state by the end of the war. This was evident in the fact that Politizdat's late Stalinist biographical output was almost entirely limited to reissues (and, in 1946, a new edition) of Stalin's biography. In apparent contrast to this absence of biography in Politizdat, when LRP revived, its first post-war plan was headed by a list of party and revolutionary heroes, including Sverdlov, Kalinin, Ordzhonikidze and Kirov. However, the top priority articulated by its editor M. Penkin in his 1947 explanation of the plan to party authorities was in fact biographies of *Russian* heroes, such as distinguished scientists, alleged inventors and writers; such books, he explained:

> [M]ust foster patriotism and a sense of national pride in youth. One of its main aims is to glorify Russian culture, to propagandize the great contribution of the Russian people to the treasures of the world of culture. For that reason, when choosing names, particular attention is devoted to Russian figures. The publisher strives to ensure that the young reader is free of veneration of the West and is conscious of the great merits of Russian science and technology, literature and art before the whole of humanity and feels pride in them.[25]

Bolshevik biography after the *Short Biography* is D. Ershov, *Ivan Vasil'evich Babushkin*, Moscow, 1939.

[23] Semanov, *Katalog*, pp. 103–06.

[24] S. V. Bakhrushin, *Ivan Groznyi*, Moscow, 1942; V. Snegirev, *Ivan Tretii i ego vremia: obrazovanie russkogo natsional'nogo gosudarstva*, Moscow, 1942; V. V. Danilevskii, *Aleksandr Nevskii*, Moscow, 1943. On the revival of Russian heroes, see David Brandenberger, *National Bolshevism: Stalinist Mass Culture and the Formation of Modern Russian National Identity, 1931–1956*, Cambridge, MA, 2002; Kevin M. F. Platt and David Brandenberger, *Epic Revisionism: Russian History and Literature as Stalinist Propaganda*, Madison, WI, 2006.

[25] RGASPI-m, f. 42, op. 2, d. 1228, l. 1 and *passim*.

This list of heroes, which Penkin had redrafted after serious criticism of his original plan for its excess of foreign 'remarkable people', was in line with the Russian nationalism and chauvinism that dominated late 1940s ideology and propaganda, but also fitted with the series' traditional emphasis on culture rather than politics.

Even though the number of Bolshevik biographies planned for the post-war decade was small, Molodaia gvardiia failed to reach even this modest target. It did not commission authors to write biographies for several of the subjects identified in the plan, such as Kirov, Kalinin and Sverdlov, and biographies that were successfully assigned were then delayed by onerous review processes.[26] In fact, in the first decade of its post-war revival, LRP published just two biographies of Bolsheviks: the pre-Revolutionary heroes Bauman and Babushkin, long since identified by Lenin as priorities for biographies and so already the subject of several biographical accounts.[27] Both of these biographies were by Mikhail Novoselov, whose previous biographies had included a much earlier (and shorter) biography of Bauman.[28] A third text, a biography of Frunze by the writer Viacheslav Lebedev, author of a 1940s *povest'* about Frunze and of several other Bolshevik biographical stories, was started in 1946, before either of Novoselov's texts, but not published until well after them, in 1957.[29]

All three of these late Stalinist Bolshevik biographies were long (over 300-page) birth-to-death chronicles of their heroes' lives. Like Socialist Realist literary texts of the time, they emphasized influences on the formation of revolutionary consciousness and the acquisition of typical Bolshevik traits of 'firmness', 'calmness', resilience and self-sacrifice (including in the realm of intimate relationships, though this was barely covered in the texts). Despite these fundamental similarities, the editing — and the final versions — of all three texts illustrate that the criteria applied to late Stalinist Bolshevik biography and its exploration of character were demanding, but also heterogeneous, if not contradictory.[30] This suggests that, despite the apparent stagnation of Bolshevik biographical production

[26] RGASPI-m, f. 42, op. 2, d. 1228, l. 1.
[27] For example, D Ershov, *Ivan Vasil'evich Babushkin*, Moscow, 1939; V. I. Lenin, *Ivan Vasil'evich Babushkin*, Moscow, 1940; S. D. Mstislavskii, *Grach, ptitsa vesenniaia: povest' o N. E. Baumane*, Moscow, 1946.
[28] M. A. Novoselov, *Nikolai Ernestovich Bauman: 1873–1905*, Moscow, 1951; M. A. Novoselov, *Ivan Vasil'evich Babushkin, 1873–1906*, Moscow, 1954.
[29] M. Anan'ev, V. Lebedev, *M. V. Frunze, 1885–1925*, Moscow, 1957. Compare V. Lebedev, *Komandarm: povest'*, Leningrad, 1940.
[30] Materials on commissioning and editing of LRP texts, and correspondence with Soviet authorities, form the vast majority of available materials in the LRP archive, most of whose whereabouts or even survival remain unclear.

(akin to the 'film famine' of the late Stalin years), the fundamental question of how to represent personality convincingly — even Bolshevik leaders' personalities, with their strong tendencies to hagiography and standardization — remained subject to genuine discussion and disagreement in the early post-war years.

The only post-war LRP Bolshevik biography to be published in Stalin's lifetime, Novoselov's biography of Bauman, was criticized by internal reviewers mainly for its excessive attention to the hero's childhood and its 'saccharine', 'pre-Revolutionary style' account of his family background, and the author was urged to 'strengthen the formulation of general political questions of the history of the party' while 'restricting [the text] strictly to the domain of party-historical literature'.[31] The latter instruction for redrafting suggested that biographies had an important general educational function and that the narrative of party history had been firmly established a decade after publication of the *Short Course*. At the same time, the editors relied heavily on Old Bolshevik knowledge of the distant pre-Revolutionary past, meaning that such reviewers could enrich the historical context with their personal memories (for example, Elena Stasova corrected the description of pre-Revolutionary prisons in both of Novoselov's biographies).[32]

The requirement for lives to be placed in broader context also applied to Novoselov's slightly later biography of Babushkin, to which a preface was appended on publication, after the author failed to provide enough of the revolutionary background requested by reviewers. It was authored by the prominent historian Anna Pankratova (also an internal reviewer of both manuscripts) who intended its narrative of the broader changes to the proletariat during the hero's lifetime 'to help young readers to understand correctly and evaluate the role of Babushkin as a proletarian revolutionary of a new type'.[33] Strikingly de-individualizing for an introduction to a biography, the para-text represented an extreme variation on Lenin's identification of Babushkin as a model of the professional revolutionary type.[34] However, internal reviewers also praised both of Novoselov's texts for the emotion that they infused into the individual hero's life story, acclaiming the Bauman text for 'rising to passionate pathos' and praising the Babushkin biography for 'forcing the reader to relive the fate of its hero' rather than just recounting life events (in this, Novoselov was greatly aided

---

[31] RGASPI-m, f. 42, op. 2, d. 1239, ll. 3, 8.
[32] Ibid., l. 12; RGASPI-m, f. 42, op. 2, d. 1255, l. 55.
[33] RGASPI-m, f. 42, op. 2, d. 1255, ll. 48–50.
[34] Novoselov, *Ivan Vasil'evich Babushkin*, pp. 5–15.

by Babushkin's own memoirs, heavily cited in order to dramatize the hero's thoughts and feelings).[35]

These twin, and competing, criteria of historical background and personal drama were also applied to Lebedev's biography of Frunze, but took far longer to be realized. The first version submitted in 1946 was deemed a complete failure by all its internal reviewers, including one, a certain Bobunov, who wrote an extraordinary 144-page denunciation. Part of the problem lay in the subject matter itself. Unlike the short, pre-Revolutionary lives of Bauman and Babushkin, Frunze's life stretched well beyond 1905, taking in the Revolution, Civil War and NEP era; his death in the early Stalin era was shrouded in controversy; and, despite publication of some biographical accounts in the 1920s and 1930s, he lacked a canonical biography of the kind that the biographer of Bauman or Babushkin could draw upon (such as Lenin's obituary of Babushkin). Lebedev's first attempt was accused of failing to evoke either context or character satisfactorily. In contrast to Novoselov's critics, some reviewers deemed the amount of historical background excessive for a text that should focus above all on a single individual, rather than replicating general party history texts.[36] At the same time, the historical context that *was* necessary to understand Frunze's life had to be stripped of errors and infused with greater understanding of party and military history, based on the *Short Course*.[37] The military reviewers of the manuscript were especially critical of Lebedev's 'military helplessness and illiteracy' in writing about the Civil War and about Frunze as a military commander and strategist.[38]

Yet as important as these multiple historical misunderstandings was the biographer's failure to grasp the hero's *character*. Unlike the limitations that reviewers placed on Novoselov's account of Bauman's childhood, several reviewers of this text saw the virtual absence of childhood scenes as one of its worst flaws. Nonetheless, their differing views of subject formation during childhood led them to propose different revisions. The Frunze military academy historian Timoshkov criticized the fact that the 'formation of the child's personality [*lichnost'*]' focused only on family background, with 'nothing about the political and socio-economic situation in Turkestan, which certainly shaped Frunze', thus taking a conventional Marxist-Leninist view of the influence of the social

---

[35] RGASPI-m, f. 42, op. 2, d. 1239, l. 2; RGASPI-m, f. 42, op. 2, 1255/45.
[36] RGASPI-m, f. 42, op. 2, d. 1642, l. 103–15.
[37] RGASPI-m, f. 42, op. 2, d. 1230, l. 7; d. 1642, ll. 103–14.
[38] RGASPI-m, f. 42, op. 2, d. 1230, l. 10; d. 1642, ll. 98–102, 103–10.

environment on the personality.³⁹ By contrast, the reviewer Bobunov saw the family as the key locus of subject formation, reiterating the point several times in his monumental critique: 'One can't describe his life and works without mentioning anything about family, which undoubtedly influenced the formation of his character,' he claimed, while appealing to Lebedev to describe the full range of Frunze's relatives and their emotions: 'what were they like? Did Mikhail love them, and if he did love them, why?'⁴⁰ In a more forceful formulation later in his review, Bobunov termed the lack of information about Frunze's early life 'the most serious gap in the manuscript, its most significant flaw. It's unthinkable to give a detailed description about the life and works of a great man without having shown his childhood and youth in detail, which was when the foundations of the conscious, thinking person were laid'.⁴¹

This view of the personality also led Bobunov to criticize the manuscript for failing to 'uncover the inner world of Frunze', the 'spiritual' and 'moral' aspects of his character. In a strikingly holistic view of the Bolshevik self, he listed the many aspects of 'Frunze the person' (*chelovek*) that the biography had not covered: his personal life (*lichnaia zhizn'*) and Frunze the family man (*sem'ianin*), as well as Frunze the comrade, the leader and the military commander. In not showing Frunze in all these domains of his life, Lebedev had blurred the outlines of his personality (*lichnost'*), failing to evoke his unique features and his 'integrated' character, and painting only a few 'brushstrokes' of a biographical 'portrait'.⁴² Bobunov's response was thus intended not only to point out the text's errors, but also to provide a model of the holistic biographical enquiry that such a figure truly deserved.

These proposed revisions were enormous in scope and bewilderingly inconsistent, but were nonetheless initially scheduled for completion within a mere month. After revisions in spring 1947 and summer 1948 failed to satisfy editors, Lebedev requested a co-author in 1949, and Konstantin Anan'ev (who had published multiple books on the Civil War), was brought on board with the aim of bolstering the military aspects of the biography in particular.⁴³ The pair embarked on further research,

---

³⁹ RGASPI-m, f. 42, op. 2, d. 1642, ll. 98–102.
⁴⁰ RGASPI-m, f. 42, op. 2, d. 1230, ll. 9–18.
⁴¹ RGASPI-m, f. 42, op. 2, d. 1230, l. 18.
⁴² RGASPI-m, f. 42, op. 2, d. 1230, ll. 5–7, 65, 76.
⁴³ On this saga, see RGASPI-m, f. 42, op. 2, d. 1642, passim., and especially ll. 166, 175. 192, 201–03.

including fieldwork, and produced a new version within a year.[44] Reviews in 1951 still found the work unsuitable for publication, however: one reviewer, the military historian Sidorov, observed that the manuscript 'gave the impression that you're reading a book not about Frunze, but articles about Soviet history, and the narrative of historical events in many places is of poor quality, simplistic'.[45] Though the manuscript finally went to press in 1952, it was further delayed by editors' lingering anxieties about its historical coverage.[46] Soon after, however, the death of Stalin meant that 'all the material had to be re-assessed in light of the latest guidelines, adding new criticisms to the old ones', and the Secret Speech then further delayed publication, in order to prioritize biographies of newly rehabilitated cult victims.[47] Compounding the authors' woes, and fuelling their escalating complaints to Molodaia gvardiia in the mid-1950s, the commissioning editors also voided the previous contract and asked the authors to adapt the manuscript into a *povest´*, in one sign of how quickly literary quality came to the fore after Stalin's death. Indeed, the authors' acceptance of the final set of demands reacted to this stylistic volte-face with some exasperation: 'One cannot but note,' they observed acidly in June 1956, 'that at the start of work on the book about Frunze, there could have been no talk of a *povest´*, and all the efforts of the author to make the book about Frunze even slightly artistic were simply cut off by the editors.'[48]

The final text, published in 1957, covered Frunze's military career in much more detail than the original text, and also now contained a long section on Frunze's childhood and a later section on his hobbies and friends, but his own child and wife were not mentioned until the last third of the text, and then only very briefly. The author therefore only partly answered the appeals for Frunze's multiple identities to be covered, and satisfied the requirements of the *povest´* even less. Indeed, in the same year that this account of Frunze's life came out with LRP, a popular Stalin-era *povest´* about his Civil War exploits was reissued in a large print-run, highlighting the LRP's text's shortcomings in style and characterization.[49]

These editing practices in the late Stalinist and early post-Stalinist period suggest that historical accuracy — construed as fact-checking against the canonical historiography — was paramount in biography and that historical context played a central role in the narration of individual

[44] RGASPI-m, f. 42, op. 2, d. 1642, l. 200.
[45] RGASPI-m, f. 42, op. 2, d. 1642, ll. 103–15.
[46] RGASPI-m, f. 42, op. 2, d. 1642, ll. 160–61.
[47] RGASPI-m, f. 42, op. 2, d. 1642, ll. 160–61, 22–25.
[48] RGASPI-m, f. 42, op. 2, d. 1642, ll. 1, 22–25, 217.
[49] N. Vigilianskii, *Povest´ o Frunze*, Moscow, 1957 (1941).

lives; without correct and comprehensive general historical analysis, biographies would not be passed for publication. Indeed, all three of these biographies in their final form contained extensive analysis of general historical and political background, alternating with the party activities of the individual hero. In the Babushkin biography, the only post-war text published before Stalin's death, such historical analysis was heavily influenced by the *Short Course* and the *Short Biography*, though these texts' influence waned quickly in early post-Stalinist biographies.

In addition to this intertwining of individual and context, however, biography was also supposed to evoke personality so that its readers could develop a personal connection to the subject. The paramount importance of an emotional response to texts had long been enshrined in the Soviet notion of 'agitation', and had been a key factor dictating the turn to less faceless heroes in the 1930s.[50] These principles, already present in late Stalinist biographical propaganda, grew markedly in importance in the early post-Stalin period, as the later shift in criteria for the Frunze biography suggests. Ultimately, however, and despite the substantial disagreements about psychology and personality amongst their reviewers, these post-war texts presented their heroes' personalities in very similar ways, especially after the youngest years. They all charted coming to consciousness, documented the 'forging' of revolutionaries through trials such as prison and exile, promoted devotion to the cause over family or personal life, and celebrated the 'professional revolutionary' type. Such standardization of both the Bolshevik personality and the Bolshevik biographical narrative began to attract criticism even before some of these biographical projects had been completed, from Stalin's death onwards.

Debating Biography after Stalin's Death
The death of Stalin had profound effects on party propaganda, which were then accelerated by de-Stalinization from the mid-1950s onwards. Alongside hostility to the 'cult of personality', and in partial compensation for its effects, the first post-Stalin decade saw the (re)emergence of hundreds of 'personalities' from historical neglect or stigmatization: from the enemies of the recent terror to the hundreds of Old Bolsheviks whose contribution to the Revolution and Lenin era had been distorted or silenced in the *Short Biography* and *Short Course*. This drive to expand the biographical canon accelerated markedly after Khrushchev's appeal at the 1961 Twenty-Second Party Congress for elite cult victims' life stories to be rescued from decades

---

[50] Lenoe, *Closer to the Masses*; Brandenberger, *Propaganda State in Crisis*.

of oblivion. In this decade of biographical renewal, these far-reaching changes to content and expansion of the roster of biographical subjects largely overshadowed analysis of the genre and its poetics. However, once the ideas of expanding the biographical canon and of (re)identifying the Leninist era as the regime's key usable past were accepted, the problem of effective, entertaining and edifying narration of these new heroes' lives and personalities moved quickly up the agenda.

In the early years after Stalin's death, a number of high-profile criticisms of Bolshevik biography — especially the post-war LRP texts examined in our previous section — appeared in the Soviet press. These included a letter of complaint about the series' unsystematic choices and small numbers of Bolshevik heroes, apparently sent by ordinary readers to the main Soviet history journal, a common technique used to signal a policy shift.[51] Press reviews of the small number of published post-war Bolshevik biographies similarly lamented their limited numbers, but also increasingly pointed out their narrative flaws.[52] They expressed a growing intolerance of their 'dry', 'colourless' language and their unimaginative form.[53] Bolshevik biographies stood accused of adopting a 'protocol-like' tone, and an enumerative, informative style, compiling and listing facts and events rather than organizing them into a more inventive narrative form.[54] Another problem was that Bolshevik heroes' childhoods and the early formation of their personalities, as extensively dramatized in the Babushkin biography for example, consistently generated more 'involving' and 'bright' narrative and gave a better sense of the heroes' 'psychological makeup' than the account of their later careers, which tended toward the 'protocol' style of reporting facts, often in rapid succession (*skorogovorka*).[55] This, asserted one 1955 critical overview of LRP, was exactly contrary to what should happen: the post-Revolutionary era merited more 'brightness' and 'uplift' than all other periods.[56] As such, LRP was falling well short of party requirements; its Bolshevik biographies were failing to touch the minds *and* hearts of Soviet readers.

---

[51] A. Melnikov and F. Feigina, 'O serii knig ZhZl', *Voprosy istorii*, 9, 1955, pp. 108–09.

[52] Other complaints about small numbers of Bolshevik biographies include I. Riabov, 'Narodnyi geroi', *Partiinaia zhizn'*, 23, 1955, pp. 71–76; G. Prusova, 'Zhizn geroia: primer dlia molodezhi', *Voprosy istorii KPSS*, 3, 1958, pp. 216–19.

[53] B. Raevskii, 'Soldat revoliutsii', *Neva*, 8, 1955, pp. 180–81; 'Narodnyi geroi Russkoi revoliutsii', *Molodoi kommunist*, 6, 1955, pp. 126–27; Prusova, 'Zhizn' geroia — primer dlia molodezhi'; Riabov, 'Narodnyi geroi'.

[54] Ibid.; Prusova, 'Zhizn' geroia — primer dlia molodezhi'.

[55] Raevskii, 'Soldat revoliutsii'.

[56] Riabov, 'Narodnyi geroi'.

These early post-Stalinist criticisms suggested that biography had not yet (or not recently) been practised as a genre in its own right: authors had merely engaged in recapitulation (*pereskaz*) of the hero's party and state record.[57] At most, they had been practitioners of 'life description' (*zhizneopisanie*), and compilers of 'biographical data', rather than experts in the craft of biography, alleged one critical article in the authoritative journal *Kommunist*.[58] By the late 1950s, the pressure on LRP to increase its coverage of Bolsheviks, but also to create convincing 'images' (*obrazy*) of their personalities, was intense: at the end of the decade, an article in the newly founded official party history journal reviewed all of the Bolshevik biographies that had come out in the late 1940s and 1950s, and praised the recent growth in numbers, but concluded that the new output lacked psychological and narrative interest. The recent biographies of Frunze and Kuibyshev still exhibited a familiar divide between interesting narratives of childhood character formation and the dry account of later party work with no sense of individual 'features'. Overall, too, LRP biographies still failed to penetrate the 'inner world' of their heroes.[59]

These were far-reaching demands, but initially publishers responded with familiar Soviet measures: changes to plans and quotas, and bouts of *kritika* and *samokritika*. Under pressure from concerted press criticism, LRP included more Bolshevik figures in their publication plans for the series of the late 1950s and early 1960s.[60] The former dominance of Russian heroes was thereby much reduced, and the goals of the series shifted away from Russian patriotism and towards 'great revolutionaries' and Bolsheviks who 'give models of self-sacrificing service of the people and are an inspiring example for youth'.[61]

Politizdat, though it had been formally criticized much earlier than LRP, in a Central Committee (CC) resolution of December 1953 criticizing its general party history failings, needed first to move to publishing biographies in significant numbers. Internal meetings in the second half of the 1950s lamented the many 'notable figures' neglected during the long lapse in its biographical publishing.[62] The biographical sketch, in particular, promised to appeal to a much broader audience and needed

---

[57] Ibid.; Prusova, 'Zhizn' geroia — primer dlia molodezhi'.
[58] 'Knigi o geroiakh Oktiabria', *Kommunist*, 15, 1958, pp. 123–28.
[59] Prusova, 'Zhizn' geroia — primer dlia molodezhi'.
[60] RGASPI-m, f. 42, op. 2, d. 1281, l. 2.
[61] RGASPI-m, f. 42, op. 2, d. 1281, ll. 10–14.
[62] RGASPI, f. 623, op. 1, d. 187, l. 193, *passim*.

to be deployed more fully.⁶³ As these discussions of biography and 'mass literature' continued, Politizdat started planning and publishing biographical series (notably 'Heroes and Feats' and 'Tales of the Tasks and People of the Party', as well as 'Heroes of Labour') and then put out at least fifteen individual biographies and collections of sketches about Bolsheviks in the first half of the 1960s, outdoing LRP's eight Bolshevik biographies published in the same period.⁶⁴ The two publishers' virtually simultaneous drives to prioritize Bolshevik and Revolutionary biography unsurprisingly led to duplication across their plans, with rival biographies of figures including Frunze, Kirov and Ordzhonikidze published in close succession.

However, despite the early emergence of a new discourse of psychological portraiture, early post-Stalinist changes to biography did not focus much on improving the evocation of personality; this was mainly due to the intense disruption to the broader Soviet historical narrative that biographers, as in the Stalin era, had to use to frame the lives of biographical subjects. This was evident, as we have seen, in the latter stages of the tortuous editing of the LRP Frunze biography, where the pervasive instability in party and military history consistently outpaced the authors' revisions. It also caused the next LRP Bolshevik biography, of Kuibyshev, to be significantly delayed.⁶⁵ Pavel Berezov, a biographer with many sketches and short biographies of Bolsheviks to his name, was commissioned to write the Kuibyshev biography in 1955, but the first round of reviews, within months of the Secret Speech in summer 1956, found its treatment of the individual problematic in several respects, traceable to Stalin-era practice.⁶⁶ On the one hand, the biography 'enumerat[ed] the actions of Kuibyshev, instead of showing them concretely'.⁶⁷ On the other hand, though, Kuibyshev was 'divorced from his surroundings' and shown as 'a leader [*vozhd*'] standing above the masses', in the vein of the now denounced 'cult of personality'.⁶⁸ Only after multiple rounds of editing was the reworked biography deemed acceptable and finally published in 1958. While superficially stripped of the *kul't lichnosti*, Berezov's text nonetheless largely stuck to the Stalinist

---

⁶³ RGASPI, f. 623, op. 1, d. 193.

⁶⁴ RGASPI, f. 623, op. 1, d. 273 (discussion of 40 series in Politizdat, many of them biographical). The 'Tales of the Tasks' series was often praised (RGASPI, f. 623, op. 1, dd. 218, 284, 295).

⁶⁵ P. I. Berezov, *Valerian Vladimirovich Kuibyshev, 1888–1935*, Moscow, 1958.

⁶⁶ One letter from the author to the series editor refers to the 1946 commissioning of a Kuibyshev biography, which was never published despite being approved (RGASPI-m, f. 42, op. 2, d. 1504, ll. 19–20).

⁶⁷ RGASPI-m, f. 42, op. 2, d. 1504, ll. 21–28.

⁶⁸ RGASPI-m, f. 42, op. 2, d. 1504, ll. 9–13, 17, 19–28, 30.

template, endowing the hero with stock traits (calmness, a strong will) and enumerating the stages of his party involvement chronologically and exhaustively. Only in the insistent lyrical motif of Kuibyshev's love for writing poetry, and the 'in medias res' opening, could the reader glimpse the textual innovations that would proliferate over the next decade.

In the 1960s, as problems of quantity were addressed with the insertion of multiple new Bolshevik biographies into publishers' plans, and as the broader narrative of Leninist and Stalinist history started to stabilize into a steadier background for biographical accounts, the question of how to write a compelling life and evoke character loomed much larger. In his first plan of the 1960s, LRP's editor-in-chief pledged to tackle the chronic problems of unsystematic coverage of party heroes and 'dry', 'grey', 'standardized' and linguistically 'inexpressive' biographies.[69] While improved coverage of revolutionaries was to be assured by increasing the number of such subjects from the nine featured in the 1957–61 plan up to thirty-five, language and form would improve through better editing and reviewing, including a pledge to respect the 'individuality and creative manner' of each author.[70] Meanwhile, in Politizdat in the same period, criteria for good and bad biographical practice began to be formulated: biographies should be broadly gripping (*zanimatel'nyi*), entertaining (*uvlekatel'nyi*) and emotionally affecting (*volnuiushchii*). The list of what biography should *not* be was longer, and sharper in its criticisms. Now that biography was so much more prominent in Politizdat's plans, it could not afford to be of poor quality, yet the genre was so difficult that it might 'torture' inexperienced authors and end up full of clichés.[71] As in the earliest post-Stalin criticism, texts must not be 'grey', 'dry' or 'bureaucratic' in tone, which had by now come to mean listing facts in boring succession and thus replicating the party *anketa* or the press obituary (*nekrolog*). The 'artistic depiction' of personality had now become critically important.[72]

Such psychologization depended on a willingness to broaden both the typical authorial cohort and the generic limits of Bolshevik biographies (to take in literary techniques). One obstacle to such expansion was the fact that many post-Stalin biographies in both LRP and Politizdat were still written by historians and academics, notably employees of the Institute of Marxism-Leninism, and by those who had started work as

---

[69] RGASPI-m, f. 42, op. 2, d. 1281, ll. 10–14.
[70] Ibid.
[71] RGASPI, f. 623, op. 1, d. 284, ll. 289.
[72] RGASPI, f. 623, op. 1, d. 284, l. 285; Tsentral'nyi arkhiv sotsial'no-politicheskoi istorii Moskvy (hereafter, TsAOPIM), f. 819, op. 1, d. 32.

biographers in the Stalin era.⁷³ Manuscripts were still reviewed mainly by such figures too, who concentrated on monitoring factual accuracy and adherence to the party line, rather than assessing narrative quality (which they were ill-equipped to do in any case). The need for an injection of literary excellence into biography was recognized in Politizdat as early as the mid-1950s; thereafter, the identity of the required 'masters of the pen' slowly crystallized, as did the necessary practical links with literary organizations.⁷⁴ As these writers started to write for Politizdat, they also began to range into genres beyond the LRP-style quasi-academic biography and the life summary used in agitprop. The most significant generic innovation came in one of the first major biographical ventures at Politizdat to involve significant numbers of members of the writers' and journalists' unions: a series of five biographical anthologies, each containing roughly twenty-five short stories about Leninists and Old Bolsheviks. These collections, which opened with the 1963 anthology *At the Sources of the Party*, fused the discontinued tradition of biographical collections and dictionaries with the genre of the biographical tale, both types of biography that had been much more popular in the Lenin era and early Stalinism than in the recent past.⁷⁵

Overall, then, Politizdat responded to the criticisms of the 1950s with a more multi-faceted approach to biography than Molodaia gvardiia, where the biographical template of LRP (the comprehensive, documentary-based text) had been set years earlier and was still adhered to assiduously in the sensitive realm of Bolshevik biography. Politizdat's shortage of previous biographical experience liberated it somewhat from this weight of tradition, and, as the next section explores, allowed its texts in particular to include new approaches to psychological portraiture.

The New Bolshevik Biographies
In their pursuit of more convincing psychological portraiture, critics of biography have often urged biographers to move away from a 'chronicle' form and towards a more selective and imaginative presentation of moments when the subject's personality is sharply illuminated.⁷⁶ Until

---

⁷³ For example, A. Melchin (biographer of Kosior) was a historian at the Institute of Marxism-Leninism.
⁷⁴ TsAOPIM, f. 819, op. 1, d. 22; TsAOPIM, f. 819, op. 1, d. 34.
⁷⁵ L. D. Davydov, *U istokov partii: rasskazy o soratnikakh V. I. Lenina*, Moscow, 1963.
⁷⁶ This was one of the key appeals of Lytton Strachey and other 'new biographers' of the 1920s. Marcus, *Dreams of Modernity*; Hoberman, *Modernising Lives*. It was also central to Irving Stone's arguments in favour of the biographical novel: Irving Stone, *The Biographical Novel*, 1957.

the emergence of postmodernist approaches, however, the use of fictional techniques *per se* remained beyond the mainstream of Western biographical practice, and was typical only for the often maligned sub-genre of the *biographie romancée*.[77] In the first post-Stalin decade, the chronicle form attracted increasing criticism, but was still widely employed, especially by LRP. Publishers also began to view literary techniques as a panacea for the ills of Bolshevik biography; in time, fictionalization would flourish, especially in Politizdat, but its texts of the early 1960s displayed a cautious embrace of literary techniques in its first attempts to access the inner life and 'soul' of the subject.

Despite the strong critical consensus that had formed within a few years of Stalin's death against summarizing and enumerating — and thus ultimately only 'describing' — a life, the majority of post-Stalinist biographies in both Politizdat and LRP remained chronologically linear and comprehensive. Only a few of the shortest biographies dared to select episodes of the hero's life (such as some stories in Politizdat's Leniniana collections, including a tale about Kalinin that focused only on the few years when he worked in a factory, and the sketches about Bauman and Babushkin in the same volume, which covered only a few years each).[78] This comprehensive coverage was shaped partly by the template of Stalin's biography, and partly by the well-established 'cradle to grave' narrative tradition of LRP. It also reflected an abiding belief in biography's informational and educational function, which was slow to be challenged, partly due to the moral importance in the Khrushchev era of resurrecting the 'truth' about stigmatized figures. Indeed, it was in the flurry of biographies of Stalin cult victims that Politizdat published in the early to mid 1960s (including full-length biographies of Kosior and Tukhachevskii, and sketches of figures such as Gamarnik, Postyshev, Rudzutak and Skrypnik in the Leniniana collections) that this principle of information compilation and painstaking biographical reconstruction was most clearly in evidence.[79] A parallel might be drawn between Nathaniel Knight's study

---

[77] On the often pejorative attitude to novelized biography in the 1950s and 1960s (and beyond), see the contemporary analyses: Stone, *Biographical Novel*; Carl Bode, 'The Buxom Biographies', *College English*, 16, 1955, 5, pp. 265–69; and the retrospective analysis of the genre's eventual rise to respectability in Michael Lackey, *The American Biographical Novel*, London, 2016. On the desire, even amongst literary-minded critics of the period, to keep biography from straying into fiction (setting the limit at the novel*istic* biography), see Edel, *Literary Biography*; Kendall, *The Art of Biography*.

[78] Davydov, *U istokov partii*, pp. 9–30; Davydov, *Partiia shagaet*, pp. 117–31.

[79] Aleksandr Ivanovich Todorskii, *Marshal Tukhachevskii*, Moscow, 1963; A. I. Mel′chin, *Stanislav Kosior*, Moscow, 1964; L. D. Davydov, *Partiia shagaet v revoliutsii: rasskazy o soratnikakh V. I. Lenina*, Moscow, 1964.

of the scholarly biography in this issue, and this attempt to resurrect the party's old guard through careful compilation of surviving evidence.

However, biographers tried to introduce structural change and dramatization despite this continuing tendency to recount the whole life. Some texts of the early 1960s began to experiment with the 'in medias res' technique in order to grip their reader at the outset, narrating an episode from the middle or end of a life as a way to characterize the hero in action, or at a key turning point, before returning to birth and early childhood to embark on the chronological narrative proper. Pavel Podliashuk's Politizdat biography of Inessa Armand opened with the heroine in the midst of a police search of her apartment; while the trope of police harassment continued a long tradition of Bolshevik biographical writing, the scene also concisely characterized her as calm, strikingly beautiful and devoted to her children, even under extreme stress. Before returning to the start of her life, the biography took the second of 'two frames of a picture not yet taken, of the life and activities of Inessa Armand, the start and the end of her path': this time, of Armand's funeral, which intensified these tropes of love for the revolution and the family.[80] Anna Itkina's biography of Aleksandra Kollontai, also for Politizdat, began her narrative with the heroine travelling to Russia on a train in 1917, experiencing the triumph of Bolshevism on home soil for the first time with a sense of 'excitement' (*volnenie*).[81] This was a personal high-point as well as a key juncture in party and Russian history; it immediately evoked the heroine's emotional investment in revolution, a theme explored throughout the rest of the text. In both these cases, the contrast with the bald report of birth that opened Stalin's *Short Biography* was clear. In an even more striking contrast to Stalinist narrative, the opening to Mukhadze's biography of Ordzhonikidze for LRP plunged the reader straight into the hero's tragic falling-out with Stalin and suicide in 1937, in order to set the leitmotif of its hero's willingness to 'look truth in the eye', before the narrative zoomed backwards to bucolic scenes of Sergo's Caucasian childhood.[82]

In contrast to these attempts to grip the reader from the start, biographies still usually ended in a formulaic way, with descriptions of death followed by reassurance of the continued 'life' of the hero in collective memory. This still, however, compelled biographers to confront

[80] Pavel Isaakovich Podliashuk, *Tovarishch Inessa*, Moscow, 1963, p. 7.
[81] A. Itkina, *Revoliutsioner, tribun, diplomat*, Moscow, 1964, p. 6.
[82] I. Dubinskii-Mukhadze, *Ordzhonikidze*, Moscow, 1963, pp. 3–6. This material about the suicide had also been the sample material submitted to the press as part of the book proposal, and Mukhadze described the death as the most important aspect of his research for the text.

their hero's death, even though this was a sensitive issue for many of those newly included or prioritized in the biographical canon. Terror victims' deaths were normally attributed to the 'cult of personality', rather than to specific agents, and authors were instructed to avoid a 'lachrymose' tone.[83] However, there remained considerable variation in dramatization of such deaths: Politizdat's and LRP's rival biographies of Kirov and Ordzhonikidze infused very different levels of detail (and bloodshed) into their narratives of the heroes' murder and suicide, as did the various sketches of cult victims in the Leniniana collections.[84]

A more noticeable change from Stalinist poetics was the greater personalization of the biographer's attitude to the subject, moving away from the *ex cathedra* style of the *Short Biography*; the biographer's admiration of his subject was supposed to trigger the reader's own attachment to the Bolshevik hero. The Old Bolsheviks and former colleagues of the biographical subject, increasingly hired as biographers in the early 1960s, brought a personal knowledge of their subjects' personalities, serving to humanize and even sentimentalize their biographical accounts. Itkina's biography of Kollontai, for example, drew on her close work with the heroine, which both authenticated and personalized the account, helping her to create a 'warm' portrait of her former boss.[85] Todorskii's biography of Tukhachevskii for Politizdat likewise emphasized from the outset that he had worked closely with the Marshal (to the extent of being implicated himself in the 'all-Army tragedy' of the late 1930s) and grown to love him, as he hoped contemporary readers would too.[86] Old Bolsheviks, especially the influential Elena Stasova, also provided paratexts for several

---

[83] RGASPI-m, f. 42, op. 2, d. 1662, l. 5.

[84] The Politizdat biography of Kirov devoted ten pages to a suspenseful account of Kirov's (unidentified) assassin (S. Krasnikov, *Sergei Mironovich Kirov: zhizn' i deiatel'nost'*, Moscow, 1964, pp. 193–202), whereas Sinelnikov's biography was very brief about it (Sinelnikov, *Kirov*, p. 363). Kirillov's biography of Ordzhonikidze for Politizdat analysed the historiography of his death (G. Kirillov, *Ordzhonikidze-Sergo. Biografiia*, Moscow, 1963, p. 321). The LRP editor, Korotkov, had urged Mukhadze to be cautious on the subject, as 'not everything known [about the death] can be published' (RGASPI-m, f. 42, op. 2, d. 1664, ll. 17–18), and the biography ultimately devoted three dramatic pages to the suicide (Mukhadze, *Ordzhonikidze*, pp. 4–7). In the numerous sketches about cult victims in the second Leniniana volume, accounts ranged from detailed narratives of the arrests to standardized phraseology about the cult of personality (Davydov, *Partiia shagaet*).

[85] Itkina, *Revoliutsioner, tribun, diplomat*, p. 3; p. 28 (one of their first conversations); p. 75 (her personal impressions of one of Kollontai's speeches), and p. 126 (their last meeting before Kollontai's death).

[86] Todorskii, *Marshal Tukhachevskii*, pp. 3–4. Compare Mukhadze's claim of personal knowledge of Ordzhonikidze in his proposal (RGASPI-m, f. 42, op. 2, d. 1664, ll. 1–2).

works including the Kollontai and Armand biographies and Politizdat's Leniniana anthologies, inviting readers to share her personal, emotional connection with the biographical subjects while also authenticating the biographies' claims to 're-create' (*vossozdat´*) their subjects' personalities.[87]

The Bolshevik personality itself was also represented in new ways, indicating the post-Stalinist imperative to humanize the subjects and indeed to reflect a more complex notion of the human self. Some biographies, though far from all, allotted more space to describing the subject's *lichnaia zhizn´*, such as their marriage and children (the subjects' own childhoods were covered to a similar degree as in the biographies of the 1950s examined earlier). Reinforcing traditional gender stereotypes, family and children featured most prominently in new biographies of prominent Bolshevik women, such as Kollontai and Armand, whose 'personal [*lichnaia*] drama' was featured at some length (albeit without confronting their challenging ideas about sex and gender, or Armand's true relationship with Lenin, described only as close friendship and mutual assistance). Armand's biographer conceded that motherhood and children 'aren't inscribed at first glance into her image as a professional revolutionary', but claimed that Inessa's maternal devotion was in fact an important facet of her biography.[88] The domestic life of male revolutionaries was still largely elided, however. Mogilevskii's biography of Leonid Krasin for Politizdat contained just one, belated reference to his marriage and wife ('by this time, he was already married'), while the two publishers' biographies of Kirov both shrank the role of his wife to almost nothing, with Sinelnikov asserting outright that 'the most immaterial thing for him was the strictly personal [*lichnoe*]'.[89] However, one story in the *At the Sources* collection anchored its narrative around marriage, with Lenin and Krupskaia helping Bauman to propose to his partner (an episode not covered in the earlier LRP biography of Bauman, despite its considerable length).[90]

Another 'personalization' technique that now featured in some biographies was the inclusion of information about the subject's hobbies and (always scant) leisure time. Such information was usually brief and might leap from dietary preferences (in the case of Kirov) to love of

---

[87] Itkina, *Revoliutsioner, tribun, diplomat*, p. 4; Podliashuk, *Tovarishch Inessa*, pp. 3–4 (Stasova claims to 'remember the multi-facetedness of Inessa'); Davydov, *U istokov partii*, p. 5.

[88] Itkina, *Revoliutsioner, tribun, diplomat*, pp. 48–49, 99; Podliashuk, *Tovarishch Inessa*, pp. 60, 65 23, 39, 52–54, 73.

[89] B. Mogilevskii, *Nikitich*, Moscow, 1963, p. 64; Sinel´nikov, *Kirov*, p. 352; Krasnikov, *Kirov*, pp. 67–68 (sole references to wife).

[90] Davydov, *U istokov*, pp. 20–30.

music or theatre (a common sign of *kul'turnost'*, shared by Kirov, Kosior, Kollontai, Armand), or deep feelings about nature (a trope also present in some 1940s and 1950s texts, such as the Bauman biography, but more lyrically expressed in new biographies including those of Kollontai, for whom nature was 'a requirement of the soul', and Ordzhonikidze, inspired by the beauty of the Caucasus).[91] It often, therefore, had the paradoxical effect of hiving off the 'personal' into the text's periphery and reinforced the primacy of politics.

However, there were also attempts to personalize the political itself as a realm of emotional experience and personal drama. This emphasis on the profound impact of ideology on the 'soul' was not new in Bolshevik discourse, which had often imagined coming to consciousness in spiritual and quasi-religious terms, but the ways in which the 'soul' was dramatized in early post-Stalinist biographies stretched across a wider emotional and psychological range.[92] Some still paid little more than lip service to the new requirements for emotional sincerity, such as Mogilevskii's biography of Krasin, which referred only rarely, and vaguely, to the state of his 'soul' without further elaboration.[93] However, others took the idea of the 'soul' of the subject more seriously, trying out new methods to explore it. Romantic and Promethean tropes featured in some texts' dramatization of coming to consciousness, reflecting the broader Khrushchev-era revival of *romantika*.[94] One of the first Politizdat biographies by a literary writer, Irina Guro, sought to dramatize Anton Kostiushko's emotionally tumultuous journey to revolution through the metaphor of a boat turning to ride into the storm (echoed later in a description of him as a 'lone voyager' on the stormy seas of revolution), and later, with the imagery of the hero opening his wings to set flight into freedom.[95] Another literary writer who started to write for Politizdat at this time, Arsenii Rut'ko, directly drew on Gor'kii's revolutionary Romanticism in his sketch about Krzhizhanosvkii for the *At the Sources* collection. The hero was characterized as a 'dreamer'

[91] Krasnikov, *Kirov*, pp. 187–89; Sinelnikov, *Kirov*, pp. 356, 359, 129–34; Podliashuk, *Tovarischch Inessa*, pp. 80–82; Mel'chin, *Kosior*, p. 53; Itkina, *Revoliutsioner, tribun, diplomat*, p. 19; Mukhadze, *Ordzhonikidze*, p. 18.
[92] Igal Halfin, *From Darkness to Light: Class, Consciousness, and Salvation in Revolutionary Russia*, Pittsburgh, PA, 1999; Igal Halfin, *Terror in My Soul: Communist Autobiographies on Trial*, Cambridge, MA, 2003; Jochen Hellbeck, *Revolution on My Mind: Writing a Diary under Stalin*, Cambridge, MA and London, 2006.
[93] Mogilevskii, *Nikitich*, pp. 33, 109.
[94] Katerina Clark, '"Wait for Me"'; Pinsky, 'Origins of Post-Stalinist Individuality'; Serguei Alex Oushakine, '"Sotzromantizm" and Its Theaters of Life', *Rethinking Marxism*, 29, 2017, 1, pp. 8–15.
[95] Irina Guro, *Podvig Antona Kostiushko*, Moscow, 1961, pp. 7, 73.

(*mechtatel'*), through the use of the Gorkyan motif of a childhood campfire exploding into the national conflagration of revolution. The sketch ended, however, by extrapolating the Romantic trope of the lone dreamer into a 'type': all the Old Bolsheviks commemorated in the Leniniana project were dreamers of the same ilk.[96]

Other biographers used techniques drawn more from realism than Romanticism (though many combined both, as remained typical in post-Stalinist Socialist Realism). In the biographies of Kollontai and Armand, in a further reflection of the gendering of the new biographies, the 'soul' featured particularly frequently in accounts of the heroines' involvement with revolution. Both were depicted as emotionally sensitive to injustice, with this distress propelling them instinctively toward the party (as much as learning from what they had read, which earlier texts, such as the 1950s Bauman and Babushkin biographies, had shown as the main influence on revolutionary consciousness). Passages of free indirect discourse (adapted carefully from diaries) dramatized the troubled state of Kollontai's 'soul' as she observed the problems of pre-Revolutionary society. Podliashuk, meanwhile, explicitly refused to impose a linear narrative on the account of Armand's development into a revolutionary; there was no single turning point (*rubezh*) that transformed her, but rather a process of personal development that the biographer must compose 'like a mosaic-maker' from the sources available.[97] In both these cases, and in most other biographies of the time, the biographers continued to emphasize the strong documentary foundation to their claims about personality, only showing inner life where they had concrete evidence for it.[98]

The attempt to infuse the process of coming to consciousness with affect was perhaps most visible in Poltizdat's Leniniana project, which explicitly positioned itself as a first foray into a new type of Bolshevik biography: in her foreword to the second volume (published in 1964), Stasova denied that the sketches in the collection were 'life descriptions' (*zhizneopisaniia*), but described them instead as intimate explorations of how each figure had developed a love of revolution and Lenin(ism).[99] Lev Davydov, editor of the series, attempted to set an example for this type of biography with

---

[96] Davydov, *U istokov partii*, pp. 188, 200.

[97] Itkina, *Revoliutsioner, tribun, diplomat*, pp. 7, 9–11; Podliashuk, *Tovarishch Inessa*, pp. 17, 7, 11, 1314.

[98] For example, Lev Davydov's description of his largely failed attempts to locate evidence for the content of Kurnatovskii's conversation with Lenin: Davydov, *U istokov partii*, pp. 222–23. Compare Podliashuk's meta-narrative of trying to fill the 'gaps' (*probely*) in sources: Podliashuk, *Tovarishch Inessa*, pp. 9, 17.

[99] Davydov, *Partiia shagaet*, pp. 120–40.

BOLSHEVIK BIOGRAPHY FROM STALIN TO BREZHNEV 169

his sketches about Kurnatovskii and Dzhaparidze in the first and second volumes respectively. While acknowledging that it was hard to access the 'movements of the soul', especially of Dzhaparidze whose 'life [was] as big as the ocean', he tried to show how the heroes had fallen in love with the revolution, and with Lenin as its leader.[100] The sketch about Kurnatovskii opened with the hero spending the night in heartfelt conversation with Lenin in a hunting lodge. The narrative later moved back to Kurnatovskii's earlier life and the beginnings of his relationship with Lenin, and then forward to the end of his life, to trace how his feelings about the leader had intensified over the years, and to show his devotion to the revolution as highly personal, and deeply emotional.[101] Even post-Revolutionary party work was occasionally reimagined as a personal as well as political drama. Thus Kollontai's struggle with oppositionist ideas in the early 1920s was recounted largely as a 'tussle in her soul' and as another expression of her 'perpetually stormy, restless soul'.[102]

However, where such ideological drama or doubt was absent, the period after the Revolution and Civil War usually proved stubbornly resistant to dramatization, with later chapters of many biographies cantering through party posts, and clearly struggling to infuse vitality into leaders' relentlessly hard work in party control, city-planning or taxes, for example.[103] And whether or not they had traced the subject's emotional life in detail, biographies usually closed with the heroes' and heroines' (and indeed their relatives' and successors') feelings of unalloyed 'happiness' about the continuation of the Soviet cause even after their lives had ended.[104]

Conclusion: Biographical Reform and Stagnation in the 1960s
By the end of the Khrushchev era, then, Bolshevik biography had risen from almost nothing to become the fastest growing sector of Politizdat, and it had evolved into a more prominent subsection of the LRP series too. The reception of this growing and diversifying corpus of Bolshevik biographies in the early 1960s saw critics and editors identifying innovations to pursue further, even as they grew increasingly impatient about the stubborn obstacles to biographical reform.

As already established by the end of the 1950s, compilation of dry detail was now decisively unacceptable as a biographical method. This

---
[100] Ibid., pp. 124, 120.
[101] Davydov, *U istokov partii*, pp. 220–39.
[102] Itkina, *Revoliutsioner, tribunal, diplomat*, p. 107.
[103] Mogilevskii, *Nikitich*; Krasnikov, *Kirov*.
[104] Itkina, *Revoliutsioner, tribun, diplomat*; Mukhadze, *Ordzhonikidze*, p. 376.

was clear when rival biographies of Kirov published by LRP and Politizdat in the early 1960s both attracted criticism for failing to move beyond such 'compilation' and fixating on trivial details of the life, rather than 'recreating' Kirov's personality for readers.[105] Meanwhile, critics' praise for new biographies valorized above all the texts' ability to show their subjects as real, living people. The biographies of Kollontai and Ordzhonikidze, in Politizdat and LRP respectively, were both praised for resurrecting their subjects.[106] This idea was most extensively developed in a high-profile paean of praise for the *At the Sources* collection, which contrasted the 'didactic life description' of past biographies to the 'agitation' of the reader's encounters with real-life Bolsheviks via vivid sketches. For Old Bolsheviks, such as Stasova, such textual encounters revived poignant memories of revolutionary comradeship; new generations of readers, meanwhile, would fall in love with these vividly depicted personalities and would instinctively desire to emulate them. The cross-generational transmission of revolutionary values, the aim of the biographical innovation undertaken since Stalin's death, would thereby be achieved.[107]

Within Politizdat, such prominent praise — and, just as important, the high sales achieved by the Leniniana collections and biographies such as *Comrade Inessa*, quickly reissued after selling out its first run — endowed editors with greater confidence to define what its recent biographies had done right and wrong. Internal reviews of the early 1960s publications now decisively prioritized affect and the evocation of personality as the best way to achieve propaganda goals. The goal was to 're-create' a 'clear' and 'lively' image of the individual: by looking into the 'soul' of the subject, biographies would in turn touch the souls of their readers.[108] On the other hand, according to his colleague Lobarev (whose comments on biography opened this article), clichéd language and superficial characterization would 'skim along the surface of the imagination, not touching the most complex claviers of our brains'.[109] It was better for biographers to verge on the sentimental, as Itkina and Podliashuk had in their accounts of

[105] M. Nepriakhin, 'Novye biografii Kirova', *Moskva*, 4, 1965, pp. 194–95. Indeed, Sinelnikov's biography for LRP had nearly not been published, such were the concerns about the text's 'entirely inadequate depiction of Kirov the person'; when readers later wrote to Molodaia gvardiia to complain about errors, the LRP editors turned down their requests for a corrected second edition, on the grounds that the book was not of high enough quality to be reissued. RGASPI-m, f. 42, op. 2, d. 1749, *passim*.

[106] 'Iarkaia zhizn'', *Izvestiia*, 8 July 1964, p. 3; 'Pravde v glaza!', *Izvestiia*, 21 November 1963, p. 4.

[107] 'Riadom s Leninym', *Izvestiia*, 4 July 1963, p. 3.

[108] RGASPI, f. 623, op. 1, d. 285, l. 298.

[109] RGASPI, f. 623, op. 1, d. 305, l. 15.

Kollontai and Armand respectively, or to be heartfelt, as Todorskii had been in writing about Tukhachevskii, than it was to produce cold life summaries in 'officialese', as had Melchin's biography of Kosior.[110] The text that best epitomized this move away from unimaginative and unevocative biographies was *At the Sources*, praised consistently within Politizdat for achieving high sales, critical acclaim and literary quality and for representing a genuinely 'new type of artistic-political book'.[111]

Politizdat quickly moved to capitalize on the success of this Leniniana collection by publishing several successor volumes within a short period and also by hatching plans for a similar biographical initiative under the same editorship (of Lev Davydov), but on a far more ambitious scale, encompassing a greater range of 'revolutionary' subjects and book-length biographical accounts.[112] In 1963, Politizdat managers already started to discuss a series, initially entitled 'Remarkable Revolutionaries' (*Zamechatel´nye revoliutsionery*).[113] Although their new series borrowed the initial name, ambitious scope and guiding concept of the 'remarkable' from LRP, Politizdat editors soon adopted a strategy of distinguishing themselves from the older series, denouncing its failings in Bolshevik biography, and promising to compensate for them.[114] In their attempts to dispel anxieties about duplication, Politizdat editors cited LRP's ongoing failures to prioritize Bolshevik biography and to raise its aesthetic standards.[115] Requesting party and state permission for the series, they confidently described revolutionaries, and Bolsheviks in particular, as a peripheral strand and 'political appendage' in LRP, where texts were more turgid than the rest of the series' output.[116] Politizdat's new series by contrast would concentrate exclusively on revolutionaries, and would be written in 'artistic prose', building on the innovations of the Leniniana collections, such as the use of psychologization and affect, and the commissioning of literary writers.[117]

At the same time, the editors of LRP themselves acknowledged to the party authorities that its Bolshevik biographies were indeed

---

[110] RGASPI, f. 623, op. 1, dd. 298, 305.
[111] RGASPI, f. 623, op. 1, d. 294, l. 8; RGASPI, f. 623, op. 1, d. 298; TsAOPIM, f. 819, op. 1, d. 32, 33, 34.
[112] RGASPI, f. 623, op. 1, d. 288.
[113] RGASPI, f. 623, op. 1, d. 284; TsAOPIM, f. 819, op. 1, d.34; RGALI, f. 2464, op. 3, d. 141; RGASPI, f. 623, op. 1, d. 312.
[114] RGASPI, f. 623, op. 1, d. 285, 288, 293.
[115] RGASPI, f. 623, op. 1, d. 299, 306.
[116] RGASPI, f. 623, op. 1, d. 69; Gosudarstvennyi arkhiv Rossiiskoi Federatsii (hereafter, GARF), f. 9604, op. 2, d. 365; RGASPI, f. 623, op. 1, dd. 305; 306; 312; 313.
[117] For example, RGASPI, f. 623, op. 1, d. 299.

continuing to fall short in terms of both quantity and stylistic quality.[118] However, its promises of improvement were vague, and its proposals for innovation limited to publishing biographical collections as an occasional 'exception'.[119] Consequently, LRP again came under fire in the Soviet press at the start of the Brezhnev era for similar problems as had been identified a decade earlier.[120] While Politizdat's biographical innovations continued to gather pace in the early Brezhnev era, LRP's Bolshevik coverage therefore increasingly seemed backward and stagnant.

Party and state approval of Politizdat's new series — now entitled 'Fiery Revolutionaries' — came in 1964–65, despite some concerns about duplication of LRP, with its first texts published from 1968 onwards.[121] These early years of the series witnessed fierce internal contestation over genre, form and the use of imagination, which limited the series' literary innovations and its popular acclaim (as did the fact that its initial cohort was dominated by little-known specialists in Leniniana recruited from the *At the Sources* series and other Politizdat biography publishing). By the 1970s, though, the series had branched into a range of genres, most notably the biographical novel (as opposed to the artistic-documentary texts examined above). It also attracted an unprecedented number and range of celebrated literary writers (including Bulat Okudzhava, Iurii Trifonov, Iurii Davydov, Vasilii Aksenov and Vladimir Voinovich).[122]

Like many reforms to Stalinist practices in the 1950s and 1960s, both publishers' attempts to reform Bolshevik biography were driven not only by shame at past errors, but also by optimism, even utopianism — in this case, by the belief in reconnecting the population directly to the revolution's vivid cast of characters. In the first post-Stalin decade publishers and Soviet authorities alike believed that Bolshevik biographies, despite their powerful tendencies to de-personalization and their political sensitivity, could and should attempt emotionally affecting and psychologically convincing portraiture. On the one hand, these two publishers' only partly successful attempts to create such portraits offer further proof of the inherent difficulties of the genre, in particular its demands to evoke personality. On the other hand, they demonstrate that Soviet biography's

---

[118] RGASPI-m, f. 42, op. 2, d. 1281, ll. 10–14.
[119] Ibid.
[120] G Volokhova, 'Seriia biografii ZhZL', *Voprosy Istorii*, 5, 1965, pp. 128–36.
[121] RGASPI, f. 623, op. 1, d. 293; GARF, f. 9604, op. 2, d. 365.
[122] Polly Jones, 'The Fire Burns On? The "Fiery Revolutionaries" Biographical Series and the Rethinking of Propaganda in the Brezhnev Era', *Slavic Review*, 74, April 2015, 1, pp. 32–56; V. Zhukova, M. Litovskaia, 'Seriia *Plamennye revoliutiosnery*: istoricheskii roman kak vospitatel´ svobodomysliia', *Filologiia i kul´tura*, 4, 2012.

urgent need to reconnect with its readers pushed it to stretch, and eventually transgress, the generic limits (on fictionalization, for example) still constraining most Western biography of the period.

Ultimately, however, evoking the personalities of Bolsheviks and other revolutionaries was a more urgent task for Politizdat, a CC publisher dedicated to political and propagandistic literature, than for the distinctive niche that the eclectic and cosmopolitan LRP occupied within the Komsomol's main publisher. Politizdat's reforms to Bolshevik biography continued into the 1980s, while LRP's Bolshevik lives always remained one of the least prominent strands in the series. Although other, much more popular aspects of LRP, such as its coverage of cultural figures and international subjects (and its increasing use of foreign authors), made it the most important series of the late Soviet boom in biographical publishing, its portraits of revolutionaries consistently lagged behind those of Politizdat.[123] Both publishers therefore played an important role in bringing the genre(s) of biography to the forefront of critical and popular attention in the Brezhnev era, and in contributing to the period's broader debates about the significance and complexity of the individual socialist personality.

[123] Pomerantseva, *Biografiia v potoke vremeni*; Ludmilla A. Trigos and Carol R. Ueland, 'Literary Biographies in the *Lives of Remarkable People* Series (*Zhizn' zamechatel'nykh liudei*),' *Slavic & East European Journal*, 60, Summer 2016, 2, pp. 207–20.

NOTES ON CONTRIBUTORS

Angela Brintlinger is Professor of Russian Literature and Culture at Ohio State University.

Ben Eklof is Professor of History at Indiana University.

Jochen Hellbeck is Distinguished Professor of History at Rutgers University.

Polly Jones is Associate Professor of Russian and Schrecker-Barbour Fellow at University College, Oxford.

Nathaniel Knight is Associate Professor of History at Seton Hall University.

Tatiana Saburova is a Research Fellow at the Higher School of Economics in Moscow and Visiting Professor at the University of Alberta.

Ludmilla A. Trigos is an independent scholar and has taught at Columbia University, Barnard College, Drew University and New York University.

Carol Ueland is Professor of Russian and Director of the Russian programme at Drew University in Madison, New Jersey.

www.ingramcontent.com/pod-product-compliance
Lightning Source LLC
Chambersburg PA
CBHW051100160426
43193CB00010B/1258